The Life and
of the Reverend Robert Wright
(1772–1850)

Clerical Magistrate,
of Itchen Abbas, Hampshire

David Taylor

First published in 2019 by William David Taylor,
11 Jellicoe Drive, Sarisbury Green, Southampton, SO31 7NW

William David Taylor asserts the moral right to be identified as the author of this work.

A catalogue record for this book is available from the British Library.
ISBN 978-1-9161749-1-7

Artwork by Leanne Kelman   (www.lwrightdesign.co.uk)

Edited by Landmark Editorial   (www.landmarkeditorial.com)

Designed by Tim Underwood   (timund@hotmail.com)

Printed by Sarsen Press, 22 Hyde Street, Winchester, SO23 7DR

Every effort has been made to obtain permission to reproduce copyright material. The author apologises for any errors or omissions and, if notified, will make the necessary corrections in future reprints.
wdtay1948@gmail.com

Please note: The original spelling, punctuation and grammar has been retained in all quotations.

Contents

Figures (Maps and Diagrams)

Tables

GRAPHS/CHARTS

PLATES

Abbreviations

HRO   The Hampshire Record Office
TNA   The National Archives
CCED   Clergy of the Church of England Database
HL   Hartley Library, University of Southampton

Preface

In the 1980s, when I was teaching history at a Winchester comprehensive school, I decided to introduce the Schools' History Project (SHP) as an option at GCSE level. The SHP had a strong local history component and, after much thought, I decided to use the upper Itchen Valley as a site for study. The students presented some high-quality work on the parishes of Avington, Itchen Abbas and Easton and built up a bond with the local residents who allowed them to study their houses.

The school benefitted from its proximity to the Hampshire Record Office, the first in the country to employ an education officer. The students were shown how to use the catalogues in the record office, which enabled them to order their own documents and study independently. Without exception, they found it a very enriching experience and it was, indisputably, the most rewarding period of my teaching career.

It was at this time that I first 'encountered' the Reverend Robert Wright, a clerical magistrate and the rector of Itchen Abbas from 1803–1850. Finding out about his life, however, was problematical. There was little in the way of original source material readily available at the time other than generic items such as the Itchen Abbas tithe map, Ordnance Survey maps, census returns and trade directories. Also available were the surviving Itchen Abbas parish documents such as churchwardens' accounts and parish registers plus information gathered from local monuments, gravestones and oral evidence. Jessie E. Corrie's *Records of the Corrie Family*, published in 1899, however, provided extremely useful information about Wright and his extended family. There was just one known copy of this valuable source, which was kept in the 'stack' of the local history room at the Jewry Street Library in Winchester. Readers had to ask for it by name and wait for the librarian to fetch it. This was also the location to research the *Hampshire Chronicle* on microfilm, but it was necessary to pre-book the electronic reader to avoid disappointment. The logistics of local history research were very challenging in the 1980s!

I left teaching in 1993 to work in educational publishing and my Robert Wright 'material' was deposited in the loft at home, where it lay dormant for a number of years. My enthusiasm for the upper Itchen Valley was unexpectedly reignited over 20 years later by a chance internet search which unearthed an article written by Andrew Rozefelds of the Tasmanian Museum and Art Gallery in Hobart. Rozefelds had used *St John the Baptist in Itchen Abbas: A Short History of a Church and its Community in the Upper Itchen Valley*, a booklet I had co-authored with Penny Claisse in 1992, to help compose a fascinating article on the Reverend William Webb Spicer, rector of Itchen Abbas from 1850–1874. This chance event illustrated the power of the internet and I decided to rescue my Wright material and see what else I could discover using the worldwide web. Shortly afterwards, I was provided with an additional incentive when I came across the magnificent *Complete Diaries of a Cotswold Parson*, the edited diaries of the Reverend Francis E Witts, a clerical magistrate of Upper Slaughter, Gloucestershire and a contemporary of Robert Wright. The diaries provided the perfect backcloth against which to construct a parallel biography of the Itchen Abbas cleric.

Robert Wright has still been a difficult person to research mainly because he left no private papers; he was either too disorganised or too busy to bother with record-keeping. The internet, however, has proved an invaluable tool in the search for sources to uncover information about Robert Wright's life. Unlike in the 1980s, it is now possible to download census returns and tithe maps, and explicit searches can reveal some excellent material and leads. For example, the internet facilitated a meeting with Susie Edmonds, a direct descendant of the Wright family. Susie still possesses Victorian toys which had belonged to the children of Robert John William Wright, son of Robert Wright. Despite a gap of almost 170 years, the people involved in this story are not so far from us as we might think.

I would like to acknowledge the inspiration provided by historian, Ruscombe Foster, author of *The Politics of County Power*. His work provides an excellent and authoritative discussion of the Hampshire Quarter Sessions and county politics during the Robert Wright era. The publications of Dr Barry Shurlock have also served to spur me on. His latest book, *The Speaker's Chaplain and the Master's Daughter*, is superb and emanates from a love of the Georgian period; it is a fine example to any would-be local history author.

The commitment of archivists and librarians never ceases to amaze me.

I have received courteous and expert service from a large number of dedicated people over the years. The staff at the Hampshire Record Office have been exemplary and have always been prepared to help me with any problems. I express my sincere thanks to the archivists at the Hartley Library at Southampton University where the Wellington Papers are deposited. Gratitude is also extended to the staff of the Shakespeare Birthplace Trust in Stratford-upon-Avon and the Church of England Record Centre.

I have relied heavily on several websites in researching the story of Robert Wright. Among them are:

www.ancestry.co.uk

www.britishnewspaperarchive.co.uk

www.thegenealogist.co.uk

www.theclergydatabase.org.uk

These websites have been invaluable in enabling research to take place at home, thus saving money and time in having to travel to libraries and archives.

I am very happy to acknowledge the generosity of the Bartons' Local History Group, who allowed me access to the documents on their website. Online discussions with Stephen Grieve concerning the people of Itchen Abbas in the nineteenth century also proved to be thought-provoking and informative.

I must also pay tribute to my past history students at the Henry Beaufort School in Winchester who embarked with me on this journey over 30 years ago; their enthusiasm and *joie de vivre* has stayed with me long into retirement.

I express my sincere gratitude to my long-suffering and supportive wife, Pat, who has had to live with Robert Wright for far too long.

I have attempted to place the life of Robert Wright firmly within the context of his times which resulted in my having to research a wide variety of subjects, including Church history and the law. I have little academic prowess and I sincerely apologise for any errors that I have unwittingly made in the construction of the narrative. In the words of Dr Barry Shurlock, 'tolerance ... is asked of those with specialist knowledge'.

David Taylor
Sarisbury Green, March 2019.

Leading Figures and Their Titles

Reverend Robert Wright (1772–1850)
Rector of Itchen Abbas and clerical magistrate on the Hampshire bench from 1808 to 1850. Referred to as Wright or Robert Wright throughout.

Reverend Robert John William Wright (1803–1887)
Son of Robert and Elizabeth Wright. Curate of Itchen Abbas and Ovington, chaplain at the county gaol from 1836 to 1853 and vicar of Selston, Nottinghamshire from 1856 to 1887. Referred to as RJW Wright throughout.

Richard Temple-Nugent-Brydges-Chandos-Grenville (1776–1839)
Styled Earl Temple from 1784 to 1813 and then Marquis of Buckingham from 1813 to 1822. He was created the first Duke of Buckingham and Chandos in 1822.

Lady Anna Eliza Brydges (1780–1836)
Daughter of the third Duke of Chandos and Anna Eliza Gamon. She married Richard Temple-Nugent-Brydges-Grenville in April 1796, and he added 'Chandos' to his surname. Lady Anna was the first Duchess of Buckingham and Chandos from 1822 to 1836.

Richard Plantagenet Temple-Nugent-Brydges-Chandos-Grenville (1797–1861)
Only child of Richard Temple-Nugent-Brydges-Chandos-Grenville and Lady Anna Brydges. Styled Viscount Cobham from 1797 to 1813, Earl Temple from 1813 to 1822 and Marquis of Chandos from 1822 to 1839. He became the second Duke of Buckingham and Chandos in 1839. In 1819 he married Lady Mary Campbell (1795–1862), daughter of the fourth Earl of Breadalbane, but the marriage ended in divorce in 1850.

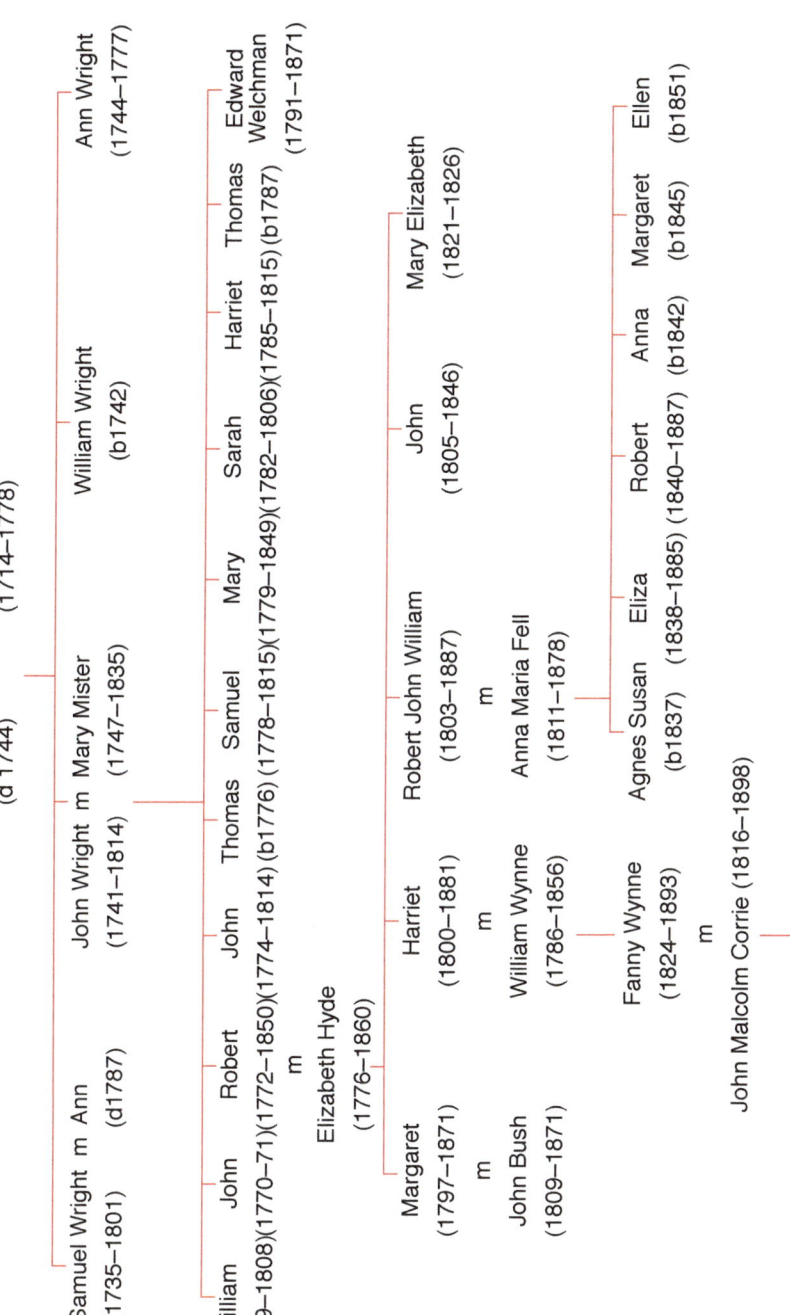

Figure 1: *Wright family tree (Source: Jessie E Corrie and Shakespeare Birthplace Trust).*

Introduction

On Saturday 30 March 1850 a 22-year-old domestic servant journeyed the four miles into Winchester from the small village of Itchen Abbas. Her name was Louisa Hughes and she had been sent to register the death of her employer, the Reverend Robert Wright, who had died at home the previous Tuesday 26 March. Louisa had been present at Wright's death and she passed on the relevant information to the registrar, EH Chiddy, who recorded the cause of death as 'old age'.[1] On 30 March 1850 the *Hampshire Chronicle* carried a brief entry in its announcement column:

> Died on Tuesday, at Itchen Abbas, near this city, aged 78, the Rev Robert Wright, 37 years Rector of that parish [sic], and for many years an acting magistrate for this County.[2]

Wright had, in fact, been the rector of Itchen Abbas for 47 years and his service on the Hampshire bench amounted to 42 years in which he made a more than substantial contribution to administering the county and dispensing justice. When the Easter Quarter Sessions met in Winchester on 8 April 1850, however, there was no official mention of Wright's death. No doubt the attending magistrates from all parts of the county would have discussed Wright's demise in private conversations, but there was no public tribute for a person who had carried out his duties as a Justice of the Peace for Hampshire so energetically and consistently for such a long period of time.

In terms of primary sources, a small number of notebooks and diaries kept by magistrates at this time have survived, but Robert Wright was not one for keeping records and there are no *personal* documents appertaining to his career as a member of the Hampshire bench. Any investigation of his life, therefore, involves searching for primary sources elsewhere.

Fortunately, a few letters he wrote have survived in the Bolton and Baring archives and they throw some light on his character and opinions. Local newspapers, such as the *Hampshire Chronicle* and *Hampshire Advertiser*, also carry detailed accounts of Quarter Sessions proceedings and reports of speeches made by Wright at various Hampshire functions. In addition, the parish registers for the four Hampshire parishes Robert Wright served provide some evidence of his career as a clergyman and several property deeds have survived giving some details of his private dealings in real estate. All of these sources, valuable as they are, leave gaps and often prompt more questions than answers.

However, there is one invaluable source entitled *Records of the Corrie Family*, written and published in 1899, by Jessie E Corrie, the great-granddaughter of Robert Wright. The book is a compilation of family stories handed down through the generations and as such depicts Robert Wright in a favourable light. This source facilitates a reconstruction of Wright's life but it is difficult not to agree with Corrie when she expresses regret that 'We have no written record of Great-grandfather's life in those days, nor of the friendships he made'.[3]

It is obvious that Wright was admired within his family, with Corrie stating confidently that 'in all the memories that have endured of him there is not one of any unkind action'.[4] The reality, however, was that he also had a number of disagreeable personality traits, including truculence and stubbornness, and his demeanour was changeable depending on the circumstances and situation.

Corrie also claims that the lower classes regarded Wright as the 'poor man's friend' and she tells the story of John Hughes (alias Smith), an itinerant traveller who was sentenced to death for horse stealing in 1825.[5] According to the tale, Wright appealed against the death sentence but was unsuccessful. The authorities, however, agreed to release the body for burial rather than sending it for medical research and Wright arranged for the body to be buried adjacent to the yew tree in Itchen Abbas churchyard.

Corrie cites a second story of when Wright was ambushed one dark night as he rode home from Winchester, a journey that he undertook regularly. The assailant hurriedly disappeared into the hedgerow when he learned the identity of his potential victim, exclaiming 'the friend of the poor'.[6] As the only witness to this event, apart from the robber, was Wright himself, we may need to exercise caution as to its reliability. In addition, Corrie does not give us any indication as to the date and year that this incident was supposed to have occurred.

These legendary stories have been repeated and embellished over the years by the authors of articles for popular historical magazines and websites, but there are few citations to support the content. Although the assertion that Wright was 'the poor man's friend' has remained, a deeper investigation into Wright's life reveals a much more enigmatic and complicated man than previous writers have depicted. Sometimes he displayed a degree of paternalistic compassion, but he was also capable of taking an unforgiving stance towards the poor, particularly in the aftermath of the agricultural riots of 1830.

The Reverend MR Austin, in describing the stereotype of a Georgian clergyman in the late eighteenth and early nineteenth centuries, commented:

> The position of most Church of England clergy in this period was to uphold the laws and institutions of the State, as it was the State which protected the Church. Thus, they were opposed to Reform [which directed their attitude to a range of social questions] and to religious toleration. Politically, they supported the Tories.[7]

As Wright's story unfolds, it becomes clear how closely he fitted this stereotype. In general, he was mostly concerned about preserving the Georgian values he had been brought up to believe in and this motivated him to reject any kind of reform or change. As the clamour for political, economic, social and religious reform grew louder after 1815, his opposition increased in equal measure. Whether we judge Wright to be the 'labourers' friend' or more a 'pillar of the establishment', it is high time that a full account of his remarkable life and career was added to the historical record.

NOTES

1 General Register Office, Certified Copy of an Entry of Death, Robert Wright, 1850. On the death certificate the informant is named as 'Louisa Youse'. She must have been misunderstood by Chiddy when she said her name and it has been misspelt. In the 1851 Census for Itchen Abbas she is enumerated as 'Louisa Hughes' and is a servant to Wright's widow, Elizabeth.

2 *Hampshire Chronicle*, Saturday 30 March 1850, p. 2.

3 Corrie, Jessie Elizabeth, *Records of the Corrie Family AD 802–1899*, Part 2, Mitchell and Hughes, 1899, p. 43.

4 *Ibid.*, p. 42.

5 *Ibid.*, pp. 35–36.

6 *Ibid.*, p. 35.

7 Austin, MR Rev., 'The Church of England in the County of Derbyshire 1772–1832', unpublished PhD thesis, University of London, 1969, p. 220.

A Georgian Upbringing

Robert Wright was born in Shipston-on-Stour in 1772, the third of eleven children produced by the marriage of John Wright (1741–1814) and Mary Mister (1747–1835).[1] John Wright described himself as a 'gentleman' and would have been well known in the small market town (population 1,293 in 1801) which was then within the borders of Worcestershire.

Located on the route of the old A34 between the cities of Oxford and Birmingham, Shipston was well placed to benefit from the expanding construction of turnpike roads in the last quarter of the eighteenth century, and a number of coaching inns in the

Plate 1: *John Wright (1741–1814) of Shipston-on-Stour (Jessie E Corrie).*

town, such as The White Bear and The George, enjoyed prosperous times. Shipston's economy had traditionally been based on its sheep market and shag weaving, both of which were beginning to decline. The coaching age thus provided a timely economic boost for the town.[2]

John Wright's last will and testament, dated 3 December 1812, provides us with a number of clues as to his social status, and he was best described as a 'middling' sort of gentleman.[3] In this will Robert Wright was gifted the advowson (the right of presentation to a living) of Itchen Abbas, which had been bought for £3,850 in 1802.[4] John Wright left leasehold land of 1.5 yardlands (about 45 acres) in the open fields of Shipston to his son Samuel Wright, together with a pecuniary legacy of £500 and the copyhold tenancy of The George Inn. John's freehold land in Willington hamlet in the parish of Barcheston, one mile south east of Shipston, was handed down to his son, Edward Welchman Wright. The tithe schedule for Barcheston shows this land amounted to 57 acres, 1 rood and 4 perches.[5]

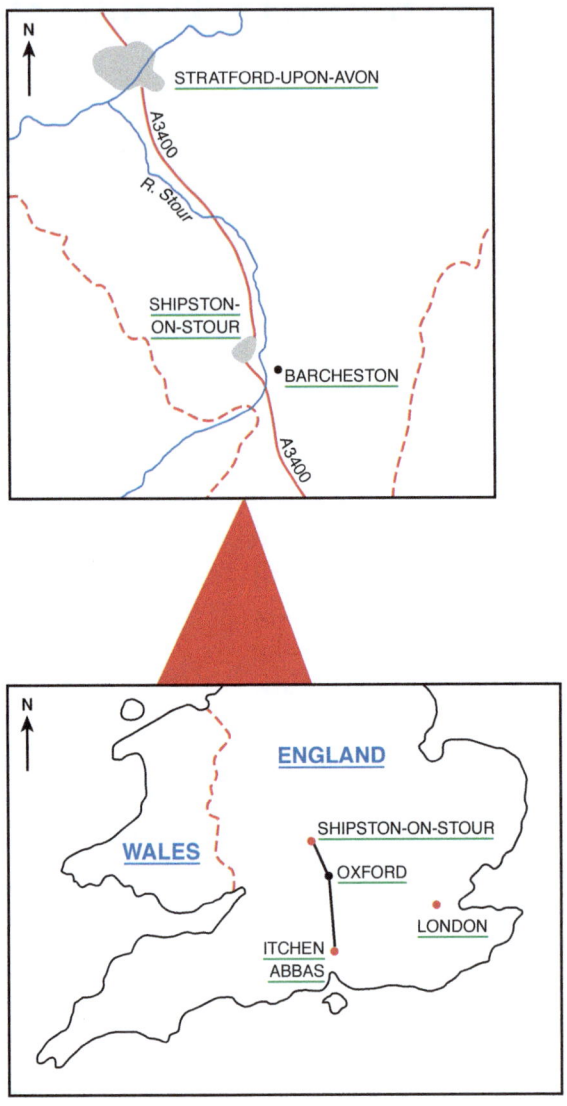

Approximate distance from Itchen Abbas to Shipston-on-Stour
= 85 miles.

Figure 2: *The location of Shipston-on-Stour.*

John Wright's wife, Mary, outlived him by 21 years and she, too, had a 'middling' estate. In her last will and testament, made on 25 January 1830, she left two messuages[6] in Limehouse, Middlesex to Robert Wright, together with a pecuniary legacy of £900. Edward Welchman, described as a doctor in medicine, received Mary's messuage situated in Shipston. She named Robert Wright, Edward Welchman Wright, Mary Ann Wright (her daughter) and Richard Mister (her nephew) as executors of her will.[7] There was thus sufficient wealth within the family to claim the status of middling gentry.

There would have been discussions within the family about the careers that the sons, in particular, would enter. The eldest son, Samuel Wright (1769–1808) joined the army and became a lieutenant colonel in the 30th Regiment of Foot, but he died in Malacca[8] on 16 August 1808, aged 38 years.[9] A second son, John, born in September 1770, survived just eight months, leaving Robert as the eldest surviving son.

The importance of social standing was instilled into Robert Wright from a young age and he doubtless felt there was no conflict in living the life of a gentleman while vast numbers lived their lives in abject poverty. Wright was brought up to have total respect for the monarchy and the established Church of England. During Wright's lifetime, however, the Georgian status quo was challenged by the spread of non-conformity, industrialisation and the rise of the radicals who wanted the reform of Parliament. Furthermore, for 22 long years between 1793 and 1815, the French Revolution and ensuing wars with Napoleonic France hung like a huge black cloud over the British Isles. These events were to punctuate Robert Wright's life as he later attempted to hold on to the values of the old world into which he was raised.

THE YOUNG ROBERT WRIGHT ENTERS THE ANGLICAN CLERGY

In her thoroughly researched book *The Education of the Anglican Clergy, 1780–1839*, Sara Slinn informs us that:

> The families who sent their sons into the [Anglican] Church ... were ... drawn from that section of the social spectrum that was from the moderately prosperous middle sorts [successful farmers, tradesmen, skilled artisans and professionals] through to the gentry, that is those groups who could afford to give their sons an appropriate education.[10]

Plate 2: *Robert Wright (1772–1850) (Source: Jessie E Corrie).*

Plate 3: *Elizabeth Wright (1776–1860) (Source: Jessie E Corrie).*

The Wright family fitted this profile perfectly and the decision was made that Robert Wright would embark on a career in the Anglican Church, taking the classic pathway via an expensive university education paid for by his father. John Wright wished to give his son a secure financial future and he hoped the experience of university would turn Robert into a gentleman and provide access to social and clerical contacts.

The sixteen-year-old Robert Wright entered Trinity College, Oxford on 15 December 1788. There, he gained his BA in 1793 and an MA in 1809.[11] At this time the degree curriculum was limited in vision and content, and undergraduates were tempted to waste time on a range of social activities such as dinner parties and horse riding. The BA degree focused more on the classics than divinity and only if an ordinand took an MA would he receive any theological teaching.[12] An MA qualification also legally allowed a clergyman to hold livings in 'plurality' and this opened up a greater number of career opportunities for Wright. Pluralism, and as a result, clerical non-residence, was rife within the Church of England, even though many contemporaries did not approve of the practice.[13]

Robert Wright went on to be ordained as a deacon in 1794 and as a priest in 1797.[14] His first position in the Church was a curacy in the parish of Dummer, Hampshire, which he took up on 1 January 1798. In terms of entering the Anglican clergy, Robert Wright had the perfect start and his future was more or less secured.

MARRIAGE AND FAMILY

On 5 November 1795 Robert Wright married Elizabeth Hyde (1776–1860), the daughter of William and Margaret Hyde of the city of Oxford. The couple must have met when Robert was studying at Trinity College. Their wedding took place at St Martin's Church, Carfax, Oxford.

The newly-weds took up residence in Dummer, where Elizabeth gave birth to Margaret in 1797, Harriet in 1800 and Robert John William in 1803.[15] Margaret married John Bush, a surgeon, of Witney in 1830, and Harriet married William Wynne, a stationery and paper merchant, in Itchen Abbas Church on Thursday 13 January 1820. According to Jessie Corrie, Harriet chose William over his elder brother, Peter, and the two men became 'estranged' for several years.[16] William's brother John Wynne (1792–1872) was to benefit from the patronage of Robert Wright, who employed him

Plate 4: *Reverend Robert John William Wright (1803–1887).*

at Itchen Abbas as a curate in 1837 on a salary of £80 per year.[17] Harriet and William Wynne started married life at Grove Hill, Camberwell, but they later had a residence in Euston Square.[18] Margaret, known as 'Peggy' within the family, lived with John Bush in the London suburb of Clapham. Both Margaret and Harriet were cultured and educated young women who kept in close contact with their parents and their native county of Hampshire.

Robert John William was destined to follow his father into the ranks of the Anglican clergy, also taking the familiar Oxbridge route. RJW Wright matriculated at Trinity College, Oxford on 11 December 1821, aged 18, and went on to gain his BA in 1826 and his MA in 1828. He was ordained as a deacon on 21 May 1826 and as a priest on 17 June 1827. Initially, he worked under the wing of his father as a curate at Itchen Abbas and Ovington, before becoming the chaplain at the county gaol in Winchester in January 1836.[19] Five months later, on 28 May 1836, he married Anna Maria Fell, the eldest daughter of the Reverend TC Fell, rector of Sheepy in Leicestershire and prebend of Lichfield Cathedral.[20] The couple had six children (born between 1837 and 1851) and for 17 years lived in the parish of St. Faith's in Winchester before RJW Wright was forced to resign his post as chaplain in November 1853. It appears that a rift may have developed with his elderly father during the late 1840s, and the younger Wright left Hampshire to become the curate of Queenshead,[21] Yorkshire from 1854 to 1856 and then the long-serving vicar of Selston in Nottinghamshire until his death in 1887.[22]

A fourth child, John, was born in 1804 and publicly baptised twice, initially on 10 December 1804 by his father at Itchen Abbas Church[23] and then at St Mary's Church, Bloxham, Oxfordshire by the incumbent vicar on

15 August 1805. John joined the British army, and on 12 May 1846 he died in the East Indies, where he was serving as a brigade general in the Third Regiment Native Infantry (Second Belochee Division).[24] According to Jessie Corrie, the family erected a memorial tablet to John Wright in the old church at Itchen Abbas, but it was removed when the parish church was rebuilt between 1861 and 1863, and subsequently taken to Shipston.[25]

A final child, Mary Elizabeth, was belatedly born to Elizabeth, then aged 45, and Robert Wright in 1821,[26] but sadly she died at Witney in Oxfordshire on 18 March 1826, aged just five. She was buried on 22 March at Witney, which was given as her 'place of abode' in the burial register signed by the officiating minister, H Gregory.[27] The child seems to have been 'airbrushed' out of the Wright story and does not merit a single mention in Corrie's family history. There is a distinct possibility that the girl had some sort of disability, which might explain why she was hidden from sight.

Robert and Elizabeth Wright suffered their fair share of premature deaths in the family, and more tragedy ensued when their granddaughter, Mary Wynne, died from scarlet fever on 13 April 1832, aged 11.[28] In his will, Wright left instructions that his body was to be buried 'by the side of my granddaughter, Mary Wynne', in the vault under Itchen Abbas Church, which suggests there was a strong bond between the two of them.[29]

Throughout his life Robert Wright kept in contact with his extended family. There were frequent visits to Oxfordshire and London and the evidence shows that he often officiated at family baptisms and marriages. Wright had a great deal in common with his brother-in-law, the Reverend John Hyde (1774–1838), who was a pluralist and a 'much respected' clerical magistrate on the Oxfordshire bench.[30] They shared the same Tory politics, but interestingly both wished to improve the treatment of 'lunatics'. No doubt, the two of them would have had much to discuss when they met.

Jessie Corrie paints a picture of Wright as a popular father figure within the confines of the family who was also well loved by the local population. She described his distinctive appearance in the following manner:

> He was the picture of an old-fashioned gentleman with upright figure and snowy white hair. He wore black silk stockings and little diamond knee buckles, the frills and ruffles of his shirts being the finest cambric, and generally fastened with either a small gold or cornelian brooch in the form of a circle.[31]

The image fitted the ideas and attitudes that Wright held dear. Continuity with the old, rather than social and religious change was an absolute vision that Wright held on to throughout his life.

NOTES

1 Shakespeare Birthplace Trust (Stratford-upon-Avon), ER20/146/1–3, Genealogical Collections.

2 *Shipston-on-Stour Conservation Area*, published by Stratford-upon-Avon District Council, 1992. Shag weaving was the production of long, rough pile suitable for rugs and carpets.

3 Prerogative Court of Canterbury Wills, John Wright, Probate dated 23 May 1814 (www.ancestry.co.uk).

4 HRO, 23M69/E/T2, The advowson of Itchen Abbas, Bargain and Sale for £3,850, 1 November 1802.

5 Willington Tithe Schedule, 1839 (www.thegenealogist.co.uk). There are 40 perches to a rood and 4 roods to 1 acre.

6 'Messuage', a word derived from Anglo-Norman French to describe a dwelling house with outbuildings and attached land.

7 Prerogative Court of Canterbury Wills, Mary Wright, Probate dated 24 April 1835 (www.ancestry.co.uk).

8 The city of Malacca, a former British territory, is situated in south east Malaysia (www.lonelyplanet.com).

9 Shakespeare Birthplace Trust, *op. cit.*

10 Slinn, Sara, *The Education of the Anglican Clergy 1780–1839*, Boydell Press, 2017, p. 44.

11 *Oxford University Alumni, 1500–1886*, Volume IV (1715–1886), p. 1,615 (www.ancestry.co.uk).

12 Slinn, Sara, *op. cit.*, p. 51.

13 'Plurality describes the situation when one priest [holds] two or more benefices [parishes], which are in other respects independent' (www.crockford.org).

14 CCED (www.theclergydatabase.org.uk).

15 HRO, 65M72/PR2, Dummer Parish Register, Baptisms, Marriages and Burials, 1740–1812.

16 Corrie, Jessie Elizabeth, *op. cit.*, p. 51.

17 HRO, 21M65/E6/12/130, Copy curate's licence, John Wynne BA, Curate of Itchen Abbas, 18 May 1818.

18 Corrie, Jessie Elizabeth, *op. cit.*, p. 53.

19 *Oxford University Alumni, 1500–1886, op. cit.*, p. 1,615.

20 *Salisbury and Winchester Journal*, Monday 13 June 1836, p. 2.

21 Queenshead was later renamed Queensbury, and in 1870–1872 was described by John Marius Wilson as a 'large village and chapelry ... 3½ miles NNE of Halifax station'.

22 *Crockford's Clerical Dictionary 1868*, p. 739 (www.ancestry.co.uk).

23 HRO, 23M69/PR2, Register of Baptisms, Marriages and Burials for Itchen Abbas, 1699–1812.

24 *Hampshire Chronicle*, Saturday 1 August 1846, p. 1.

25 Corrie, Jessie Elizabeth, *op. cit.*, p. 40.

26 HRO, 23M69/PR5, Register of Baptisms for Itchen Abbas, 1813–1942.

27 Church of England Deaths and Burials, 1831–1965, Witney St Mary, 1813–1832 (www.ancestry.co.uk).

28 Corrie, Jessie Elizabeth, *op. cit.*, p. 3.

29 HRO, 23M69/E/T28, Copy of the Will of Reverend Robert Wright, Rector of Itchen Abbas, proved by the PCC, 27 May 1850.

30 *Oxford Chronicle and Reading Gazette*, Saturday 15 December 1838, p. 4.

31 Corrie, Jessie Elizabeth, *op. cit.*, p. 9.

Parish and Church: Robert Wright, the Rural Clergyman

CURATE OF DUMMER (1798–1804)

Little is known about Robert Wright's time at Dummer, apart from a complaint he made to Thomas Hall, a local magistrate, about the theft of hedge wood from one of his fields in the village during the autumn of 1798. The angry Wright instructed his servant Benjamin Webb to collect some evidence by keeping a close watch on the hedge in question. Thomas Hall examined Webb who told him that he had witnessed William Knight, a labourer, breaking a fence and pulling up the hedge, the property of Robert Wright. Knight appeared before Hall and admitted the offence. He begged the forgiveness of Wright and promised not to commit any further misdemeanours. The magistrate imposed a fine of five shillings and there the matter concluded.[1] Wright's indignation at the law being broken was a portent of things to come. One imagines that Knight would not have crossed Wright a second time!

On a happier note, three of Robert Wright's five children were born at Dummer and spent their infancy in the quiet north Hampshire village. Wright formally resigned his 'charge as curate of Dummer' on 5 July 1804 to take up his new position as rector of Itchen Abbas.[2]

ARRIVAL AT ITCHEN ABBAS

Located in the upper Itchen Valley, four miles north east of Winchester, the manor of Itchen Abbas appears in the Domesday Survey of 1086, and between this date and the dissolution of the monasteries in 1539 it was, for the main part, in the hands of St Mary's Abbey, Winchester.

Following the dissolution of the monasteries, the manor of Itchen Abbas became the property of William Paulet, the first Marquis of Winchester, in whose family it remained until 1820. The Paulets (styled 'Powlett') became

17

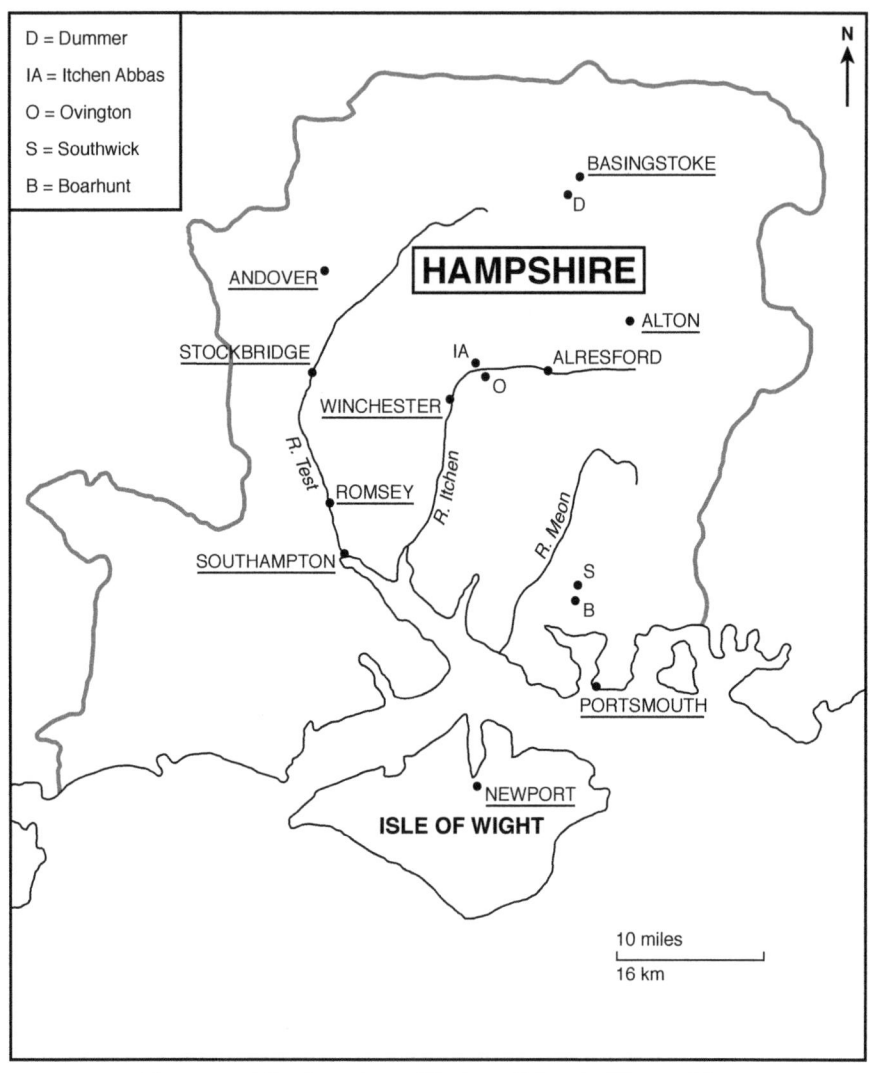

Figure 3: *The location of Itchen Abbas in Hampshire.*

Dukes of Bolton and sold the property to the Marquis of Buckingham for the sum of £60,000.[3] The Marquis, who was created the first Duke of Buckingham and Chandos in 1822, died in 1839 and Itchen Abbas passed to his son. However, by 1847 the second Duke of Buckingham and Chandos was in such deep financial trouble that he was obliged to sell much of his land. The manor of Itchen Abbas was bought jointly by the estate of Lord Ashburton (deceased) and John Shelley.[4]

Robert Wright was active in Itchen Abbas from 1800 and in 1802 his father, John Wright, purchased the advowson from the Reverend Charles Powlett the Elder for the sum of £3,850.[5] It was common practice at the time for advowsons to be considered 'valuable pieces of property' and 'they could be bought, sold or mortgaged'.[6] It is not known how John Wright knew that the living of Itchen Abbas was for sale and available, but his decision to purchase it turned out to be inspired. With his father the patron of a highly desirable parish, Robert Wright was now in a position that most aspiring clergymen could only dream of. Those without the right connections and support, however, struggled to find such a lucrative living and many had to settle for a poorly paid curacy. *Table 1* shows that the six parishes of the upper Itchen Valley, with the possible exception of Ovington, were all relatively prosperous. It is Itchen Abbas that heads the list, with each parishioner 'worth' £2-3s-2d per annum to the rector.

Parish	Value	Per Head	Area	Pop
	£	£	(acres)	1861
Avington	270	1.66	1794	162
Easton	620	1.36	2926	455
Itchen Abbas	468	2.18	2100	214
Itchen Stoke	320	1.08	2694	295
Martyr Worthy	488	1.88	1974	259
Ovington	150	0.98	1270	152

Table 1: *Values of upper Itchen Valley livings in the mid-nineteenth century (Sources: William White's 1859 Trade Directory and Census Returns for 1861).*

Robert Wright was officially presented to the Bishop of Winchester as the next rector of Itchen Abbas in 1803. The entry in the administration records of the Bishop of Winchester stated:

On the 15th January 1803 Robert Wright Clerk AB was admitted & instituted to the Rectory of Itchin Abbas [Abbas Itchin] in the County of Southampton & Diocese of Winchester void by the Resignation of Robert John Sayer Clerk the last Incumbent on the Presentation of John Wright the elder of Shipston upon Stour in the County of Worcester Esquire the Patron thereof.[7]

WHAT SORT OF A PARISH WAS ITCHEN ABBAS?

In 1801 the parish of Itchen Abbas had a population of just 185 souls.[8] The predominant economic activity in the parish involved mixed agriculture and associated occupations such as blacksmiths and wheelwrights. Sheep and cattle were kept on the well-drained downland above the river and in the valley below. John Duthy wrote that:

> The soil around the village, and along the vale, is of the same mild tender loam; ... excellent turnip and barley land; and, in fact, productive of all kinds of grain, pulse and green crops. Higher up, towards the north, the soil is stronger, and more retentive, but well calculated for wheat and oats. [9]

The landscape is famous for its natural beauty and over the years writers have consistently commented on its idyllic location. In 1908 DH Moutray Read informed his readers that 'it is not land to be hurried through, this vale of Itchen'.[10]

THE 1803 GLEBE TERRIER

With a new incoming rector, the Bishop of Winchester ordered the compilation of a new glebe terrier which would list the customary property, land and tithes that were attached to the living. Such a document was drawn up by the rector and churchwardens and usually verified by a senior parishioner before it was sent to the Bishop's registry. A glebe terrier was important as a means of reasserting the rights of the incumbent, thus avoiding any argument about the assets of the benefice.

'A Terrier of the Glebe Lands and Tythes belonging to the Rectory of Itchen Abbotts; also of the lands belonging to the Rural Prebendary in the same Parish taken in the Year 1803'[11] has survived and provides an excellent insight into the assets of the living. In addition to the land belonging to the parish, the terrier set out the living accommodation provided for the rector, which was described as follows:

> A Mansion House with Barns, Stables and Dove House, Orchards and Gardens ... converted to pleasure grounds estimated at an acre according to the place, taken by the Rev Dr John Burton, formerly Rector, who also provided a writ ad quo dominum to turn a common footpath leading down the court and Garden across Dell's Close.[12]

The rector was also the owner of the tithes, whereby landowners and tenant farmers had to give the equivalent of one-tenth of their annual produce to the incumbent. The terrier recorded that the 'Parsonage is endowed with all manner of Tithes- Corn, Hay, Wool, Wool and Lamb, whiting of Cows, Calves, Piggs, Eggs, Hops, Mills, Colts, Apples, Pears and other fruits whatsoever'.[13]

The glebe terrier of 1803 stated that land belonging to the church consisted of:

> Four little meadows ... [a] parcel called cloak mead ... [two] parcel[s] called Burley Brook ... [and] Chalk Mead. ... Also a small arable field, about an acre ... [and] a field called Priestlands, 18 acres more or less. [Also] parcels of land called 12 acres more or less ... [and a field called] ... Platt 15 acres more or less.

> The Rural Prebendary consists [of] ... A small field called Prebend Barn Close, 3 quarters of an acre ... a field called Eight Acres ... [and] a field called Prebend Down 10 acres more or less.[14]

William Marsh, who had lived in the parish for 50 years, verified the terrier as being 'correct'. It is not known whether Wright received his tithes in kind or money (or both) and there is no record of an annual celebratory 'tithe supper' being provided by the rector for the farmers as happened in some parishes. However, there did not appear to be any contentious issues and the rights of the incumbent appeared to be firmly established as customary lore within the parish.

ROBERT WRIGHT, THE PLURALIST

Hampshire parishes

On 7 August 1813, Robert Wright was inducted by the Bishop of Winchester to be the prebend of Itchen Abbas, in addition to his status as rector. This allowed him the privileges of a prebendal stall in Winchester Cathedral, prebendal land in Itchen Abbas and a prebendal income or pension.[15]

Wright proceeded to become a pluralist, a practice that was common in the Church of England at the time. From 1817 he held, as well as Itchen Abbas, the living of nearby Ovington:

> A dispensation has been granted to the Rev R Wright, Domestic Chaplain to the Most Noble the Marquis of Buckingham, to hold the living of Ovington, with Itchen Abbas, in this county-Patron, the Bishop of Winchester.[16]

Jessie Corrie states that Wright never resided in the rectory at Ovington.[17] Perhaps this was the case on a permanent basis, but he and wife, Elizabeth, were enumerated as staying there on census night, Sunday 6 June, in 1841.[18]

Wright also simultaneously held Southwick and Boarhunt, two parishes to the east of Wickham. This was regarded as acceptable because the four livings were in contiguous pairs (although separated by 30 miles). Jessie Corrie records that the Wrights spent time at Southwick in the winter months and rented a large house called The Oaks because the parsonage was deemed too small to accommodate the full household.[19] She describes how the journey from Itchen Abbas to Southwick was undertaken in the family barouche:

> Great-grandpapa [Robert Wright] sat upon the box and drove his pair of trusty cobs. I say 'drove', but to be strictly truthful, the reins generally hung over the old gentleman's arms, and his eyes would be fixed upon a book; or else, when talking to the occupants of the carriage, he would turn round and sit with his feet dangling over the wheel.[20]

Boarhunt is two miles south of Southwick and Wright liked to walk between the two villages. They were donative livings under the 'peculiar jurisdiction' of Thomas Thistlewayte, the lord of the manor of

Southwick.[21] This meant Thistlewayte had the right to appoint a clergyman to the parishes without a licence from the Bishop of Winchester, who had no episcopal power in such livings. The salary was 'arbitrary' and decided by the lord of the manor, who was also the tithe owner.[22] There is, regrettably, no record of the amount that Wright received for his work at Southwick and Boarhunt.

Wright had a very good, informal relationship with Thistlewayte. In 1827 Thistlewayte was having problems with a Mr Swann who was opposing the closure of a footpath and road in the parish. Swann had even attended the Quarter Sessions in Winchester to lodge a complaint, but Wright, as chairman of the Footpaths Committee, told him that no injury had been caused to the public and he dismissed the case. Wright wrote to Thistlewayte and asked:

> Why my dear fellow, do you not get two magistrates to certify to the Sessions that the roads in question are useless and unnecessary and have been legally shut up? I shall be most happy to lend you my assistance. I would never be beaten from my purpose by such a Ragamuffin.[23]

In a postscript, Wright chides Thistlewayte for not telling him that his daughter was expecting a child. He indignantly complains that he was told the news when he met one of Thistlewayte's servants in Winchester. However, he warmly congratulates the family and tells Thistlewayte that if he is ever in need of company he is welcome to visit 'one of the most impudent scamps in the county of Hants!'[24] The letter is special because it is one of the very few pieces of evidence to illustrate that Wright had a lively sense of humour.

For his part, according to Corrie, Thistlewayte used to hand Wright pieces of paper during church services to remind the forgetful rector of the time they were dining.[25] Furthermore, Wright was gifted the abbot's sofa and chair from Southwick Priory which had been dissolved by Henry VIII in 1539.

The neglected parish of Steeple Barton in Oxfordshire

Robert Wright's fifth parish actually brought him into disrepute. On 5 November 1808 the *Oxford University and City Herald* reported that:

The Rev Robert Wright BA is instituted by the Bishop of Oxford to the vicarage of Steeple Barton, in the county, on the presentation of William and Mary Mister.[26]

The Wright family was related to the Mister family by marriage. William and Mary Mister were joint patrons of Steeple Barton together with the Duke of Marlborough and Henry Hall (lord of the manor) and Wright obtaining this living was a good example of the patronage system at work.[27] Those who had the right connections had a big advantage over other individuals when looking for a parish to serve. Wright held the parish until his death in 1850 but allegedly visited Steeple Barton just once to read himself in! The parish provided approximately £100 per annum, tithes and 75 acres of glebe, and qualified Wright for the vote in the county of Oxfordshire. He employed non-resident curates on a salary as low as £40-£50 a year. There was often no service on a Sunday and the parishioners felt abandoned and frustrated.[28]

In 1837 Robert Wright was the subject of a letter written to the *Oxford Chronicle and Reading Gazette* by an anonymous correspondent with the pen name of 'Mr Timothy Homespun'. During the general election of that year, three Tory candidates were returned for the three Oxfordshire seats. These three Tory candidates were anti any form of free trade, anti-Catholic and anti any kind of non-conformity. These were views held by Robert Wright, an ultra-Tory, who was against any sort of change in the existing order. 'Homespun' states that he had examined the votes and found that the Reverend Robert Wright had posted from Southampton, 'to record his vote'. He continued sarcastically:

This Minister of a reformed religion [Wright] holds the living of Barton Steeple ... and the Parish Clerk, who has been in office 20 years, has never yet seen his Rector's face.[29]

In addition, Wright had made a declaration when he was presented to the parish in 1808 in which he promised the parishioners that he was fully committed to his cure. 'Homespun' ends his letter with some harsh words:

Such promises Mr Wright and many other non-residents made, and their fulfilment of them has been to absent themselves entirely from their cures during twenty years, having service performed once a week by a Curate, also non-resident, which performance they appear to think a tenure by which they hold their livings.[30]

Wright had totally ignored the cure and needs of 600 people and had used his vote in Oxfordshire county elections to further his own political views.[31]

In 1848 Wright received a letter from an exasperated Samuel Wilberforce, the Bishop of Oxford, which contained a rather belated rebuke:

To the Rev R Wright

61 Eaton Place, April 5 1848

Rev & Dear Sir,

The state of your Parish of Steeple Barton has been brought strongly before me by some of the most important of its inhabitants; & I feel bound to call on you to provide for it a Resident Curate with full double duty in the Church.

I am anxious that no time should be lost in making this arrangement.

I am, Rev. and Dear Sir, Very truly yours,

S. Oxon.[32]

Wilberforce's letter was disregarded by Wright and had no effect whatsoever. The Bishop sent two more letters calling for Wright to appoint a resident curate, but again there was no response. It is hard to avoid the conclusion that Wright was used to doing things his own way and immune to any sort of criticism, even if it came from someone in authority such as the esteemed Bishop of Oxford.

By the time Wright died on 26 March 1850, the value of the parish had risen to £150 per year as a result of the tithes being commuted, but the glebe house was in a state of disrepair and uninhabitable. The church building itself had also been neglected. Nevertheless, a group of 27 parishioners petitioned the Duke of Marlborough to present the Reverend Robert Wynne (1823–1881), the grandson of Wright, to be the next incumbent. Wynne had served some time as the parish curate and the petition described him as 'zealous, active and a talented Clergyman'.[33]

The Duke of Marlborough took no notice of the petition, and on 22 September 1850 the Reverend Arthur Hercules Packenham, MA was inducted into the church of Steeple Barton, probably much to the relief of many local people.[34] Repair work was carried out on the church and 'congregations increased somewhat, [but they] were still unsatisfactory in 1854'.[35] The 1851 Ecclesiastical Census of Great Britain, enumerated on Sunday 30 March 1851, illustrated the poor state of the parish, which had resulted from the neglect it suffered during the period that Robert Wright held the living as the absentee incumbent. Ninety-one persons were recorded as attending morning worship, but they had to be accommodated in the chancel as the rest of the church building was unsafe. Evening services had to be held in the church of neighbouring Wescott Barton, with 136 people attending. The rector of Wescott Barton even included a note with his census return explaining it was impossible to give an average attendance for this parish during the previous year because people from Steeple Barton had been allowed to attend services such was the state of dilapidation of their own church. Furthermore, the Primitive Methodist Chapel in Wescott Barton appeared to be enjoying more popularity, with Henry Brook, the minister, quoting the average attendance as 130 at the morning service and 136 in the evening.[36] It may have been that some people had changed their allegiance from the Anglican Church to non-conformity.

If Steeple Barton was typical of a parish that had an absentee incumbent over a period of 42 years then it is small wonder that pluralism was seen as a serious abuse by those who wished to reform the Anglican Church.

CONDUCTING CHURCH SERVICES AND CEREMONIES

There is no written evidence of how Wright organised his church services or how often he administered Holy Communion. We do know, however, that he failed to provide the double duty (two church services each Sunday) that was demanded by the parishioners of Steeple Barton, leaving many exasperated and incensed. Similarly, we do not know the style of Wright's preaching, but it was more than likely to have included the themes of discipline, obedience and deference.

The only sources that have survived are the various baptism, marriage and burial registers from his four Hampshire parishes, which suggest that he carried out these ceremonies (sometimes called 'surplice duties') regularly up to 1840.[37] After this date he was inactive at Southwick and Boarhunt, delegating ceremonies to curates and locums. Using the registers, Robert Wright officiated at 796 ceremonies during his long career, assisted mainly by his curate son, RJW Wright *[see Table 2]*.

	RW	RJWW	Locums	Not Known	Totals
1801-1810	25	0	4	0	29
1811-1820	115	0	24	0	139
1821-1830	191	62	24	0	277
1831-1840	310	125	58	12	505
1841-1850	155	1	9	0	165
Totals	796 (71.39%)	188 (16.86%)	119 (10.67%)	12 (1.08%)	1115 (100%)

Table 2: *Officiating clergy at baptisms, marriages and burials in the parishes of Itchen Abbas, Ovington, Southwick and Boarhunt, 1801–1850 (Source: HRO Parish Registers).*

The registers give the impression that on occasion Wright took ceremonies in both Itchen Abbas and Southwick on the same day. This could just have been possible if the first event was in the early morning in one parish and the second in the evening. The journey was possible in that time using turnpike roads for the whole distance, probably travelling in the family barouche. However, a word of caution should be heeded as Wright was a poor record keeper. His method for filling in the registers was to keep a rough list of ceremonies on scraps of paper and then copy them up when he had time. There is evidence to prove that he often forgot! For example, there is an entry in the Itchen Abbas baptism register made by William Webb Spicer in 1851 informing the reader that 'the late rector, the Reverend Robert Wright' had omitted 16 names. It is very probable that Spicer had found the information on scraps of paper which had been left inside the cover of the register to be recorded at a later date. Spicer dutifully wrote the missing baptisms, dating from 1831 to 1849, into the register.

The various registers of the four parishes also show that Robert Wright recorded ceremonies that had been performed by his son and vice versa. In addition, analysis of the registers is made difficult by poor presentation and illegible entries. Consequently, the statistics in *Table 2* can only provide an impression of Robert Wright's clerical activity.

ITCHEN ABBAS AND THE WARS AGAINST FRANCE, 1793–1815

The wars against France were an issue in the upper Itchen Valley. Up to 300 French prisoners of war were held at Alresford and Bishops Waltham, and with the area being so close to Portsmouth, there was always the possibility of invasion, especially before the defeat of the French fleet at Trafalgar in October 1805.[38] Measures to be adopted in the event of an invasion were published by the government and Wright would have been expected to keep his parishioners informed, both from the pulpit and, from 1808, in his role as a magistrate. The tension was demonstrated by the shocking murder of an exiled French priest who had been taking the air at Oram's Arbor in Winchester.[39] Furthermore, in 1812 two Alresford men, John Goulding and John Hilson, were committed to the Assizes charged with assisting French prisoners to make good their escape back to France.[40]

After the British and Prussian victory at Waterloo on 18 June 1815 the clergy in the Winchester diocese received a letter from the Bishop requesting them to read a message from George III urging people to contribute to a fund to support the families of the injured and dead.[41] Robert Wright responded to this request and a collection was organised in Itchen Abbas. On Monday 25 September 1815 the *Hampshire Chronicle* reported: 'The following sums have been collected for the … relief of the sufferers at the battle of Waterloo- Itchin Stoke, £3-0s-0d [and] Itchin Abbas, £5-9s-6d per Rev R Wright'.[42]

The war years from 1793–1815 had brought unprecedented prosperity for landowners and farmers. In 1812 wheat was selling for a record price of £6-6s-6d per quarter and the high cereal prices encouraged the widespread enclosure of land in the south and east of England. In Itchen Abbas more land was brought under the plough with the enclosure of the common between 1811 and 1814. These were boom years for the farmers, but not for the labourers, who discovered that their wages did not keep pace with the rising prices.

At the end of the French Wars, however, there was widespread distress for both the farmers and the labourers. About 250,000 servicemen returned home and flooded the labour market, but there was little work available. The government attempted to help the farmers by reintroducing the Corn Laws in 1815, which banned the import of foreign grain until the domestic price reached £4 per quarter. This had the effect of keeping the price of bread artificially high and added to the distress of the labourers, who applied for parish poor relief in high numbers. Farmers found it more difficult to meet their tithe payments to the clergy, which would have affected Robert Wright. As a farmer himself, therefore, Wright would have suffered from the lower grain prices after 1815 and may have experienced some resentment from the local farmers who were still expected to pay him one-tenth of their produce each year. Apart from parish relief, the labourers were not given any help and many found it almost impossible to feed their families.

There is no record of living conditions in Itchen Abbas and the level of distress. The population of the parish increased from 192 souls in 1811 to 254 in 1821, a rise of 32 per cent. It is not known whether this was caused by returning soldiers or, possibly, an influx of itinerant travellers. There would have been work in the parish between 1811 and 1814 to construct roads and fences as part of the enclosure of Itchen Abbas common, but this was only a temporary phenomenon. Judging from later comments made by Robert Wright about the increasing cost of poor relief in the parish, it can only be assumed that there was a good deal of hardship for the labourers in the locality. Wright's feelings towards the labourers were ambivalent but he displayed solid support for the farmers in their efforts to survive their own distress.

BEATING THE BOUNDS OF ITCHEN ABBAS, 1826

Much of the spiritual and pastoral work in Itchen Abbas was being carried out by Wright's son, the Reverend Robert John William Wright (1803–1887), who had become the curate of Itchen Abbas in 1826 and was also employed as a locum in his father's three other Hampshire parishes.[43] RJW Wright was paid a salary of £300 per year, which was extremely generous. As a general rule of thumb, in parishes worth over £400 per year, such as Itchen Abbas, a curate could expect to earn about one-fifth of this amount.[44]

RJW Wright was made to earn his salary by his father. Between 7 and 9 November 1826 RJW Wright organised a three-day perambulation of the boundaries of Itchen Abbas, aided by Arthur Octavius Baker, steward to the first Duke of Buckingham and Chandos (owner of Avington Park, the manor of Itchen Abbas and land in Easton), and several other locals who had knowledge of the customs and geography of the parish.[45] This exercise was usually undertaken at Rogation in late April/early May, so this particular perambulation in Itchen Abbas was carried out very late in the year. Before the production of printed maps, beating the bounds was the traditional method – dating back to Anglo-Saxon times – for confirming the parish boundaries. RJW Wright's detailed account of the route taken included an explanation of how potential disputes were solved:

> At many doubtful and disputed places temporary sticks were placed and Mr Baker, the Steward of the said Manor, agreed that in those places strong oak piles should be put down by the Duke of Buckingham to make a lasting and clear boundary.[46]

Reaffirming the parish boundary was important in that it helped to establish the value of the tithes and prevent encroachment from neighbouring parishes. RJW Wright, at the age of 23, would have been dependent upon the opinions of the senior members of the perambulation party, who had knowledge of the traditions and customs of the parish. No doubt Robert Wright was busy with his work as a JP but delegating the perambulation to his son suggests a degree of trust that the job would be conscientiously completed.

ATTEMPTS TO IMPROVE EDUCATION IN ITCHEN ABBAS

When Robert Wright took up his post in Itchen Abbas, the state played no part in educating the nation's poor; it was not seen as a priority and some in authority thought that schooling the masses could lead to 'revolution'. Elementary schools, therefore, had to be provided by individual benefactors and voluntary groups; inevitably, they were few in number and unevenly distributed.[47] Often there were no schools in a district, particularly for educating the poor. In 1818 a Select Committee of the House of Commons was established to inquire into the provision of education for children nationwide. Questionnaires were distributed to parishes and the local incumbent usually answered them. Robert Wright duly made a return in which he stated that the parish had no educational endowments and he painted an educationally bleak scenario when he wrote:

> All the poor children of this parish and those of Ovington and [Itchen] Stoke, amounting altogether to 60, are instructed at the rector's expense. The poor, of themselves, have no sufficient means of education, but are desirous of possessing them.[48]

He continued to explain that the nearby parishes of Avington and Easton were more fortunate in that they had schoolrooms supported by Lady Anna Eliza Brydges. Wright, however, appeared to be reluctant to get fully involved in providing schooling for the poor and the amount of money he expended on education was minimal. Despite this, it is likely he would have agreed with the Reverend Frederick Iremonger of Wherwell, the secretary of the Hampshire Society for the Education of the Poor, who wrote in 1813:

> The experience of the last twenty years has spoken to us in a language which cannot be resisted; it has proclaimed the awful truth that without the sound principles of Religion in the mass of the people, there can be no stability to government, no security for any of the comforts of social life ... There must be religious education for fear of revolution ... [There must be] a strict attention to sound religious principles by which the poor may be trained up in early life to know their duty, to know their proper place in society, to honour and respect those who are placed over them; and thus, as far as possible, an opportunity may be afforded to the diligent and active to obtain the rewards of good conduct, by increased comfort, and perhaps advancement in life, while, at the same time, the several orders, degrees, and distinctions in society are preserved.[49]

In 1833 a second return was sent to Parliament reporting an improvement in the situation in Itchen Abbas, in that it now possessed:

> One Day and Sunday School, containing 40 children of both sexes ... endowed with £365 per cent consols, and ... further, supported by voluntary contributions.[50]

The endowment referred to was that of Nathaniel Bailey, gentleman, who had died in August 1823. In his will, dated 5 June 1823, Bailey stated his legacy was to be 'received half yearly by the Minister and applied in teaching six poor boys and six poor girls belonging to the parish' and to employ 'a proper schoolmistress for that purpose'.[51] He also desired that Louisa Stanbrook (1792–1858) of Itchen Abbas should be appointed to this position immediately after his death. Louisa just happened to be his daughter, who was married to Job Stanbrook, an agricultural labourer, of Itchen Abbas.

In August 1833 Parliament voted the sum of £20,000 for the 'purpose of education'[52] to be used nationally 'to supply half the cost of building new schoolhouses'.[53] The money was to be equally shared by two church societies, namely the National Society for Promoting the Education of the Poor in the Principles of the Established Church Throughout England and Wales (formed in 1811) and the non-conformist British and Foreign Schools Society (formed in 1814).[54] The parish of Itchen Abbas had already been formally affiliated with the National Society in June 1832 on the application of the curate, RJW Wright, who consented to use the 'National System of teaching ... in the Liturgy and Catechism of the Established Church'.[55] RJW Wright first applied for a grant from the National Society in the same month, but it appears there was a breakdown in communication between the Archdeacon of Winchester, RJW Wright and the National Society, as the application had to be resubmitted in December 1833. In describing the reason a grant was needed for the parish, RJW Wright explained that 12 children were educated under the auspices of Bailey's charity but there was no schoolroom. The parish needed financial aid to provide education for up to 40 boys and girls in one room. A schoolteacher was to be paid £20 per annum (£10 from Bailey's charity and £10 from donations), but currently teaching took place in the main body of the church with the children sitting on stools and it was an unsatisfactory arrangement. The intention was to build a schoolroom using flint and thatch, sized 24 feet long by 14 feet wide and with a height of 8 feet, where the children would be instructed in 'learning the Catechism and Scriptures'.[56] RJW Wright had also previously stated that the schooling they received would teach them to 'understand their duty to God and their neighbour'.[57] The ground for the new school was to be donated on lease by the present mistress (Louisa Stanbrook) and the first Duke of Buckingham and Chandos. The entire cost of the new building and fittings would be £30, but the only way of meeting the expense was £15 promised by the rector and 'what may be granted through the National Society'.[58] In an addendum, RJW Wright put a further gloss on the planned acquisition of land:

> The ground upon which the Itchen School is to be built is now in the occupation of the Mistress of the School and is hers for her life. She would grant a Lease for that period and the Duke of

Buckingham would renew it for the purpose of the school as it would revert to him.[59]

Although the application was signed 'R.J.W. Wright, Curate', RJW must have had detailed discussions with his father, Robert Wright, about the case they should put forward to the National Society. In the second application, however, just £30 of aid was requested compared with £40 in the original. A weakness in the application was the absence of an accurate plan and it also lacked a professional estimate from a local builder to provide a more realistic costing.

RJW Wright's bid for a grant does not appear to have been successful. The application form was not endorsed with the amount of aid granted by the National Society which was the usual procedure.[60] *White's Trade Directory* for 1859, however, states that a schoolroom was built in 1834 but such a building is not shown on the 1839 tithe map for Itchen Abbas.[61] A room may have been built on the side of Job and Louisa Stanbrook's cottage, plot 186 on the tithe map. This same plot has the annotation 'Endowed School' on the large-scale (25-inch) Ordnance Survey map of 1870 *[Figure 4]*.

Despite RJW Wright's efforts, it was not surprising his bid for aid failed, as the National Society had only £10,000 at its disposal for the whole country, forcing it to prioritise. According to the historian HC Barnard:

> 'Preference was given to applications from larger cities and towns, and for schools with accommodation for not less than 400 pupils … the poorer, and therefore more necessitous, country districts were neglected'.[62]

A similar application to the National Society was submitted at the same time by the Wrights for grant aid towards a new schoolroom on a plot of land near the rectory in Ovington. The application, however, lacked clarity and was also unsuccessful.

RJW Wright, however, did manage to secure a more modest sum of money from the localised Hampshire Society for the Education of the Infant Poor which had limited funds raised from subscriptions and donations. A meeting of the Society in March 1834 allowed £15 to the schools at Itchen Abbas and Ovington. RJW Wright most probably used a proportion of this money to help finance the building of a new schoolroom at Itchen Abbas.

In 1839 plot 186 was a cottage occupied by Job Stanbrook. No endowed school is marked on the tithe Map.

In 1848 the plots marked 178, 183, 185, 186 and 187 on this map and the tithe map (above) were purchased by Lord Ashburton's estate from the second Duke of Buckingham and Chandos. No endowed school is marked on the 1848 map.

The 1870 Ordnance Survey Map (25 inches to 1 mile) shows the endowed school clearly marked on the site of plot 186. In 1875 this school was replaced by the Itchen Abbas Board School, which was built on a site to the north of The Plough Inn.

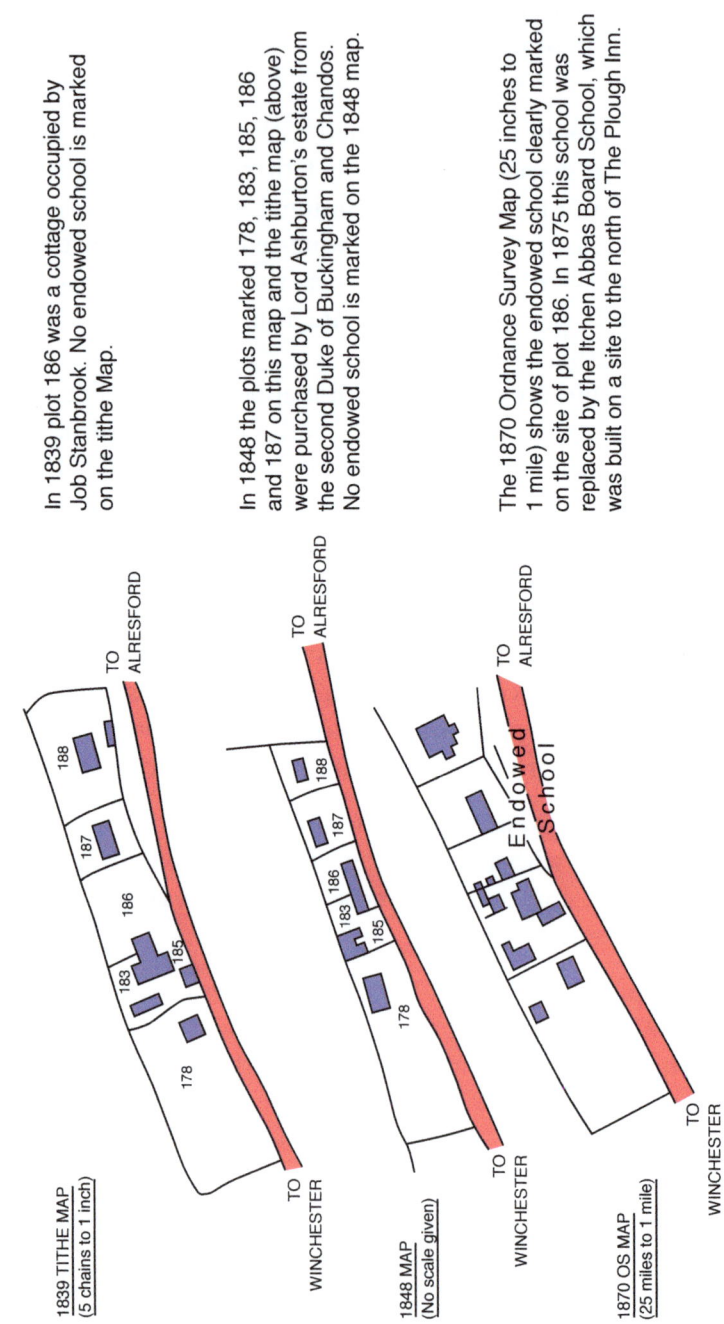

Figure 4: *The site of RJW Wright's endowed school.*

In 1836 RJW Wright left his post as curate and Robert Wright made no further attempts to advance the cause of education in the locality. Unlike the Reverend Samuel Best of Abbotts Ann, near Andover, Robert Wright could not be considered a visionary when it came to educating the poor. The Elementary Education Act of 1870 confirmed that the education in Itchen Abbas remained inadequate. The terms of the act forced the parish vestry, reluctantly, to form a School Board to build a new school financed out of the rates.[63]

BUILDING A NEW GALLERY IN ST JOHN THE BAPTIST'S CHURCH

From the 1830s there was pressure from groups within the Church of England to regain prestige as a result of its reputation being damaged by pluralism, absenteeism and apathy among some of the clergy. Not enough new churches had been built to keep pace with the increasing population and this, together with the practice of pew-renting, had led some in the lower classes to turn their backs on the Anglican Church.[64] There was also the additional threat of dissenters, such as the Methodists, taking worshippers away. There was little open dissent to the Anglican Church in Itchen Abbas, but the church building itself was in a state of decay and the Wrights saw improving the accommodation as desirable. In the aftermath of the 1830 agricultural riots Robert Wright needed to reassert his authority in the parish and one way of achieving this would be to improve church attendance. This would allow him to promulgate the message that the labourers needed to accept their place in society and be obedient if they wished to have the help of the parish poor fund when they fell on hard times.

On 15 June 1832 RJW Wright applied to the Incorporated Society for Promoting the Enlargement, Building and Repairing of Churches and Chapels, established in 1818, for a grant to finance the building of a new gallery at the west end of the church. He explained that the church had 100 sittings of which only 40 were free, thus revealing a clearly defined social hierarchy in the village:

> The body of the church contains Pews for the different Houses and
> … everyone above the rank of a Cottage has its seat. The lower end
> of the Church is set apart below the Pews for free sittings for poor
> women and in general they are filled by them or their children.

There are no sittings for the labouring poor men except some forms in a confined part of the chancel where they cannot well hear and are just out of sight of the Minister. There is no room in this place for half the men who usually attend church if they were to attend altogether ... inattention in the younger men receives no check, [and] may in some way be encouraged by the secluded position of the seats ... I see no possible remedy ... but in building a Gallery for which the nature of the lower end of the Church is well adapted which will cost £30. Having no means to provide this sum I am inclined to appeal to the Society for their assistance.[65]

The application form was completed by RJW Wright but signed by his father. Unwittingly, perhaps, the Wrights had revealed that relationships with the lower orders and the 'paupermen' were strained, and even if they did attend church, they did not listen to the words that came from the pulpit. It would be interesting to know how frequently the Wrights paid visits to the poor in their homes but there is no way of finding this out. There may have been this sort of contact in the event of a death or illness in a family; otherwise the poor were expected to attend church regularly to be considered as deserving of support. In one instance, Wright referred to a parishioner as an 'idle frequenter of beershops who never attended his church',[66] which provides further evidence that the rector did not relate to the needs of the labouring poor in Itchen Abbas.

The application to support the new church gallery had to be scrutinised and approved by the Archdeacon of Winchester, Charles Hoare, who was resident at Farnham Castle in Surrey. As with the application for aid to the National Society, there then seems to have been some misunderstanding and the application form went missing. The matter lay dormant and unattended for 16 months before any action followed. On 30 October 1833 RJW Wright was obliged to write again to the Incorporated Society:

Itchin Abbas
Hants
Dear Sir

Some months ago I made an application to the Incorporated Society for enlarging Churches to contribute some aid towards giving accommoda-

*tion to our poor Parishioners. You were kind enough to forward me the
printed Forms which I filled up and made out a plan … and forwarded
them altogether to the archdeacon. Owing to a slight mistake in the
number of sittings, the forms were returned to be rectified and, being sent
again to the archdeacon, were by some means mislaid or lost. May I beg
the favour of some more forms which I will … submit in due order.*

I am dear sir
Yours truly
R J W Wright.[67]

It looks as if the application had been lost in the Archdeacon's office
but RJW Wright had not followed it up and thus the long delay. More
forms were sent to Itchen Abbas, and were completed and resubmitted on
15 November 1833. The new forms required more details about the parish
and thus provide some interesting additional information. It stated the
church was built in about 1000AD and its dimensions were 60 feet long, 20
feet wide and 30 feet high with a tower. In order for it to accommodate a
congregation of 100 it must have been a squeeze, not to mention the damp,
the draughty windows and the loose floor tiles that needed to be repaired
regularly.

RJW Wright explained that some new pews were erected in part of the
church in 1830 at a cost of £100 and there was no appetite in the parish
to make large voluntary contributions towards financing a new gallery.
They had, however, managed to get the Duke of Buckingham and Chandos
to provide the timber (which saved an estimated £4) and the rector was
willing to provide £5 to match the £5 collected from the parishioners.
James Bignell, a local carpenter, had been invited to draw up plans and
provide a quotation for building the gallery. He estimated £30 to complete
the work, but added a further £5 when he was told that the Incorporated
Society required kneeling ledges to be built on to the seats. An exasperated
RJW Wright explained:

It has been with great difficulty that the Parish have been
persuaded to contribute but even £5 and we cannot hope for any
further assistance from them … The only further exertions that
can be made are to apply to the Society for assistance.[68]

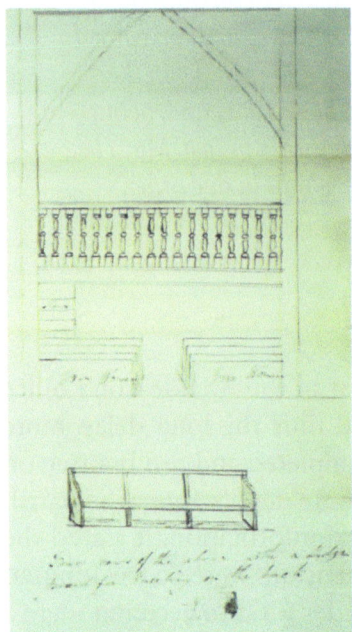

Plate 5: *Bignell's new gallery, built in 1834 (Source: Lambeth Palace Library, ICBS 1456).*

This second application was forwarded to the Archdeacon for checking and proved to be successful. On 18 September 1834 RJW Wright wrote to the Incorporated Society, on behalf of his father, and said that Bignell had completed the gallery and forty new free sittings in four rows had been added to the church. *[Plate 5]*

The church now had 140 sittings, of which 80 were free and 60 appropriated. An inscription recognising the role of the Incorporated Society was erected in the church and a certificate sent to London stating that the work had been carried out 'according to the Plan and declarations submitted to the Incorporated Society'. The certificate contained the signatures of James Bignell (builder), Andrew Twitchen (churchwarden), John Dagwell (churchwarden), William Rogers (farmer) and RJW Wright (officiating minister).[69]

It appears that the whole cost of £35 was paid by the Incorporated Society, as the churchwardens' account book shows that on 25 August 1835 the sum of £5 was paid to Mr Robert Wright towards the gallery. The rector had actually taken back the money he had previously donated! There was also an untruth in the second application: it was stated that the new pews built in 1830 for £100 had, in fact, cost just £34-9s -6d![70]

Despite this major improvement, the infrastructure of the church was in long-term decay and money was constantly being spent from the church rates on repairing the tower, tiling and leaking window casements. The path leading to the church was muddy, overgrown with nettles and needed attention on a regular basis, plus whitewash had to be applied frequently to the interior walls. An examination of the churchwardens' account book reveals a number of references to repairs that were required to keep the building functioning. Between May 1822 and March 1849 a total of

Plate 6: *Itchen Abbas Church during the time of Robert Wright, painted by Rachel Morse (after Jessie E Corrie and Isobel Sanderson).*

Plate 7: *The rebuilt church of St John the Baptist in Itchen Abbas today. It was consecrated on 30 May 1863 (Source: Author).*

£92-12s-5d was paid to local craftsmen to carry out repairs. Clearly, it was a battle of attrition for Robert Wright's churchwardens to keep the building in any sort of acceptable condition.[71] *[Plate 6]*

These measures, however, were mere 'fire-fighting' and it fell to the next rector, William Webb Spicer (1850–1874), to bring about the demolition of the decaying building and the erection of a new church. *[Plate 7]*

CHARITY AND PATERNALISM

A rural clergyman was expected to display a degree of charity and paternalism and there were times when Robert Wright obliged. He was capable of empathising with the plight of pauper lunatics and he sanctioned poor relief when he believed it was a deserving case. Any altruism, however, was tempered by the fact that he sometimes contributed to charity to further his own reputation or impress others. Paternalistic charity was something that the clergy could choose to exercise in particular cases rather than being a wider commitment to helping society in general. Only those who were deemed to be 'deserving' were likely to receive any aid from orthodox clergymen such as Robert Wright.

In some parishes the rector, aided by his wife, encouraged the poor to be thrifty and they established self-help clubs to provide, for example, clothing and fuel. There is no record of this occurring in Itchen Abbas until 1874, when Septimus Gillson became the rector.[72] In fact, Robert Wright's wife, Elizabeth, is mainly missing from the historical record except for references made to her by Jessie Corrie, who remembers her with great fondness: 'Great grandmamma was a wise and gentle old lady, and her life must have been a happy and busy one'.[73]

Mention of specific acts of ad hoc charity by Robert Wright can be located in the local newspapers. An early example was in February 1809, when the parish of Itchen Abbas gifted two guineas to the county hospital in Parchment Street, Winchester, with Robert Wright adding one guinea of his own.[74]

Wright supported attempts to establish a Hampshire Auxiliary Bible Society to provide the poor with bibles both domestically and abroad. The main mover of this initiative was Wright's neighbour at Avington House, the Marquis of Buckingham and Chandos, later the first duke.[75] Very quickly, affiliated bible societies were established countywide. The Duke of Wellington, Sir Thomas Baring and the Bishop of Winchester were influential in the movement for a number of years, but by the mid-1830s interest was dwindling and the local press no longer carried reports. Robert Wright's interest appeared to be limited, at least in terms of holding any office such as auditor, treasurer or secretary. He also played no active part in promoting the Education of the Infant Poor in the Principles of the Established Church. Even in his own parishes the matter of education was delegated to his curate son.

At this time there were numerous thatched cottages, which were susceptible to catching fire and in 1817 a number of homes were damaged when fire broke out in Kings Worthy. In such cases, in the absence of insurance for the properties, the locals usually rallied around to provide financial support to the victims. The fund for Kings Worthy reached £196-3s-6d before Sir Henry Rivers of Martyr Worthy donated £5-3s-0d but Robert Wright could only manage £1.[76]

Lord Palmerston of Broadlands was a benefactor to the town of Romsey where he helped to fund the opening of the first boys' National School in 1835. Interestingly, the *Hampshire Chronicle* advertised a sermon that was to be given, 'in Romsey Abbey on Sunday 30 September 1827 by the Reverend Robert Wright, prebend and rector of Itchen Abbas, in aid of the funds of Romsey National School'.[77] Perhaps Palmerston invited Wright to perform the sermon and, as it started at 10.30 a.m., one wonders if he stayed the previous Saturday night as a guest at Broadlands. Presumably, there was no payment for Robert Wright's time, but his contribution would have greatly raised his profile within the county.

Orphaned and bastard children and those from poor families were chargeable to the parish and they were expensive to provide for. One way of getting these unfortunate children off the poor rates was to pay a fee to willing employers to take them on as apprentices. Robert Wright was keen to support this practice and he was a member of the Charitable Society of Aliens, which raised money to fund the apprenticeship system. The society promoted itself as a body that was 'establishing the philanthropic principles of apprenticing out poor children'[78] and held fund raising events in Winchester. One such event was the annual 'feast' whereby, after divine service, the trustees and stewards and their friends attended a dinner at a local hostelry. Members of the local gentry, such as Sir Thomas Baring, the first Duke of Buckingham and Chandos and the Earl of Northesk, donated the food and drink, which included game, venison and wine. At one feast in 1828, the considerable sum of £153 was raised in annual subscriptions and donations. The feasts were also attended by hand picked boys, who had been apprenticed under the auspices of the society as part of a public relations exercise designed to show that they had benefitted from the experience. This may have been the case for some individuals, but others found themselves with hard masters who were only interested in getting cheap labour.[79] Robert Wright was an active steward of these events and delivered the sermon on at least one occasion. The wheel often turned full circle, however, when unhappy apprentices were brought before him as a magistrate charged with absconding, for which he usually imposed a punishment of one month's imprisonment with hard labour.

Robert Wright was a director and auditor of the Hampshire Friendly Society which held four meetings a year in Winchester. Friendly Societies usually catered for skilled workers who paid a weekly contribution into a fund in exchange for benefits in the event of unemployment or sickness. Magistrates often played a role in administering such societies, particularly those with accounting skills. It is difficult to ascertain how committed Wright was to the Hampshire Friendly Society, but in 1830 it appeared to be a thriving organisation with 1,100 members and a surplus of over £5,408 in its favour.[80]

On 11 March 1837 a serious fire broke out in neighbouring Itchen Stoke, destroying three cottages and making three families (including five children) homeless. According to the *Hampshire Advertiser*, an old woman had held a candle too close to the thatch in her washhouse, and although a fire engine was despatched from Avington House it arrived too late to save the cottages. The dwellings were the property of the Duke of Buckingham and Chandos and were located in a detached portion of the parish of Itchen Stoke, close to Hampage Wood. A local subscription was launched to help the unfortunate homeless and it was reported that the Reverend and Mrs Wright had made a 'handsome donation'.[81] As the amount was not specified, it is possible that the information was supplied to the newspaper with the purpose of portraying Robert Wright as a paternalistic friend of the lower classes.

During the 1830s the Temperance Movement gained momentum throughout England and Wales, and Hampshire was no exception.

Temperance societies were established in Gosport, Portsmouth, South-ampton, Alton, Romsey and Andover, possibly as a response to the increasing number of beershops. In 1836 a Church of England Temper-ance Society in Winchester was advocated by Archdeacon Hoare and RJW Wright lent his enthusiastic support. His father, too, would have approved of this initiative, given his strong opposition to the Beershop Act of 1830 and its perceived detrimental effect on good behaviour and encourage-ment of petty crime. On Wednesday 21 December 1836 RJW Wright gave a lecture to the Mechanics' Institute in which he extolled the benefits of being teetotal with the intention of preparing the ground for the establish-ment of a temperance society.[82]

By late 1838 the Temperance Society was functioning in Winchester, but one of its meetings in the Guildhall was marred by the violent behaviour of a number of people who gatecrashed the venue. In February 1839 RJW Wright made an application for the society to hold monthly meetings in the Guildhall, but he had to guarantee the good conduct of the members by 'signifying that the admission should in future be by means of tickets'.[83] The society survived this uncertain start and was still in existence in the 1880s.

PASTURES NEW FOR RJW WRIGHT

By 1835 RJW Wright may well have wanted a new challenge from working as a mere curate. An interesting post became available early in the year when the Reverend Thomas Fielder Woodham resigned as chaplain at the county gaol and bridewell in Winchester. Supported by his father, RJW Wright applied for the position and was elected to the post by the county bench on 5 January 1836. The new post meant moving away from Itchen Abbas and relocating to the city of Winchester. The salary was £300 per annum, the same as he received for acting as curate for his father. In the meantime, it had been agreed that RJW Wright was to inherit the advowson and prop-erty attached to it in Itchen Abbas when Robert Wright retired or passed away.[84] The long-term future looked secure for the hard-working curate, but his immediate future was away from Itchen Abbas. Robert Wright wrote an open testimonial to the authorities in which he was effusive about the strength of his son's application for the post:

It is impossible for anyone to be more diligent and faithful in infant and adult teaching in the parishes he has under his care. His first qualification is devoting his time almost exclusively to his duty with patience and perseverance, under many discouragements he has to contend with. His next is, in possessing, a faculty of appealing clearly, simply, and with some power, to the minds of those under his care. Having been almost entirely under my own roof for some years, he has had much experience in the various cases of crime that have afforded me ground for more commitments than almost any other Magistrate on the Bench: whereby he may be able to identify at once with criminals the origins and progress of those circumstances that have brought them to their unhappy condition; and having resided chiefly in a country parish, he has an advantage approaching such cases as chiefly fill our County Bridewell.[85]

The testimonial also revealed an intolerant attitude towards another Christian group, with Robert Wright declaring:

His [RJW Wright's] doctrine is highly spiritual, sound and free from the peculiarities which are commonly called Calvinistic: and I beg to observe, as no light recommendation, that he will not dismiss any Bridewell culprit from his care under any delusions of Antinomianism.[86]

This is an interesting comment as Robert Wright has been labelled a latitudinarian, broad-church clergyman, but his disparaging remark about Calvinism suggests that if it suited his motives he could be somewhat intolerant of other Christian viewpoints which differed from his own. Whether it was true of his son, however, is open to question, as his subsequent career suggested he was much more liberal and progressive than his father.

The loss of his curate brought about an increase in the parish workload for Robert Wright, as an analysis of the various parish registers illustrates *[see Table 3]*. In the period from June 1826 to May 1836, RJW Wright officiated at 43.3 per cent of the combined baptisms, marriages and burials in the four parishes of Itchen Abbas, Ovington, Southwick and Boarhunt, compared with 51.3 per cent performed by his father. However, in the period

1826-1836	I Abbas	Ovington	Southwick	Boarhunt	Totals
RW	74	22	63	72	231 (51.3%)
RJWW	43	43	80	29	195 (43.3)
Locums	6	9	5	3	23 (5.3%)
Not known	1	0	0	0	1(0.2%)
1836-1846	I Abbas	Ovington	Southwick	Boarhunt	Totals
RW	86	50	78	21	235 (78.9%)
RJWW	0	1	3	0	4 (1.3%)
Locums	21	18	8	12	59 (19.8%)
Not known	0	0	0	0	0 (0.0%)

Table 3: *Robert Wright's ministry with and without the assistance of RJW Wright as curate. The figures show the total number of baptisms, marriages and burials conducted. (Source: HRO Parish Registers).*

from June 1836 to December 1846, Robert Wright's workload increased to 78.9 per cent and only 1.3 per cent of the officiating was performed by his son (the remaining 19.8 per cent of ceremonies were covered by locums). Robert Wright, it appears, had much less time available to provide any regular pastoral care for the inhabitants of Ovington, Southwick and Boarhunt.

Five months after taking up his new post at the county gaol in Winchester, RJW Wright married Anna Maria Fell, the eldest daughter of the Reverend TC Fell of Sheepy in Leicestershire.[87] For the first time in his life he was to be living under his own roof and free to be 'his own man', but he was to find the role of prison chaplain demanding and demoralising. The chaplain's journal suggests that the post took its toll on a man who started out with optimism and, perhaps misplaced, idealism. He carried out his role fastidiously and tried hard to make improvements.

On 19 May 1840 RJW Wright tried to persuade the Duke of Wellington to present a petition to the House of Lords to abolish the convention of demanding that offenders should enter a plea of 'guilty' or 'not guilty' before being tried in a court of law.[88] RJW Wright claimed that the petition had the support of many influential legal people and Robert Peel himself had been approached to present the same petition to the House of Commons. Wellington, however, was unwilling to become involved and believed the proposed change in the law was not necessary and would fail to get much support. There the matter ended.

Between November 1840 and April 1841 RJW Wright tried to persuade the Duke of Wellington to support the formation of a Hampshire House of Refuge for prisoners who had completed their sentences.[89] The forward-thinking chaplain was concerned about the high rates of reoffending and wanted more done to rehabilitate offenders and reintegrate them back into society. He sent the Duke examples of good practice he had found in Exeter and Middlesex and suggested that a House of Refuge in Hampshire could be funded by subscription and inviting leading members of the gentry and clergy to contribute. RJW Wright proposed the Duke should be the patron and informed him that:

> Many criminals are discharged from prison, especially young females and others not hardened in crime, who, during their imprisonment, have made good resolutions to leave vagrant lives and dishonest practices … But being too frequently at a long distance from home and discharged from prison without any means of returning, they are driven either to commit acts of vagrancy, by begging, or thrown upon their former sinful practices for subsistence.[90]

The idea was radical and enlightened and proved too much for the Duke of Wellington to absorb. He wrote to RJW Wright on 8 April 1841, informing him that he considered it 'necessary that success should be certain or probable' but he felt that 'failure was certain'.[91]

Perhaps the lack of progress on these two issues was a cause of disillusionment with RJW Wright's work as chaplain, because a report in the local press on 12 November 1842 stated that he was about to be presented by John Fleming for the living of Arreton on the Isle of Wight and that 'Mr. Wright, in consequence, intends to resign the county chaplaincy'.[92] Unfortunately as it turned out for RJW Wright, this move did not materialise and his career as prison chaplain was to end dramatically in 1853 when he was forced to resign.

THE TITHE COMMUTATION ACT OF 1836 AND ITS IMPACT ON ITCHEN ABBAS

Tithes had been a constant cause of friction between the clergy and farmers for many years. The Tithe Commutation Act for England and Wales, passed in August 1836, introduced a rent charge based on the average price of grain over a period of the previous seven years. HME Holt informs us that the act spelt the end of an outdated tithing system which had become the cause of much rural unrest and established a Tithe Commission in London to supervise the business of commutation.[93]

George Parrott, steward to the first Duke of Buckingham and Chandos,[94] called a meeting to take place in Itchen Abbas Church on 3 September 1838 for the purpose of 'making an agreement for the General Commutation of tithes within the limits [of Itchen Abbas]'.[95] The meeting was adjourned presumably because the discussions were lengthy, and a second meeting was held at Avington House on 7 September when a successful conclusion was reached. Subsequently, the valuer, Thomas Beards of Avington, confirmed the details of what had been agreed and sent a written report to London. After this, a survey was made of the parish and a large-scale map (66 yards to 1 inch) drawn up, with a schedule that detailed the landowners, occupants, acreage, land use and the amount payable in annual rent charge.[96] The Itchen Abbas map, dated 2 February 1839, has the following caption:

> We the undersigned Tithe Commissioners for England and Wales do hereby certify this to be a copy of the Map or Plan referred to in the Apportionment of the Rent charge in lieu of Tithes in the Parish of Itchen Abbas in County of Southampton. As witnessed our hands; W[illia]m Blamire, R[ichar]d Jones.[97]

The 1839 tithe map for Itchen Abbas is a valuable source that provides a wealth of evidence about the parish. It confirms Robert Wright as a man of relative substance within the locality being the second largest landowner in the parish after the first Duke of Buckingham and Chandos (see Table 4). The Duke owned almost 2,000 acres compared with Wright's 84 acres, 1 rood and 27 perches of land, most of which was rented out to William Rogers, who grew arable crops on 56 acres. The rectory house and grounds were leased to William Campion, a gentleman of independent means.

Wright himself rented Dell's Close, situated behind Itchen Cottage, his residence, from the Duke of Buckingham and Chandos. By this time, Wright had managed to purchase the freehold of Itchen Cottage and had thus again enhanced the size of his holdings in the parish. In all there were 2,099 acres 3 roods and 35 perches of land within the parish that were subject to tithes, of which 1,629 acres and 3 roods were used to grow arable crops, 139 acres and 39 perches were used as meadow or pasture, and 263 acres and 17 perches were woodland. The total amount of rent charged in lieu of tithes payable to the tithe owner, Robert Wright, was £468 per annum.[98] *[Table 4]*

Landowner	Occupier	Plot	Name	Cultivation	Quantity (ARP)
Buckingham & Chandos Duke of	Wright Robert Rev	193	Dell Close	Arable	05.03.12
Wright Robert Rev	Himself	190	Itchen Cottage		00.01.21
Wright Robert Rev	Himself	191	Garden		00.02.12
Wright Robert Rev	Himself	192	Way to the Stables		00.02.00
Wright Robert Rev	Campion Wm Esq	201	Lawn	Pasture	04.01.31
Wright Robert Rev	Campion Wm Esq	202	Grove		01.00.30
Wright Robert Rev	Campion Wm Esq	222	Cottage&Walled Garden		00.02.36
Wright Robert Rev (Glebe)	Rogers William	37	Prebend Down	Arable	18.03.00
Wright Robert Rev (Glebe)	Rogers William	70	Barton	Arable	13.02.00
Wright Robert Rev (Glebe)	Rogers William	69	Barton	Arable	13.00.29
Wright Robert Rev (Glebe)	Rogers William	76	Priestlands	Arable	08.00.25
Wright Robert Rev (Glebe)	Rogers William	77	Priestlands	Arable	09.02.24
Wright Robert Rev (Glebe)	Rogers William	230	Ozier Bed Plat	Pasture	00.02.19
Wright Robert Rev (Glebe)	Rogers William	225	Ozier Bed		00.01.39
Wright Robert Rev (Glebe)	Rogers William	200	Peat Bed		00.01.09
Wright Robert Rev (Glebe)	Rogers William	94	Doctors EightAcres	Arable	08.00.28
Wright Robert Rev (Glebe)	Holmes Charles	195	Farthings Cottage		00.01.13
Wright Robert Rev (Glebe)	Campion Wm Esq	203	Rectory House&Premises		01.02.05
Wright Robert Rev (Glebe)	Garrett James	206	Paddock	Pasture	01.01.07
Wright Robert Rev (Glebe)	Garrett James	207	House&Garden		00.01.04
Wright Robert Rev (Glebe)		156	Church&Churchyard		00.01.15

Key

A=Acres; R=Roods; P=Perches   40 Perches = 1 Rood;   4 Roods = 1 Acre

Table 4: *Details of land in Itchen Abbas relating to Robert Wright (Source: HRO Itchen Abbas tithe schedule, 1839).*

On Monday 11 July 1842 a notice was published in the *Hampshire Chronicle* advertising a meeting to commute the tithes in Ovington. The notice was signed by a Henry Howard, who described himself as 'the duly authorised agent of the titheowner, the Reverend Robert Wright'.[99] Why it had taken this long to put the act into effect in Ovington is unknown. An assistant tithe commissioner, William Wakefield Atree, was placed in charge of hearing the evidence over a series of meetings. Most of the

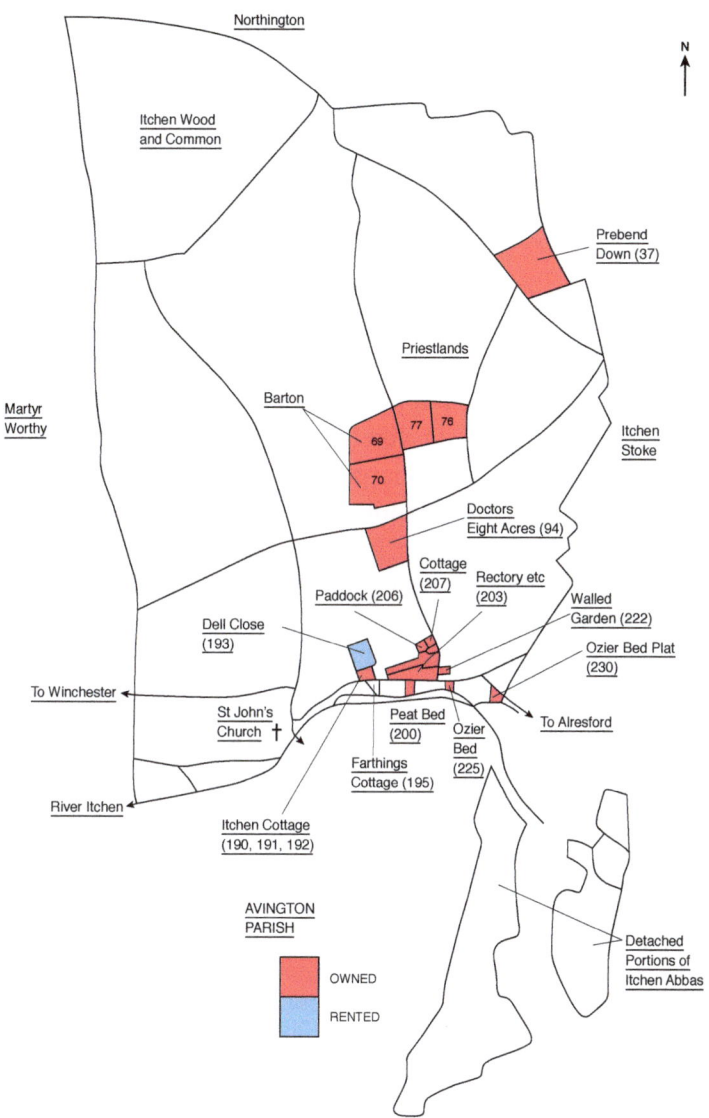

Figure 5: *The location of Robert Wright's land in the parish of Itchen Abbas (Source: HRO Itchen Abbas tithe map, 1839).*

tithes had been subsumed into an enclosure agreement of 1811 and only about 100 acres remained which were not tithe free. The rent charge was not finalised until 1846, when the nominal sum of £7-7s-0d per annum was awarded to the rector as tithe owner.[100]

DISSENTING VOICES IN ITCHEN ABBAS

On 2 February 1842 a surprise development took place in Rectory Lane (also known as Beare's Lane) in Itchen Abbas when James Garrett, a tenant farmer, was granted a Certificate for a Dissenters' Meeting House.[101] The location was given as 'the house of James Garrett' and the tithe schedule shows that Garrett rented the house from Robert Wright! It seems extraordinary that this could have happened considering Wright's total opposition to non-conformity, but it is likely that the initiative involved just a few individuals. If there had been a large number of dissenters then a chapel of worship would have been required and there is no indication that this was the case. In terms of religion, Itchen Abbas remained firmly under the control of Robert Wright and the established Church of England. When James Garrett died in December 1846 his funeral took place in Itchen Abbas Church and the service was ironically conducted by Wright!

NOTES

1   HRO, 44M69/G3/836, Complaint of Robert Wright, clerk of Dummer, against William Knight, 29 October 1798.

2   HRO, 65M72/PR2, *op. cit.*

3   Thompson, FML, *English Landed Society in the Nineteenth Century*, Routledge and Kegan Paul, 1963, p. 37.

4   HRO, 11M52/768, Deeds of the Itchen Abbas Estate, purchased by the estate of Alexander Baring, Lord Ashburton (deceased) from the trustees of the (second) Duke of Buckingham and Chandos, in 1848–1852, dated 8 March 1848.

5   HRO, 23M69/E/T2, *op. cit.*

6   Bowes, David John, 'The Church of England in East Yorkshire from 1743–c.1840 with Particular Reference to Economic Matters', unpublished PhD thesis, University of Hull, 2006, p. 151.

7   HRO, 21M65/E2/494, Presentation Deed, Itchen Abbas rectory: Robert Wright BA, 14 January 1803.

8   Page, William (Ed.), *The Victoria History of the Counties of England: Hampshire and the Isle of Wight*, Volume 5, Dawsons of Pall Mall, 1903, p. 447.

9   Duthy, John, *Sketches of Hampshire and the County adjacent to the River Itchen*, Lawrence Oxley, 1972, p. 234. Originally published in 1839 and Duthy, as a Hampshire Justice of the Peace, dedicated the book to the Duke of Wellington and the magistrates of the county.

10 Moutray Read, DH, *Highways and Byways in Hampshire*, Macmillan, 1919, p. 95.

11 HRO, 21M65/E15/66/1, Itchen Abbas Glebe Terrier, 1803.

12 *Ibid.*

13 *Ibid.*

14 *Ibid.*

15 CCED, *op. cit.*, Robert Wright, Person ID 109190.

16 *Hampshire Chronicle*, Monday 17 March 1817, p. 4.

17 Corrie, Jessie Elizabeth, *op. cit.*, p. 41.

18 TNA, HO107/404/16, 1841 Census for Ovington (www.ancestry.co.uk).

19 Corrie, Jessie Elizabeth, *op. cit.*, p. 15.

20 *Ibid.*, pp. 14–15.

21 *Ibid.*, p. 17.

22 HRO, 21M65/E7/1/178, Return of non-residence and places of worship: Southwick 1810.

23 HRO, 4M53/219–321, Correspondence between R Wright, Chairman of the Roads and Bridges Committee, William Gunner and Thomas Thistlewayte concerning the stopping up of roads in 1827.

24 *Ibid.*

25 Corrie, Jessie Elizabeth, *op. cit.*, p. 37.

26 *Oxford University and City Herald*, Saturday 5 November 1808, p. 3.

27 Bartons' History Group, Steeple Barton Vestry Minute Book, 1836–1851 (www.bartonhistorygroup.org.uk).

28 Bartons' History Group, typed notes from *A History of the County of Oxford*, Volume XI (www.bartonhistorygroup.org.uk).

29 *Oxford Chronicle and Reading Gazette*, Saturday 12 August 1837, p. 1.

30 *Ibid.*

31 *Ibid.*

32 Pugh, RK and Mason, JFA (Eds.), *The Letter Books of Samuel Wilberforce*, Buckinghamshire Record Society, 1970.

33 Bartons' History Group, Steeple Barton Vestry Minute Book, 1836–1851 *op. cit.*

34 *Oxford University and City Herald*, Saturday 28 September 1850, p. 2.

35 Bartons' History Group, typed notes from *A History of the County of Oxford*, Volume XI, *op. cit.*

36 TNA, HO129/160, Ecclesiastical Census of Great Britain, 1851.

37 HRO, Parish Registers:
    Itchen Abbas
    23M69/PR2, Register of Baptisms, Marriages and Burials 1689–1812
    23M69/PR3, Register of Marriages and Banns 1754–1812
    23M69/PR4, Register of Marriages 1813–1835
    23M69/PR5, Register of Baptisms 1813–1942
    23M69/PR6, Register of Marriages 1838–1920
    23M69/PR15, Register of Burials 1813–1993
    Ovington
    32M69/PR5, Register of Marriages 1813–1836
    32M69/PR6, Register of Marriages 1839–1980
    32M69/PR7, Register of Baptisms 1813–1991
    32M69/PR8, Register of Burials 1814–1990

Southwick

68M81/PR6, Register of Baptisms 1813–1856

68M81/PR9, Register of Marriages 1813–1837

68M81/PR13, Register of Marriages 1837–1975

68M81/PR10, Register of Burials 1813–1926

Boarhunt

69M81/PR2, Register of Baptisms 1813–1909

69M81/PR3, Register of Marriages 1813–1836

69M81/PR10, Register of Burials 1803–2004

38 HRO, *Discovering Waterloo and the Napoleonic Wars through the Archives*, Hampshire Archives and Local Studies, not dated (www.documents.hants.gov.uk/archives).

39 *Hampshire Chronicle*, Monday 21 October 1793, p. 3.

40 *Ibid.*, Monday 17 February 1812.

41 HRO, *Discovering Waterloo and the Napoleonic Wars through the Archives*, *op. cit.*

42 *Hampshire Chronicle*, Monday 25 September 1815, p. 4.

43 *Oxford University Alumni, op. cit.*, p. 1,614.

44 Virgin, Peter, *The Church in an Age of Negligence: Ecclesiastical Structure and Problems of Church Reform, 1700–1840*, James Clarke, 1989, p. 228.

45 HRO, 23M69/PR5, Itchen Abbas Baptisms 1813–1942. The details of the perambulation have been written at the front of this register in the hand of RJW Wright.

46 *Ibid.*

47 Barnard, HC, *A History of English Education from 1760*, University of London Press, 1961, p. 2.

48 Church of England Record Centre, NS/10/4/3/2, *A Digest of Parochial Returns Made to the Select Committee Appointed to Inquire into the Education of the Poor* (Session 1818, Volume II), p. 829.

49 Geddes, Alastair, *Samuel Best and the Hampshire Labourer*, Andover Local History Society, 1981, p. 8.

50 Church of England Record Society, NS/10/4/4/2, *Education Enquiry Abstracts of the Answers and Returns made Pursuant to an Address of the House of Commons* (24 May 1833, Volume II), p. 847.

51 England and Wales PCC Wills (1384–1858), Nathaniel Bailey, Probate dated 28 August 1823 (Probate 11/674) (www.ancestry.co.uk).

52 Barnard, HC, *op. cit.*, p. 98.
53 *Ibid.*
54 *Ibid.*
55 Church of England Record Centre, NS/7/6955.
56 *Ibid.*
57 *Ibid.*
58 *Ibid.*
59 *Ibid.*
60 *Ibid.*
61 White, William, *History Gazetteer and Directory of Hampshire and the Isle of Wight for 1859*, p. 123.
62 Barnard, HC, *op. cit.*, p. 70.
63 HRO, 23M69/PV1, Itchen Abbas Vestry Minute Book 1849–1921, Meeting of 24 April 1873, np.
64 Bettey, JH, *Church and Parish: An Introduction for Local Historians*, Batsford, 1987, p. 126.
65 Church of England Record Centre, Incorporated Church Building Society, ICBS 1456 (Parts 1 and 2), 1832–1834, Gallery in Itchen Abbas Church.
66 House of Commons Parliamentary Papers, *Report from the Select Committee on the Sale of Beer with the Minutes of Evidence*, 1833, No. 416, Volume XVI, p. 18 (www.proquest.com).
67 Church of England Record Centre, ICBS 1456, *op. cit.*
68 *Ibid.*
69 *Ibid.*
70 HRO, 23M69/PW10, Itchen Abbas Churchwardens' Account Book, 1821–1916.
71 *Ibid.*
72 HRO, 23M69/PW2, Itchen Abbas Parish Account Book (2), 1885–1916.
73 Corrie, Jessie Elizabeth, *op. cit.*, p. 47.
74 *Hampshire Chronicle*, Monday 13 February 1809, p. 4.
75 *Ibid.*, Monday 8 August 1814, p. 1.
76 *Ibid.*, Monday 28 April 1817, p. 4.
77 *Ibid.*, Monday 24 September 1827, p. 4.
78 *Ibid.*, Monday 27 October 1828, p. 2.
79 *Ibid.*, Monday 27 October 1828, p. 4.

80   *Ibid.*, Monday 26 April 1830, p. 1.

81   *Hampshire Advertiser*, Saturday 18 March 1837, p. 3.

82   *Ibid.*, Saturday 24 December 1836, p. 2.

83   *Hampshire Chronicle*, Monday 11 February 1839, p. 2.

84   HRO, 23M69/E/T27, Grant: The next presentation to the living of Itchen Abbas, 1 January 1836.

85   HRO, 44M69/K7/65, Letter from RJW Wright of Itchen Abbas to the magistrates of Hampshire, with testimonial from his father, R Wright, for the position of county chaplain. Addressed to G. P. Jervoise, 1835.

86   *Ibid.*

87   *Salisbury and Winchester Journal*, Monday 13 June 1836, p. 2.

88   Hartley Library, University of Southampton, MS61 Wellington Papers 4/21/13, Letter from RJW Wright to Arthur Wellesley, first Duke of Wellington, 19 May 1840.

89   *Ibid.*, Wellington Papers 4/11/35, Letter from Reverend RJW Wright to Arthur Wellesley, first Duke of Wellington, 9 November 1840.

90   *Ibid.*

91   *Ibid.*, Wellington Papers 2/75/113–114, Letter from Reverend RJW Wright, Chaplain to the Prison at Winchester, to Arthur Wellesley, first Duke of Wellington, with a copy of Wellington's reply.

92   *Hampshire Advertiser*, Saturday 12 November 1842, p. 3.

93   Holt, HME., 'Assistant Commissioners and Local Agents: Their Role in Tithe Commutation, 1836–1854', *Agricultural History Review*, Volume 32, 1984.

94   George Parrott replaced Arthur Octavius Baker as steward to the Avington Estate in 1837. Baker was deemed to have mis-managed the estate and, in doing so, had contributed to the debts of the first Duke of Buckingham and Chandos.

95   *Hampshire Chronicle*, Monday 20 August 1838, p. 3.

96   HRO, 18M51/147, Certified copy of the Itchen Abbas Tithe Award and Schedule, 1838–1839.

97   HRO, 21M65/F7/129/2, Itchen Abbas Tithe Map, 1839.

98   Although a valuable source, tithe maps and their schedules should be evaluated as mistakes did occur. For example, a description of plot number 6 on the Itchen Abbas map was erroneously omitted from the schedule.

99 *Hampshire Chronicle*, Monday 11 July 1842, p. 3.

100 HRO, 8M61/161, Copy Tithe Award for Ovington, 1846.

101 HRO, 21M65/F2/6/43, Meeting House Certificate, 2 February 1842.

Personal, social and financial matters

A SPORTING PARSON?

Itchen Abbas was a substantial living and seemingly 'ready made' for the stereotypical Georgian country parson who spent his time hunting, shooting and fishing. David Bowes describes this clerical stereotype:

> It was easy for some clerics to see their living, and the parsonage house that went with it, as a mini-estate, to be used like other country seats, living off the fruits of the land and aspiring to a life-style equivalent to that of the landed gentry. With ... land came an increase in the esteem in which many of the clergy wished to be held. It was all a question of status, both real and imaginary.[1]

There was no doubting that Robert Wright craved status, but in other ways he did not fit the sporting stereotype. There is no evidence that he was a member of any of the county fox hunting organisations, such as the Vine Hunt located near Basingstoke, and after 1828 he did not take out an annual game certificate to enable him to shoot game. He paid the annual fee of £3-13s-6d to obtain an annual game certificate between 1821 and 1828, but his name does not appear in the lists published in ensuing years in the local press.[2]

RUBBING SHOULDERS WITH THE FAMOUS

In 1808 Robert Wright became a member of the county's Commission of the Peace and he qualified as a Justice of the Peace. Social activities, such as attending dinners and balls, were all important in raising his status and forming networks that benefitted his work as a clerical magistrate. The Wrights frequently attended functions at the Assembly Rooms, located at The Swan Inn in Alresford and socialised with the Duke and Duchess of Buckingham and Chandos, as they were styled from 1822.[3] Wright was thus a friend and a 'professional' colleague of the Duke who had a wide network of associates.

Jessie Corrie promotes Robert Wright's 'importance' within Hampshire and lists a number of high society personalities with whom he rubbed shoulders. For example, she states that he had a lifelong 'friendship' with Lord Palmerston, which began when he was the curate at Dummer:

> It must, I think, have been while at Dummer that Robert Wright's friendship with Lord Palmerston began, for the latter was born in 1784, and if my memory serves me rightly it was during his residence at his tutor's (a Mr Bromley) that he first met Great-grandfather Wright.[4]

Corrie goes on to say that Lord Palmerston gave Wright a gift of a snuffbox that had the letter 'P' emblazoned in gold on the lid. Wright would certainly have known Palmerston in his capacity as a magistrate and probably met him several times at various functions, but it is unlikely that the two met in Dummer. Although Bromley did tutor Palmerston, it was at Harrow School where he was a pupil between 1795 and 1800. There was no known reason why the young Palmerston should have visited Dummer, and it is more likely that Corrie had misinterpreted the various stories that were handed down by family members over the years.[5]

One connection that seems indisputable is that during his time as curate of Dummer Wright was an acquaintance of Jane Austen's family in nearby Steventon, where Jane's father, the Reverend George Austen, was the rector. In a letter to her sister, Cassandra, dated 5 September 1796, Jane wrote:

> I shall be extremely anxious to hear the Event of your Ball, & shall hope to receive so long & minute an account of every particular that I shall be tired of reading it. Let me know how many [attended] besides their fourteen Selves & Mr & Mrs Wright.[6]

Jessie Corrie also claims that Robert Wright was the chaplain to the Duke of Wellington and the 13th Regiment of Foot and was present on the battlefield at Waterloo on 18 June 1815.[7] An examination of the available evidence casts doubt on this claim. There is nothing in the Wellington Papers to support Corrie's words, and the parish registers show that Wright was officiating at Itchen Abbas during the month of June 1815. In the 1830s Wright found the need to write to the Duke of Wellington for advice in the course of his work as a magistrate. The correspondence does not suggest that the two men had a cordial relationship or, indeed, knew each other that well. On the contrary, Wellington's replies were curt and lacking in any sort of empathy for Wright's problems. Furthermore, chaplains in the British army were expected to leave their parishes for weeks at a time to accompany regiments in the field or be present at their garrison[8], but there is no evidence that Wright was absent from Itchen Abbas for a prolonged period. Finally, he does not feature in the comprehensive list of army chaplains active at this time which was compiled by the historian, Roy Burley, in 2013.[9] Robert Wright was, however, appointed as chaplain to the Marquis of Buckingham in 1817; this fact is verifiable.[10] The two men knew each other well and were neighbours so it was an arrangement of convenience as much as anything.

Corrie is also adamant that Robert Wright was in Italy between 1815 and 1818, 'for he travelled there with the young Marquis of Chandos'[11] (who had the title of Earl Temple at this time). Again, there is more than an element of doubt about this claim. Perhaps he *was* there for a short period of time, but the registers and Quarter Sessions attendance lists tell us that Wright was not in Italy for three uninterrupted years. Chandos was banished to Europe by his father in an effort to educate him and improve his wayward behaviour. He spent time collecting art and visiting ancient temples, but he also returned home the father of an illegitimate daughter, who took the title Countess Anna Ellen St George Chandos. Nevertheless, the Marquis of Buckingham considered the European tour a success for his son and on his return declared him to be a more mature person.[12] There is no written record, however, of Wright's opinion about the tour in general or the promiscuous behaviour of the Marquis.

Robert Wright and the Marquis of Chandos went on to become firm friends, and as ultra-Tories they agreed on just about everything. They both promoted the agricultural interest to the point of obsession and were anxious to prevent any modification to the Corn Laws that resulted in freer trade. In the opinion of the historian, David Spring, Chandos was 'a man of quite ordinary abilities … (but) was perhaps the leading protectionist in the House of Commons in the 1830s and for some time thereafter'.[13] Chandos and Wright were generally opposed to any tampering with the franchise, but the Marquis spotted an opportunity to strengthen the landed interest in county elections. Together with Colonel Charles Sibthorp, he suggested giving the vote to small £50 per year tenant farmers in the counties. When this measure was incorporated into the Great Reform Act in 1832 it won Chandos the title of 'the farmers' friend', an accolade which fed his not inconsiderable ego.[14] Given that this change was in favour of the agricultural interest, it is most likely that Wright would have approved.

Chandos was also a staunch opponent of Catholic emancipation, which was a burning political issue during the 1820s, as John Beckett explains:

> Although like his father indifferent to religious matters, [Chandos] adopted his mother's hard-line Protestant position and, doubtless encouraged by his wife [a Scottish Presbyterian], became an ardent supporter of the anti-emancipation position ... [He] came increasingly to be seen as one of the leading opponents of emancipation.[15]

Although there is no direct evidence as to Wright's feelings on the issue of Catholic emancipation, he was an orthodox Anglican clergyman schooled in traditional values and was therefore highly likely to have concurred with Chandos.

ITCHEN COTTAGE AND ENFRANCHISEMENT

When he arrived at Itchen Abbas Robert Wright took an immediate dislike to the rectory, described by Jessie Corrie as a 'large square house',[16] and instead leased Itchen Cottage from the lord of the manor, Lord Bolton, who was the governor of the Isle of Wight and the Lord Lieutenant of Hampshire until his death in 1807. It was not long before the two men were involved in a lengthy argument. To fit in with his status and image, Wright wanted Itchen Cottage and its land enfranchised but Bolton refused.[17] He was angry that the advowson of Itchen Abbas had been allowed to fall into the hands of the Wright family. In fact, Charles, the third Duke of Bolton (1685–1754) had donated the advowson as provision for one of his three illegitimate children by the actor Lavinia Fenton. The recipient turned out to be the Reverend Charles Powlett (1728–1809), curate of Itchen Abbas from 1763–1792.[18] Powlett subsequently sold the advowson to John Wright in 1802. The title deeds, which were in possession of the Wright family, proved that all past transactions involving the advowson were legitimate. Robert Wright used this to his advantage in the negotiations and offered the advowson to Bolton for the sum of £4,700 in return for his agreeing to the enfranchisement of Itchen Cottage. Bolton, however, refused to entertain this outrageous offer and the issue was temporarily shelved. The relevant correspondence in the Bolton archives shows Wright to be a shrewd and stubborn negotiator determined to advance his own ambitions.[19]

The death of the Reverend Charles Powlett in 1809 precipitated a family quarrel, and in 1810 the Court of Chancery ordered the sale of the Powletts' land in Itchen Abbas. The auction took place at The George Inn in Winchester on 27 October [20] and 474 acres of leasehold and copyhold land were bought by Robert Bird, William Burnett and William Rogers.[21] These transactions were complex, as there were a number of manorial covenants and restrictions placed on the land and the knock-on effect for Wright was to delay further the enfranchisement of Itchen Cottage.

Plate 8: *The south-facing façade of Itchen Cottage*
(Jessie E Corrie).

Wright's disagreements with the Bolton family continued. In May 1813 Wright received a surprise letter from Lady Bolton's steward at Hackwood Park, near Basingstoke, accusing him of stealing the wood from a fallen ash tree that was the property of the manor of Itchen Abbas. The letter invited the reverend to refund the value of the wood taken. In his reply, an indignant Wright retorted that the wood was rotten and the tree had fallen across his hedge, making a hole that allowed stray cattle on to his land.

His anger flowed unabated as he stated:

> I confess that after the many hundreds of pounds I have expended
> at Itchen fully relying on the enfranchisement and with ... Lord
> Bolton's written assurance that no advantage should be taken of
> me I cannot conceive it possible that I should be called upon to
> pay for a tree.[22]

By the end of the letter he had calmed down somewhat and agreed
to compensate the Dowager Lady Bolton. He was still in the process of
attempting to get Itchen Cottage enfranchised, so perhaps he did not wish
to offend Her Ladyship any further.

Wright's luck changed in 1820 when the Bolton family sold their
remaining land in Itchen Abbas to the Marquis of Buckingham, who, two
years later, was to become the first Duke of Buckingham and Chandos.
Such was Wright's determination to achieve the enfranchisement of Itchen
Cottage, he actually filed a suit in the Court of Chancery against the Duke,
claiming that the late Lord Bolton had promised that the enfranchisement
would take place. Rather than defend the case, on 11 December 1822 the
Duke agreed that 'for putting an end to the ... Suit and for settling the
differences' he would, in principle, allow Wright to buy the freehold of
Itchen Cottage. The parties had to wait until 1824 for the conveyance to
take place, which was the time when the lease held by the then holder of
the land, William Burnett, expired.[23] On 4 September 1824 the freehold of
Itchen Cottage, totalling 7 acres 3 roods and 21 perches of land, was sold to
Wright at the price of £420, the valuation having been decided by Thomas
Crawford of Avington and William Simonds (Junior) of Winchester.[24]
Wright had insisted that the valuation should be based on the (poor) state
of the property when he first moved into it, citing the many changes and
improvements he had made. The price was deemed to be fair by all the
parties and Arthur Octavius Baker, the Duke's steward based in Easton,
issued a receipt to conclude the agreement. *[Figure 6]*

Wright then wasted no time in placing Itchen Cottage and its associated
land in trust for his daughter Harriet and her husband William Wynne,
a move that was to have implications for Wright's family in the months
immediately after his decease.[25]

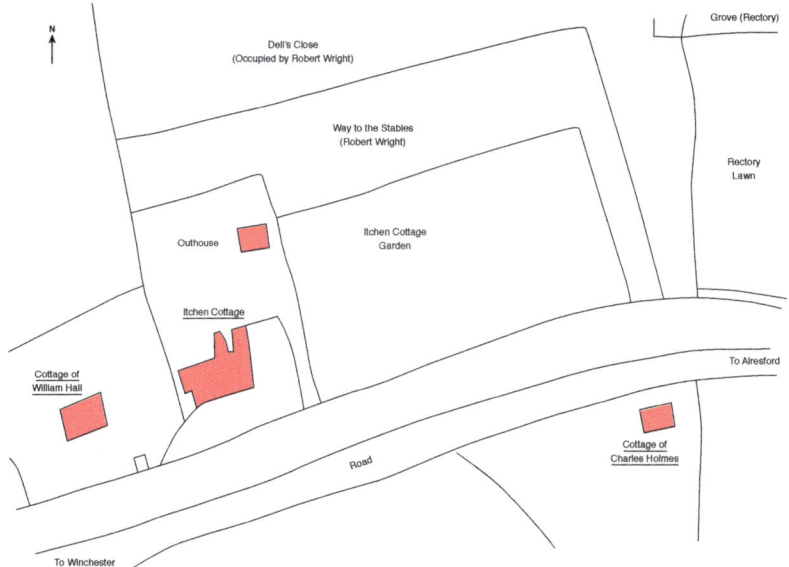

Figure 6: *The site of Itchen Cottage and its environs.*

ENCLOSURE OF ITCHEN ABBAS COMMON, 1811–14

The medieval open fields of Itchen Abbas were most likely enclosed by the private agreement of the owners of the land sometime in the eighteenth century.[26] During the French Wars (1793–1815) wheat was commanding a high price on the home market, and in 1811 the decision was taken to enclose Itchen Abbas common to bring more land into cultivation. The enclosure needed an Act of Parliament, which was passed in 1812, with George Barnes of Andover being appointed as commissioner.[27]

Those landowners wishing to stake a claim for land in the Enclosure Award had to make a formal application to Barnes and explain their reasons. Robert Wright was one of ten claimants. He stated that the rector had the right to graze ten beasts as well as sheep on the common and that he wished to be awarded land in lieu of grazing rights.[28] At various stages of the process, Barnes organised meetings in Winchester to explain his plans for new fences and roads and to invite comments and objections. No formal objections appeared to be forthcoming, even though the poor of the parish may have lost their access to the common to gather wood for fuel and graze an animal.

The Enclosure Award was made in 1814 and Wright received a total of 6 acres, 1 rood and 10 perches of common land, which he exchanged for land farmed by Robert Bird next to the glebe to the north of Itchen Cottage.[29] In this way, Wright was able to consolidate his land in one part of the village, making his farming activity more efficient and convenient. *[Figure 7]*

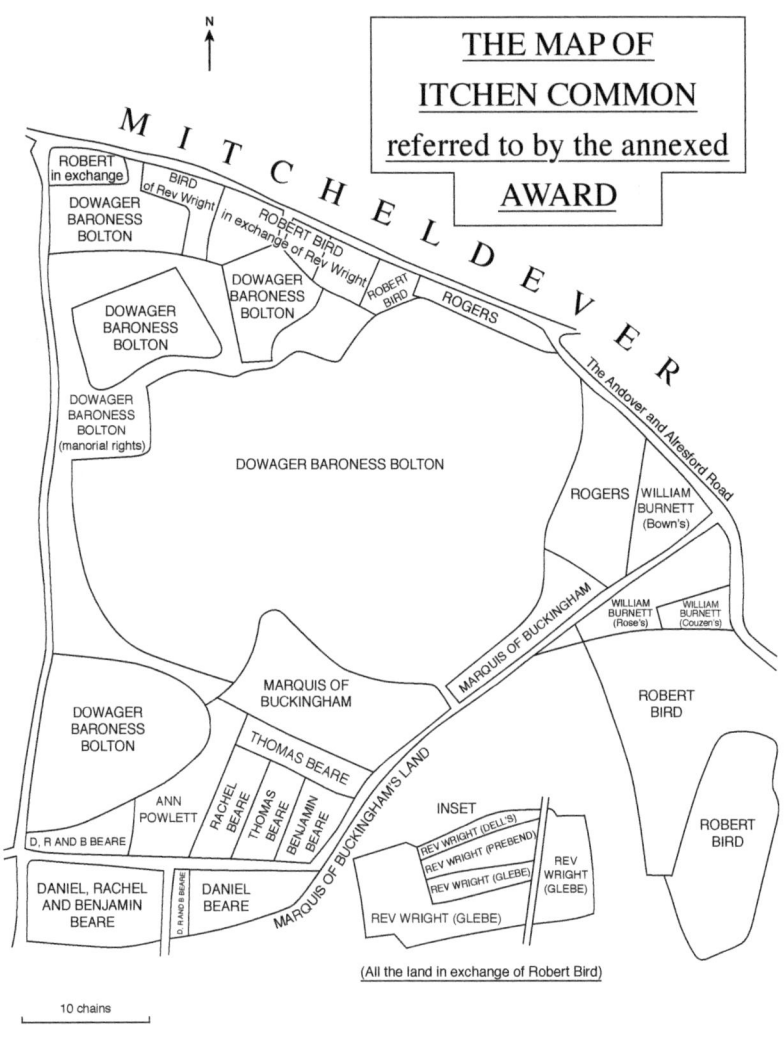

Figure 7: *Enclosure map of Itchen Abbas common, dated 1812.*[30]

WRIGHT AND LAND TAX

In August 1814 Wright took advantage of the various Land Tax Acts to redeem his annual payment of £21-19s-10d, the amount payable to the government for his ownership of the glebe and tithes. To redeem the annual payment indefinitely, Wright was instructed to make seven annual payments of £3-2s-10d until 1821. As proof that this had been done, a certificate was issued by the Commissioners of Land Tax in Westminster.[31] Another key event in 1814, on 5 January, was the granting of the advowson of Itchen Abbas to Robert Wright following the death of his father, making him both patron and incumbent of the living.[32]

WRIGHT SUPPORTS THE AGRICULTURAL INTEREST

According to Jessie Corrie, Robert Wright farmed his own glebe land and she paints an idyllic picture of the labourers being fed on stew, rice pudding and home brewed beer which were provided at harvest time by the rector's domestic servants.[33] How 'hands-on' Wright was as a farmer we do not know. In general, the clergy possessed no formal training in land management or farming techniques. Given his hectic schedule, it is likely Wright delegated tasks to others and merely supervised the work.[34] By the late 1830s he was renting out most of his land, with the majority of his time taken up by his magisterial work, which necessitated frequent absences from Itchen Abbas.

Wright did, however, find the time to take an active role in the agricultural interest at a county level. He believed that British farming should be protected from foreign competition. As a result he was concerned about calls for the Corn Laws to be modified and it was an issue that he was prepared to fight for. His strong views were probably reinforced by discussions with his close friend the Marquis of Chandos, who championed the cause of the farming fraternity.

Following the end of the French Wars in 1815, farmers experienced hard times, with plummeting cereal prices and reduced profits. By 1823 things had not improved, and when the high sheriff refused to convene a county meeting demanded by a number of freeholders, seven magistrates, including Robert Wright, took matters into their own hands and called their own meeting 'to take into consideration the propriety of petitioning Parliament ... [for] a remedy of the evils under which [farming] now labours'.[35]

The meeting, staged in the Grand Jury Room at Winchester Castle and attended by about 500 people, turned out to be a lively affair. Sir Thomas Baring, of Stratton Park, chaired the meeting, but there were a number of radicals and reformers at the gathering who were intent on putting forward an alternative view. Among them were Henry Hunt and William Cobbett, who had recently buried their differences to attend the meeting together. Hunt shouted across the crowded room to Wright and asked him if he had lowered his tithes, to which Wright answered, 'I have'. Wright went on to address the meeting in support of the 'agriculturalists', delivering an emotional rant on their behalf:

Why is the agriculturalist for ever to remain stuck in his native clay; when every lop-eared boy, as soon as his apprenticeship has ended, is dignified by the title of an esquire, and every spider brusher by the appellation of miss? Let those declaiming against the agriculturalists set us an example.[36]

Those at the meeting submitted a petition to Westminster asking for the unpopular traditional system of paying tithes to be abolished. There was no response from the government and it took 13 long years for any such change to occur in the shape of the Tithe Commutation Act of 1836.

ROBERT WRIGHT AND PERSONAL FINANCE

Robert Wright's income from his various parishes would have been well above the average for Anglican clerics at the time. It is possible to calculate that he received about £468 per annum for Itchen Abbas, £220 for Ovington and £100 for Steeple Barton, plus at least £100 for renting out the glebe land and other property each year, thereby providing a possible annual income of about £888.[37] This would have placed him in the top 20 per cent of earners in the ranks of the Anglican clergy. (His income from Boarhunt and Southwick is unknown as this was subject to a private contract made with Thomas Thistlewayte.)

However, Wright also had substantial outgoings. He spent at least £350 per year in paying his curates (Itchen Abbas, Ovington and Steeple Barton) and had the expense of a residence in Itchen Abbas and a large rented property in Southwick.[38] He employed servants and a coachman, Mark Sims, who organised the stables at Itchen Cottage.[39] Clergymen were expected to contribute to charities and schooling and the evidence shows that Wright sometimes made donations to these causes, albeit in relatively modest amounts. There would also have been rates, fees due to the Bishop of Winchester and taxes to pay but there are no readily available records that state the amounts paid. In theory, Wright had to keep the rectory houses in his parishes in good repair or risk incurring dilapidation charges from the diocesan authorities. The parsonages at both Itchen Abbas and Steeple Barton were in a poor state when Wright died, so his estate may have been faced with a bill, but again there is no evidence to confirm this.[40]

Frances Knight, quoting John Kaye (1783–1853), the Bishop of Lincoln, informs her readers that:

> The possessor of a living even of £500 a year with a family and without any private source of income, if he administers as he ought to the temporal wants of his parishioners, has little or nothing to spare.[41]

It would appear that Robert Wright maintained a high standard of living by borrowing and juggling the capital. On 15 December 1824 Wright took out a mortgage for £2,000 with William George Adam Esq of Lincoln's Inn and Sir Richard Goden Simon, Baronet, of St John's, Isle of Wight.[42] Then, on 1 March 1830, Wright remortgaged, using the advowson as security, to borrow £5,000 at 5 per cent interest from Harry Comper, alderman and banker of Chichester.[43] The payments were interest only and £125 was payable twice a year in March and September. The reason Wright required such a large amount of capital is obscure, but it may have been needed to help pay for the enfranchisement of Itchen Cottage and later to finance the building of The Elms, a large residence adjacent to the main Winchester to Alresford highway. In addition, of course, he felt he had to maintain a standard of living that matched his status. Much of Robert Wright's time was spent working as a magistrate, for which he was only paid expenses. According to Jessie Corrie, The Elms was not built until 1843, and as the house is not marked on the 1839 tithe map, this date is likely to be correct.[44] Presumably, Wright would still have had some of the capital stowed away in a bank to help pay large bills. Ownership of more freehold property would have enhanced the reverend's status among the county set and this involved taking some financial risks.

Whatever the purpose of the loans, Wright soon found himself enmeshed in another controversy and it was an old problem that returned to haunt him. Comper somehow learned that there were possible doubts as to the title of the Itchen Abbas advowson and he became nervous about the deal. In a memorandum dated 9 April 1830 he asked Wright to provide the relevant documentation to his solicitors within one calendar month to prove he owned the advowson. Comper demanded to see a list of incumbents of Itchen Abbas dating back to 1700, together with certificates for the marriage of Wright's mother and father, and for the baptisms of Wright and his two brothers. In addition, Comper wanted to see a copy of the document conveying the advowson from the Reverend Charles Powlett to Wright's father, dated 1 November 1802. Although the memorandum is in a secretary's hand, it bears the distinctive signature of Robert Wright to show that he agreed to the demands.[45]

Comper probably thought he had been 'taken in' by Wright and, unconvinced that the memorandum was sufficient to confirm the true ownership of the advowson, he took the case to the Court of the King's Bench in Westminster. He sued Wright for a debt of £10,000 (made up of £5,000 capital and the accumulated interest of 5 per cent), stating that Wright was refusing to pay the money.[46]

It looks as if Wright was made to attend the court, as the judgement in the case states that the 'Defendant in this suit [was] in the Custody of the Marshall of the Marshalsea'.[47] The outcome of the hearing was that Wright was ordered to honour the debt and pay Comper £20 in costs and 65 shillings in damages.[48] Both plaintiff and defendant had displayed a level of brinkmanship, but in reality Wright had no alternative but to pay, otherwise he would have been incarcerated in the Marshalsea debtors' prison. However, there was never any doubt about who legally owned the advowson and Comper had probably been misled by gossip and rumours that were prevalent during Wright's dispute with Lord Bolton some 25 years previously.

The records show that the dispute was settled and Wright paid £125 in interest every six months, plus some money off the capital. When he came to redeem the mortgage in 1849, he still owed £2,800 of capital.[49] The fact that Wright regularly passed judgement on numerous debtors in his work as a JP adds a strong sense of irony to this remarkable episode.

THE CONSTRUCTION OF THE ELMS

In late 1840 Wright bought a small piece of land, measuring about three-quarters of an acre, from the second Duke of Buckingham and Chandos for the sum of £25. The 1839 tithe map shows the land was used as an orchard and in the occupation of Sarah Munday, a farmer and landlady of The Plough Inn. The conveyance was by lease and release and stated that the land was to be placed in trust for the future use of Robert Wright's son-in-law, William Wynne.[50] It was also declared that Wright's 'widow, if any, shall not be entitled to dower out of the said piece of land and hereditaments'.[51]

The land was used in 1843 to construct a large house, known as The Elms, on the eastern extremity of the village. On 9 February 1844 the Bishop of Winchester issued a new licence to Wright allowing him to continue living at a 'fit and convenient house situate in [his] parish' on the condition that he kept the 'glebe house', then occupied by William Campion, in a good state of repair.[52] The new licence was due to expire on 31 December 1845, by which time The Elms would have been ready for occupation. Wright intended this house to be the new rectory and this was announced by a notice in the local press dated 28 May 1845. Wright stated that as the patron and rector of Itchen Abbas he intended to exchange the glebe house and premises for a 'certain' house which was situated on the east side of Rectory Lane (The Elms). The new property would be conveyed to the advowson of the parish 'for ever' in lieu of the present rectory house on the west side of Rectory Lane.[53] Although a substantial dwelling, The Elms was not as big or as imposing as the existing rectory house and the Bishop of Winchester did not agree to the change, so the house remained as a private residence. *[Plates 9 & 10]*

Wright may have overstretched himself financially, because in November 1847 he used the new residence as security to obtain a loan of £300 with the interest fixed at 5 per cent. The money was borrowed from George Baigent, the owner of a drugstore in Winchester and John William Jolliffe, a builder from Ryde, Isle of Wight. The terms of the agreement were strict: Wright had to insure the property for £400 and any default in the interest repayments would trigger a clause allowing the mortgagors to sell the premises.[54] Wright was already in debt to Harry Comper and this, together with events that occurred just before Wright's death, gives credence to the theory that he was living beyond his means.

Plate 9: *The south-facing façade of The Elms in the early years of the twentieth century. The house has views overlooking the River Itchen towards the parish of Avington.*

Plate 10: *The imposing south-facing façade of Itchen Abbas rectory in the early years of the twentieth century.*

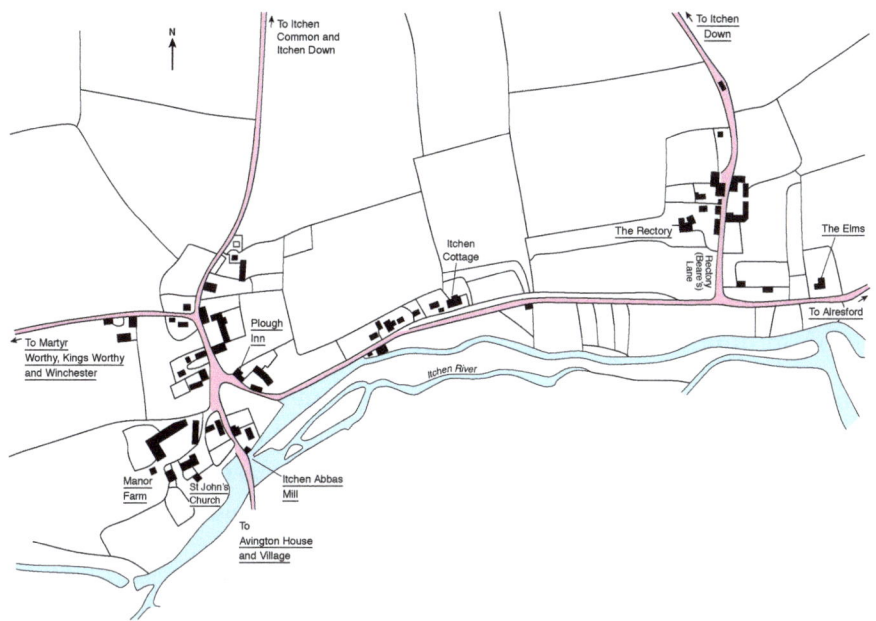

Figure 8: *The village of Itchen Abbas in about 1845.*

THE WRIGHTS, THE FIRST DUCHESS OF BUCKINGHAM AND CHANDOS, AND SLAVERY

Robert Wright was always keen to be seen with the aristocracy and it was not surprising that he forged a close social and professional association with the Dukes of Buckingham and Chandos who owned the Avington Estate. Their main family seat was the magnificent country house at Stowe in Buckinghamshire but they also owned large tracts of land in Itchen Abbas, Easton and Bighton. Richard Temple Nugent Brydges Chandos Grenville (1776–1839) became the first Duke of Buckingham and Chandos in 1822, and his marriage to Lady Anna Brydges, only heir of the third Duke of Chandos, had been arranged in 1796. The marriage turned out to be an unhappy and stormy affair and the couple lived almost separate lives for a number of years. The rift was caused by the Duke's extravagant financial dealings (and subsequent debt) as well as his infidelity.[55] The Duchess was happiest when she spent time at Avington House, where she was well known to the tenants and popular for her generosity in funding local schools and providing feasts at Christmas and other times of the year. The following report in the *Hampshire Chronicle* offers a typical example of her paternalistic attitude:

> The Duchess of Buckingham left Avington last Thursday for Stowe, having previously directed, according to annual custom, to be distributed among the poor families of Avington, and the surrounding villages, liberal portions of bread and meat. Her Grace has also presented them with blankets and various articles of clothing, adapted to the present inclement season.[56]

In another edition, the same newspaper commented that 'such well timed and unostentatious acts of benevolence are beyond eulogium'.[57]

In 1816 Lady Anna Brydges inherited the 3,344 acres which made up the Hope sugar plantation in Kingston, Jamaica. The plantation used slave labour, both domestically and in the fields; at any one time there were in the region of 350 slaves working there.[58] There appears to be a contradiction between the show of affection for the Duchess and the fact that she was the owner of a plantation using slave labour to grow, harvest and process sugar. Whether it was local knowledge within the Itchen Valley that the Duchess was involved in slavery does not generally feature in popular biographical writings. However, she was in absentia and most probably never witnessed the appalling conditions of the black slaves on the Hope plantation at first hand, relying on her agents to keep her informed. In particular, she was anxious to know about finances and the amount of sugar marketed each year.

In 1833 the British Parliament voted to end colonial slavery, with the legislation to take effect from 1 August 1834. There was to be an interim apprenticeship system so that the slaves gained their freedom gradually and plantation owners had the chance to organise the recruitment of paid labour. Field workers had to serve an apprenticeship of six years and domestic hands four years. Plantation owners were able to claim compensation from an enormous fund of £20 million made available by the British government.[59]

Dr Veront Satchell of the University of the West Indies, an expert on the history of slavery in the Caribbean, states that to manage the loss of slave labour and in anticipation of the apprenticeship system, in 1834, the

Duchess of Buckingham and Chandos sent white workers from Avington and environs to work alongside the black labour on the Hope plantation. The census population figures for the villages of Avington, Itchen Abbas, Martyr Worthy, Easton and Itchen Stoke, however, all show an increase between 1831 and 1841, which suggests that *native* inhabitants did not leave for Jamaica after 1834. Avington's population, for example, increased in size from 191 people in 1831 to 204 in 1841. It may have been the case, therefore, that some members of the large Irish travelling community in the Itchen Valley were the ones who decided to chance their luck in Jamaica.[60] The first group of white 'indentured' labourers from the Avington district arrived in Jamaica on 23 December 1834. Richard Barrett, agent and direct representative of Lady Anna Brydges, informed her that the workers 'could not have been better selected for employment in Jamaica'.[61]

More migrants were to cross the Atlantic Ocean. On 27 December 1834 the *Hampshire Advertiser* reported that a ship carrying 103 agricultural labourers, women and children had left Gravesend bound for Jamaica the previous Thursday to be 'attached to the estates of the Hon. Richard Barrett', the speaker of the Assembly there.[62] These migrants were recruited from a number of parishes but we are not told if any of them originated from the upper Itchen Valley. However, if Barrett was involved it was very likely that some of them would have been destined for the Hope plantation. The newspaper went on to make an astonishing attack on black slaves by stating that it was hoped that they would realise that if they continued 'to be slothful or refractory negroes … their places will be supplied by those who will work', meaning the incoming migrant labour.[63] Such a comment illustrates the superiority complex which many of the British had towards Afro-Caribbean people at that time.

On the arrival of these white immigrants in Jamaica, Richard Barrett wrote several letters to the Duchess telling her that the immigrants were good workers and that they in turn were happy with their conditions. He explained that he was in the process of building five cottages which would have the benefit of a sea breeze. Barrett told the Duchess the little hamlet was to be named 'Chandos'. It all sounded rather idyllic but it was in Barrett's interest to paint an idealistic picture. There was no hiding the fact that the Hope plantation was on the decline and Barrett blamed the black apprentices for this, telling Lady Anna that 'the negroes will not work' and pleading for additional white labour to be sent to Jamaica. His pleas, however, fell on deaf ears, as there were no funds available to finance ships and supplies. Once in Jamaica, many white immigrants soon succumbed to disease and several died prematurely. The scheme was nothing but a 'dismal failure'.[64]

In the early hours of 16 May 1836, Lady Anna Eliza Brydges, first Duchess of Buckingham and Chandos, died at Stowe after a period of illness, aged 56. Her body was conveyed to 'her beloved Avington for burial'.[65] The funeral took place on Wednesday 25 May at St Mary's Church 'amidst the sorrowing gaze of throngs of the surrounding poor'.[66] As well as family members, labourers, tenants and servants joined the procession to pay their respects. Reverend Robert Wright was one of the chief mourners, and his close colleague the Reverend Charles Shrubsole Bonnett of Avington conducted the service.

Plate 11: *An engraving of Avington House and St Mary's Church in 1811 by James Sargant Storer (1771–1853).*

After the death of the Duchess, ownership of the Hope plantation passed to her husband, the first Duke of Buckingham and Chandos, and then on his own death in 1839 to his son, the Marquis of Chandos, who became the second Duke. The Hope plantation continued to decline but the family was successful in securing £6,630 in compensation from the British government, which was paid to the Marquis of Breadalbane and the Hon. George Neville, who were the trustees named in the second Duke's marriage settlement.[67]

The apprenticeship system had been widely condemned as unnecessary by the slave abolition lobby in Britain. From its inception slave abolitionists had campaigned for it to be axed. On Monday 19 March 1838 a public meeting was called in the Winchester Guildhall to discuss petitioning Parliament 'for the immediate and entire emancipation of negro slaves'.[68] One of the keynote speakers was Reverend RJW Wright who attacked the plantation owners for abusing the system, saying that 'it was time that steps should be taken to procure immediate emancipation' rather than wait until 1840 as the act stated.[69] The outcome of the meeting was a signed petition sent to Parliament requesting the immediate freeing of slaves in the West Indies.[70] The intense pressure on the British government soon produced the desired outcome. James Latimer explains:

> The great degree of agitation against the apprenticeship system resulted in its being terminated two years sooner than had been directed by the Emancipation Act ... More than 600,000 [British] women signed a petition appealing to the Queen to end the apprenticeship system.[71]

By speaking in support of the immediate termination of the apprenticeship system, Reverend RJW Wright had demonstrated a liberal and compassionate side to his character. An intriguing question is whether his father agreed with RJW's contribution to the meeting, and whether the two of them were actually aware that the slavery issue was so close to home. It is hard to believe that they were ignorant of the facts, and as such RJW Wright may have risked the wrath of the first Duke of Buckingham and Chandos, his father's friend and, since the death of Lady Anna Brydges, the owner of a plantation that was heading for bankruptcy.

COMING OF AGE CELEBRATIONS AT AVINGTON

On 10 September 1844 Avington was the scene of a huge party to celebrate the 21st birthday of the Marquis of Chandos, son of the second Duke of Buckingham and Chandos. Tents were erected to accommodate the villagers of Avington, Itchen Abbas and Easton and the tenantry of the estate. The fact that the Duke was in dire financial straits at the time and on the verge of bankruptcy did not seem to affect the lavish arrangements.[72] The guests lined up at the lodge gates and marched into the grounds of Avington House accompanied by a band. It took a little time for them all to take their seats for a meal amid a noisy atmosphere. A drum roll silenced the throng and grace was said for each parish by Reverend Charles Bonnet (for Avington), Reverend Robert Wright (for Itchen Abbas) and Reverend RJW Wright (for Easton). Following the meal, strong beer was served and the speeches started. Tributes were paid to the Marquis before Robert Wright stood up and proposed a toast to the second Duke of Buckingham and Chandos, his close friend and political ally. His tribute was somewhat sycophantic and excessive in flattery:

> My friends – The toast I am about to propose is one which I feel confident will be cordially received by everyone present-it is the health of a nobleman... It is to his exertions in favour of the agri-cultural interest that you are this day enabled to partake of this festivity; for had it not been for his strong and firm attachment to the landed interest this country must have been involved in anarchy and confusion... I propose the health of his Grace, the Duke of Buckingham and Chandos, with long prosperity to himself and his friends-not with three times three but ten times ten.[73]

Robert Wright also paid tribute to the late Duchess of Buckingham and Chandos, which may well have been received with much more approval than his remarks about the Duke, a man who had cheated on his wife and spent money way beyond his means. It suited Robert Wright, however, to have him as a friend in his quest to oppose the growing demands for reform.

Following the repast, the guests danced the night away until the early hours. Four years later the second Duke, with debts estimated at £1.5 million, was forced to sell his land in the Itchen Valley jointly to John Shelley and the estate of Lord Ashburton. The change in landownership also coincided with the death of Robert Wright in 1850, ushering in a new era for the inhabitants of the upper Itchen Valley.

NOTES

1   Bowes, David John, *op. cit.*, p. 26.
2   *Hampshire Chronicle*, Monday 9 September 1828, p. 2.
3   Corrie, Jessie Elizabeth, *op. cit.*, p. 49.
4   *Ibid.*, p. 35.
5   Professor David Brown of Southampton University, an authority on the life of Palmerston, agrees that Wright and Palmerston would not have known each other when the former was resident at Dummer. (Oral evidence based on a discussion at a day conference on Palmerston, organised by the Romsey Local History Society on Saturday 29 March 2014).
6   Le Faye, Deirdre (Ed.), *Jane Austen's Letters*, Oxford University Press, 2011, pp. 7–8, Letter from Jane Austen to her sister, Cassandra, dated Monday 5 September 1796.
7   Corrie, Jessie Elizabeth, *op. cit.*, p. 3.
8   Burley, Roy David, 'An Age of Negligence? British Army Chaplaincy, 1796–1844', unpublished MPhil thesis, University of Birmingham, 2013, *passim*.
9   *Ibid.*, pp. 161–168.
10 CCED, Robert Wright, Person ID 109190, *op. cit.*
11 Corrie, Jessie Elizabeth, *op. cit.*, p. 37.
12 Beckett, John, *The Rise and Fall of the Grenvilles*, Manchester University Press, 1986, p. 114.
13 Spring, David, 'Lord Chandos and the Farmers, 1818-1846', *Huntington Library Quarterly*, Volume 33, No. 3 (May 1970), University of Pennsylvania Press, pp. 257–281.
14 *Ibid.*
15 Beckett, John, *op. cit.*, p. 14.
16 Corrie, Jessie Elizabeth, *op. cit.*, p. 10.
17 HRO, 11M49/464, Bolton of Hackwood (Powlett family, Marquesses of Winchester and Dukes of Bolton), General Estate Papers, Hampshire, Itchen Abbas and Itchen Stoke 1766–1819. Correspondence between Lord Bolton and Reverend Robert Wright.
18 Duthy, John, *op. cit.*, p. 233.
19 HRO, 11M49/404, *op. cit.*
20 *Hampshire Chronicle*, Monday 22 October 1810, p. 1.

21 HRO, Q22/1/1/241, Fawley Land Tax Assessments,
   Itchen Abbas, 1799–1800, 1806, 1808–1832.
22 HRO, 10M57/D22, Bolton Papers, Correspondence between Lord
   Bolton's steward and the Reverend Robert Wright of Itchen Abbas, 1813.
23 HRO, 23M69/E/T16, Agreement for the settlement of differences
   concerning the enfranchisement of a cottage and land in
   Itchen Abbas, 11 December 1822.
24 HRO, 23M69/E/T17, Award of Thomas Crawford of Avington and
   William Simmonds of Winchester, concerning the enfranchisement
   of a cottage, garden and meadow adjoining Itchen Abbas rectory,
   4 September 1824.
25 HRO, 23M69/E/T20, Dell's cottage and garden, and lands part of the
   rectory garden of Itchen Abbas, Trusteeship Deed, 22 December 1824.
26 In the absence of any documentary evidence, I am indebted to
   Dr John Chapman, an authority on eighteenth century enclosures,
   for his opinion on this issue.
27 *Hampshire Chronicle*, Monday 18 January 1813, p. 1.
28 HRO, 11M49/464, Itchen Abbas Inclosure Schedule
   or Abstract of Claims.
29 HRO, 11M49/E/B6/3, Copy of the Itchen Common Enclosure Award, 1814.
30 HRO, 10M57/P5, Enclosure Map of Itchen Common,
   possibly a private copy belonging to the Duke of Bolton, 1812.
31 HRO, 23M69/E/T15, Certificate of the Contract for the Redemption of
   Land Tax on Glebe and other lands in Itchen Abbas, 1814.
32 HRO, 23M69/E/T13, The advowson of Itchen Abbas, Bargain and Sale
   for 10 shillings, 5 January 1814.
33 Corrie, Jessie Elizabeth, *op. cit.*, p. 43.
34 Bowes, David, *op. cit.*, p. 136.
35 *Hampshire Chronicle*, Monday 3 March 1823, p. 3.
36 *Ibid.*
37 Smith, Mark (Ed.), *Doing the Duty of the Parish: Surveys of the Church
   in Hampshire 1810*, Hampshire Records Series, Hampshire County
   Council, 2004, pp. 171–173.
38 Corrie, Jessie Elizabeth, *op. cit.*, p. 16.
39 HO107/403, 1841Census for Itchen Abbas and HO107/1603,
   1851 Census for Itchen Abbas (www.ancestry.co.uk).

40 HRO, 21M65/210F/1, Itchen Abbas Faculty Papers, 1851.
Wright's successor, William Webb Spicer, carried out improvements
to Itchen Abbas rectory. He altered the pleasure grounds, rebuilt
the stables and 'pulled down' the kitchen and rebuilt it 'on a more
convenient site'.

41 Knight, Frances, *The Nineteenth Century Church and English Society*,
Cambridge University Press, 1995, p. 132.

42 HRO, 23M69/E/T18, The advowson, glebe, rectory and tithes of Itchen
Abbas. Mortgage to secure £2,000 and 5 per cent interest by bargain,
sale and lease for 99 years or one life, 15 December 1824.

43 HRO, 23M69/E/T23, Assignment of mortgage by lease and release,
1 and 2 March 1830.

44 Corrie, Jessie Elizabeth, *op. cit.*, p. 13.

45 HRO, 23M69/E/T24, Undertaking by Reverend Robert Wright
to deliver certain documents to the representative of Harry Comper,
9 April 1830.

46 HRO, 23M69/E/T26, Judgement in a suit for recovery of debt by
Harry Comper against the Rev. Robert Wright, Easter 1830.

47 *Ibid.*

48 *Ibid.*

49 HRO, 23M69/E/T23, Reconveyance: Discharge of Mortgage Debts,
31 December 1849.

50 HRO, 4M49/34, Conveyance by lease and release of land now used
as an orchard, formerly part of a farm called Bignell's, Itchen Abbas,
1840.

51 *Ibid.*

52 HRO, 21M65/E7/8/36, Copy residence licence, Robert Wright,
Itchen Abbas, 9 February 1844.

53 *Hampshire Chronicle*, Saturday 31 May 1845, p. 4.

54 HRO, 4M49/35, Mortgage of premises at Itchen Abbas, 2 roods,
30 perches, formerly part of a farm called Bignell's, 1847.

55 Beckett, John, *op. cit.*, pp. 103-107.

56 *Hampshire Chronicle*, Monday 28 December 1829, p. 1.

57 *Ibid.*, Monday 9 January 1826, p. 1.

58 Satchell, Veront M, *Hope Transformed*, University of West Indies Press,
2012, p. 86–87.

59 Latimer, James, 'The Apprenticeship System in the British West Indies', *The Journal of Negro Education*, Volume 33, No. 1 (Winter 1964), pp. 52–57 (www.jstor.org).

60 Satchell, Veront M, *op. cit.*, p. 91. Satchell provides no citation as to the exact identity of the people who went from the Itchen Valley to work on the Hope Plantation.

61 *Ibid.*, p. 204.

62 *Hampshire Advertiser*, Saturday 27 December 1834, p. 2.

63 *Ibid.*

64 Satchell, Veront M, *op. cit.*, p. 209.

65 Beckett, John, *op. cit.*, p. 180.

66 *Hampshire Advertiser*, Saturday 28 May 1836, p. 3.

67 Centre for the Study of the Legacies of British Slave Ownership, University College, London (www.ucl.ac.uk).

68 *Salisbury and Winchester Journal*, Monday 21 March 1838, p. 4.

69 *Ibid.*

70 *Ibid.*

71 Latimer, James, *op. cit.*, p. 53.

72 In January 1845, the second Duke of Buckingham and Chandos hosted Queen Victoria and Prince Albert at Stowe House for a three day 'sojourn'. At the time his 'finances were in ruins' and the event was considered a 'finale of supreme extravagance'. (*Stowe Through Time*, Anthony Meredith, Amberley Publishing, 2009.)

73 *Hampshire Chronicle*, Saturday 14 September 1844, p. 1.

Robert Wright, County Magistrate

The Commission of the Peace

In 1808 Robert Wright was nominated for inclusion in the county's Commission of the Peace. To qualify for nomination, it was necessary to be the owner of freehold land worth a minimum of £200 per annum.[1] Wright owned sufficient land in Itchen Abbas to qualify, thanks to his father being the patron and owner of the advowson. Without the support of an ambitious father who wished his son to progress, Robert Wright would have found it more difficult to achieve the status of a clerical magistrate.

The Lord Chancellor appointed individuals to a county's Commission of the Peace on behalf of the Crown, but he usually just rubber-stamped the recommendations of each county's Lord Lieutenant, and in Hampshire's case in 1808 this was the Earl of Malmesbury.[2] The Lord Lieutenant was technically responsible for the nomination of JPs as he was the *custos rotulorum*, or keeper of the rolls. We do not know who nominated Robert Wright, but it is reasonable to assume that his nomination would not have been advanced had Lord Bolton still been the Lord Lieutenant, given their long-standing dispute over the enfranchisement of Itchen Cottage. Robert Wright may have discussed the possibility of serving as a magistrate with the Reverend Francis Wickham Swanton (1746–1823), the respected curate of neighbouring Kings Worthy, who was an active clerical magistrate and well known in the Winchester area.[3]

Wright took the oath, named the *dedimus potestatem*[4], to become a practising magistrate at an adjournment of the Hampshire County Quarter Sessions, held at The Fleur de Lys Inn, Winchester, on the 17 December 1808. The Reverend FW Swanton and James Standerwick, Esquire administered the oath:

> I, the Reverend Robert Wright, do swear that I truly and bona fide have an estate in Law or Equity, to and for my own Use and Benefit,

consisting of the Rectory of Itchen Abbas in the County of Southampton and certain other Messuages, Lands and Hereditaments
in the same Parish of the Yearly value of three hundred pounds as
doth qualify me to act as a Justice of the Peace for the County of
Southampton.[5]

THE WORK OF THE COUNTY BENCH

Many in the Commission of the Peace did not bother to take their *dedimus
potestatem* which qualified them to become practising JPs. Ruscombe
Foster's research in Hampshire, for example, concludes that in 1821 of 283
men on the Commission only 53.7 per cent were fully qualified. Such individuals who were not qualified wanted the status of being named in the
Commission but did not want the workload that came with being a magistrate.[6] The work of county magistrates was unpaid and unrelenting, and it
comprised both administrative duties and the dispensing of justice.

The Court of Quarter Sessions

The Quarter Sessions of the Peace was a court for the whole of a county
which was summoned by the clerk of the peace and held before the
general public. The Hampshire Quarter Sessions were held at the Castle in
Winchester at Epiphany, Easter, Midsummer and Michaelmas. Full Quarter
Sessions lasted for three days; the first one was devoted to administrative
matters and the remaining time was reserved for the hearing of criminal
cases.[7] The administrative tasks included:

- appeals against removal orders, bastardy orders and rates
- upkeep of highways, footpaths and bridges
- financial accounts and setting of the county rate
- appointment of various committees and officials
- appointment of visiting JPs to the gaols and lunatic asylums
- deciding which business should be left for adjournment sessions.

Quarter Sessions Order Books recorded all the business along with a list
of magistrates in attendance in order of social standing.

The judicial role of a Justice of the Peace

A magistrate (Justice of the Peace) had the power to act on his own as an individual or with other magistrates sitting in Petty Sessions.

a) Single justice

An individual magistrate could commit a suspect to the county gaol to await trial or appear at the next Court of Quarter Sessions. He could also dispense summary justice by issuing fines or handing out immediate prison sentences for offenders he deemed guilty of offences such as drunkenness, poaching, breaching the peace or vagrancy. An individual magistrate could also serve an order for a parish to attend Quarter Sessions for failing to carry out its statutory duties such as the upkeep of roads and bridges.

b) Double justice

The law required two magistrates to appoint local officials (for example, constables), audit poor law account books, issue licences to alehouses, examine individuals as to their correct place of settlement and issue both bastardy and removal orders. They would also deal with hardened offenders who repeatedly committed serious crimes such as poaching, rioting and violent assault. They could punish offenders directly or commit them to the Quarter Sessions or Assizes (in the case of murder, for example).[8] *[Figure 9]*

ASSESSING ROBERT WRIGHT'S CONTRIBUTION TO THE BENCH

An analysis of the Quarter Sessions Order Books and the Calendars of Prisoners[9] concerning those who were held in the county gaol and bridewell in Winchester gives us some idea of the monumental contribution Robert Wright made to the work of the Hampshire bench.[10] Wright certainly craved the prestige and status of being a Justice of the Peace, but he was indis-putably not work shy. He had wasted no time in obtaining his *dedimus potestatem* and during the next 40 years he attended 156 full Quarter Sessions out of a possible 161 (96.9 per cent) as well as numerous Petty Sessions and adjourned Quarter Sessions.[11] Wright was not deterred by distance and travelled to places as far apart as Ringwood and Fareham from his home in Itchen Abbas to sit in Petty Sessions. He was by far the most active magistrate of his time and appeared to have unlimited reserves of stamina. *Table 5* shows Wright's near perfect attendance at full Quarter Sessions ranked against other committed JPs of his time.

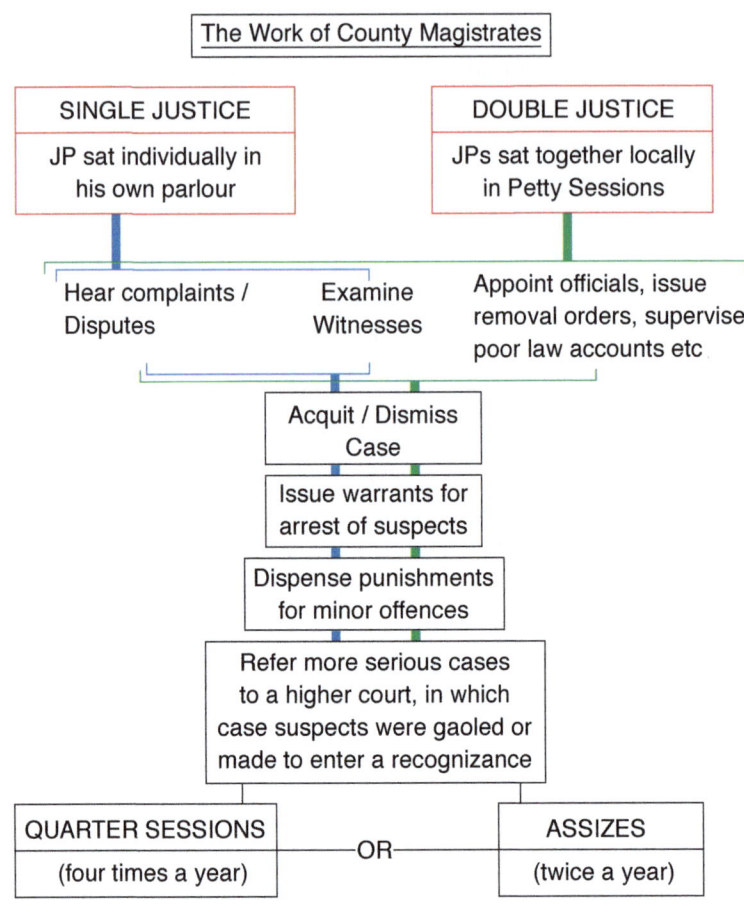

Figure 9: *The work of county magistrates.*

An analysis of the official printed Calendars of Prisoners shows that Wright dealt with a total of 579 cases which resulted in offenders being committed to gaol, either to await trial at Quarter Sessions or Assizes, or directly imprisoned for lesser offences. *Table 6* shows the breakdown of cases over the decades and indicates that Wright carried out his duties conscientiously, especially during the 1820s and 1830s when he was in his prime. Over the years, he issued more direct sentences to offenders (400) than referrals to a higher court of law (179).[12]

Name	No of QS attended	First	Last	Max QS possible	% attended
Robert Wright Clerk	156	1809	1849	161	96.9
William Hill Newbolt Clerk	70	1809	1827	74	94.6
Daniel Quarrier MD	71	1821	1843	85	83.5
William Thresher Esq	68	1829	1850	84	80.9
Edmund Poulter Clerk	73	1809	1830	92	79.3
Sir William Heatchote Bart	71	1823	1848	93	76.3
Edward W Blunt Esquire	74	1823	1848	101	73.3
Sir Thomas Baring Baronet	94	1810	1845	136	69.1
William Neville Esquire	105	1809	1850	161	65.2
George Eyre Esquire	86	1809	1848	160	53.7
John Fleming MP	68	1817	1848	130	52.3
William Grant Esquire	68	1810	1848	157	43.3

Table 5: *Best attending Hampshire JPs at Quarter Sessions ranked by percentage and contemporaneous with Robert Wright.*
(Sources: HRO Quarter Session Order Books; Hampshire Chronicle, Hampshire Advertiser, Hampshire Telegraph and Salisbury and Winchester Journal).

Decade	To QS (S)	To QS (D)	DS (S)	DS (D)	To AS (S)	To AS (D)	Total
1810-20	27	10	48	7	0	0	92
1821-30	30	20	119	35	1	2	207
1831-40	22	23	55	63	1	3	167
1841-50	18	20	36	37	2	0	113
Totals	**97**	**73**	**258**	**142**	**4**	**5**	**579**

Key
S = Offenders committed by Robert Wright acting on his own (single justice)
D = Robert Wright acting with other magistrates in Petty Sessions (double justice)
QS=Quarter Sessions;   **DS**=Direct Sentencing;   **AS**=Assizes

Table 6: *A breakdown of how offenders were dealt with by Robert Wright (Source: HRO Printed Calendars of Prisoners)*

The Calendars of Prisoners also show that Wright encountered a wide variety of crimes with poaching and theft the most numerous *[see Graph 1]*.[13]

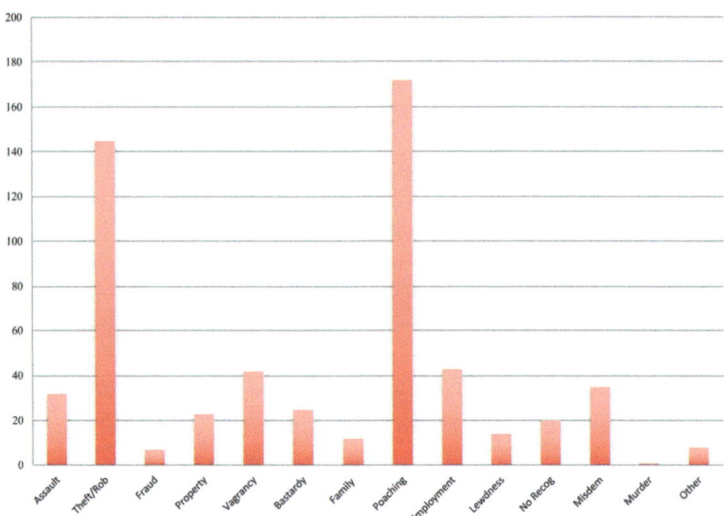

Graph 1: *Crimes dealt with by Robert Wright 1810–1849*
(Source: HRO Printed Calendars of Prisoners)

Finally, the Calendars of Prisoners afford an analysis of the total and types of punishments handed out. By far the most common punishment was up to three months imprisonment *[Table 7]*. Usually, prisoners were made to carry out hard labour during their time in prison, and some also suffered public whipping.[14]

These statistics, however, were probably only the tip of the iceberg of the work Robert Wright did as a magistrate. Unfortunately, he did not keep a notebook of the cases he heard (or at least one has not survived) and therefore the full extent of his judicial work will most probably never be known. If he acted in a similar manner to Samuel Whitbread, a Bedfordshire JP, there would have been many complaints made to him in his own parlour at Itchen Cottage which he either dismissed or mediated upon for the parties.[15] He could also have bound an offender over to keep the peace by obtaining sureties for their future conduct, issued fines or even handed out a period in the stocks. (The Itchen Abbas churchwardens' accounts show that a new set of stocks were built in the village in 1827 by the local carpenter,

Sentence	Number
Up to 3 months in prison	391
4-8 months in prison	50
Acquitted	20
No Prosecution	19
Sent to Assizes	18
1-3 years in prison	16
No Bill	16
7-11 months in prison	14
Transportation for 1-7 years	14
Recognizance	8
Case continued	6
Not known	3
Transportation for 14 years	2
Admitted evidence	1
Fined	1
Total	**579**

Table 7: *Sentences given to offenders committed to Quarter Sessions or directly punished by Robert Wright, 1810–1849 (Source: HRO Printed Calendars of Prisoners).*

James Bignell.)[16] In theory, Wright was available 365 days of the year, and he alluded to the demands of being a JP by giving the following response to a question put to him by the Select Committee on the Sale of Beer in 1833:

Question: Do you find that there are many petty offences of which no cognizance is taken?

Answer: I make up hundreds every year of my life, rather than bring them before the bench.[17]

Records of official Petty Sessions, when Wright sat with other magistrates, are also extremely sketchy and inconsistently recorded and do not allow a reliable and detailed analysis of attendance. The Calendars of Prisoners do, however, allow one to identify other magistrates who worked with Wright, either when directly sentencing offenders or when sending them to prison to await trial. Not surprisingly, the men who worked most regularly with Robert Wright lived in the vicinity of Winchester *[Table 8]*.[18]

JP Colleague	Residence	No of times working with Wright
Nevill William	Winchester	46
Yonge William Crawley	Otterbourne	42
Jarvis Stephen Raymond	Fair Oak	41
Lovell George	Crawley	21
Baring Thomas Sir	Stratton Park	18
Duthy John	Ropley	17
Wall Samuel	Worthy Park	14
Wall Charles Baring	Norman Court	9

Table 8: *JPs who worked most frequently with Robert Wright in Petty Sessions (Source: HRO Printed Calendars of Prisoners).*

Any political differences appeared to be irrelevant in magisterial work. For example, Wright, an ultra-Tory, had no problem in working closely with Sir Thomas Baring who was a staunch Whig supporter.

Wright's level of commitment can also be judged by a trawl of the Quarter Sessions Order Books to establish the amount of work he undertook in matters of routine county administration. Between 1809 and 1849 there were 247 references to Wright in relation to a range of issues, including appeals against removal orders that he had helped to initiate [Graph 2].[19]

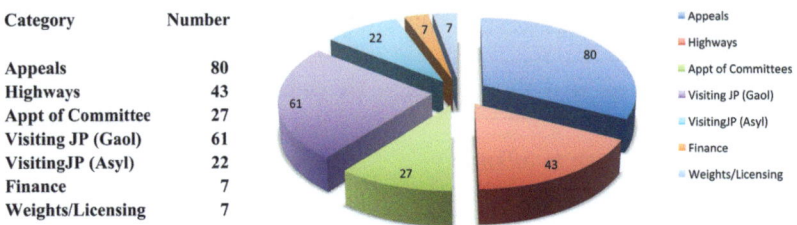

Category	Number
Appeals	80
Highways	43
Appt of Committee	27
Visiting JP (Gaol)	61
VisitingJP (Asyl)	22
Finance	7
Weights/Licensing	7

Graph 2: *Issues involving Robert Wright cited in the Hampshire Quarter Sessions Order Books, 1809–1849 (Source: HRO Quarter Sessions Order Books).*

Issue	1809-19	1820-29	1830-39	1840-49	Totals
Appt of Officials	2	9	10	7	28
Debtors	24	6	0	0	30
Highways	5	7	5	5	22
Rates	8	6	6	11	31
Parish Returns	4	4	4	9	21
Finance	1	2	6	10	19
Gaol Reports	0	1	8	6	15
Qualifying JPs	1	2	16	5	24
Advertising	1	2	0	0	3
Weights & Measure	2	0	5	0	7
Business held over	5	8	24	25	62
Other	1	2	8	9	20
Total	**54**	**49**	**92**	**87**	**282**

Table 9: *Adjournment issues involving Robert Wright, 1809–1849 (Source: HRO Quarter Sessions Order Books).*

When there was insufficient time to deal with all the business during full Quarter Sessions, adjournment sessions were held, usually in the Grand Jury Room in Winchester Castle. Here, the outstanding work was discussed by a group of JPs sitting together. The minutes of adjournments were entered into the Quarter Sessions Order Books, and an analysis shows that Robert Wright made a formidable contribution, dealing with a wide variety of issues *[Table 9]*.[20]

He was also always ready to act outside his own district if there was a shortage of JPs or to cover for magistrates who were busy with other commitments.

CLERICAL MAGISTRATES: A CONTROVERSIAL ISSUE

Period	Total attendance (All JPs)	No of attendances Clerical JPs	Clerical JPs as % of total attendance
1809-14	513	164	31.9
1815-19	613	137	22.3
1820-24	669	158	23.6
1825-29	524	89	16.9
1830-34	601	58	9.6
1835-39	786	60	7.6
1840-44	801	62	7.7
1845-50	858	56	6.5
Totals	**5365**	**784**	**14.6**

Table 10: *Attendance of clerical magistrates at Hampshire Quarter Sessions, 1809–1850 (Sources: HRO Quarter Sessions Order Books; Hampshire Chronicle, Hampshire Advertiser, Hampshire Telegraph, and Salisbury and Winchester Journal).*

Opinion was divided about clergymen serving as members of the Commission of the Peace, a position that brought considerable social prestige and status. The Duke of Wellington, who succeeded the Earl of Malmesbury as Lord Lieutenant of Hampshire in 1820, was categorically against the appointment of clergymen unless there was a shortage of suitable gentry in the locality. Wellington felt that the landed aristocracy and gentry should be the preferred option. When, in 1822, the first Duke of Buckingham and Chandos recommended the Reverend Charles Shrubsole

Bonnett of Avington, Robert Wright's neighbour, for the Commission of the Peace, Wellington told him that the only possible exceptions to his rule were 'clergymen who may have landed property in the county besides their church benefices' and turned Bonnett down.[21] The Duke also recognised the potential for conflict with a clergyman being an acting magistrate and 'was anxious to keep the clergy clear of the broils etc. in which magistrates are accasionally [sic] involved'. An analysis of attendances at Quarter Sessions *[Table 10]* shows how the influence of clerical magistrates in Hampshire declined during the years of Wellington's occupancy of the post of Lord Lieutenant. In the period 1820–1824, 23.9 per cent of all attendance at Quarter Sessions was by clerical magistrates, but by 1845–1850 it had fallen to 6.5 per cent.

Henry Brougham, the Lord Chancellor of the day, concurred, and commented:

A clerical magistrate, in uniting two very excellent and useful characters, pretty commonly spoils both ... There is the activity of the magistrate in an excessive degree; over activity is a very high magisterial offence, in my view; yet most of the magistrates distin-guished for over-activity are clergymen; joined to this are found the local hatings and likings and, generally, somewhat narrow-minded opinions and prejudices, which are apt to attach to the character of the resident parish priest; one of the most valuable and respectable, if kept pure from political contaminations.[22]

The dilemma is also succinctly explained by Peter Virgin:

[C]lerical JPs were at once judge and pastoral adviser-two incom-patible roles; he might be called upon to imprison a man for some offence on one day and then have the duty of consoling the same man's family the next. Tension and conflict were unavoidable and came to cause unease among the clergy themselves.[23]

On the other hand, an Oxbridge educated clergyman such as Robert Wright was learned, literate and often good at administrative and magis-terial work (even without formal training in the law). Wright, along with other clerical JPs, would most probably have possessed a copy of Richard Burn's *Justice of the Peace and Parish Officer*, first published in 1755, which was the JP's *vade mecum*. Providing a wealth of information relating to the law, it was indispensable to the untrained magistrate. Advice was also available from more experienced magistrates.

There was plenty of work to be done for a committed magistrate, clergyman or otherwise, and the role carried a substantial burden of responsibility. This very point was expressed in 1830 by Reverend WL Bowles, the vicar of Bremhill in Wiltshire. As a clerical magistrate himself, Bowles argued that despite some problems the roles of clergyman and magistrate did not have to be incompatible. In some localities there was no alternative to having a clergyman as a magistrate 'as there was no country gentleman within distance', and besides, Bowles wrote, 'he is as much distinguished for rectitude, integrity, and benevolence, as the best of the educated gentlemen to whom that post is entrusted'.[24]

Bowles also stated that he himself did as much as possible to defend the rights of the poor. Whether this was so in the case of Robert Wright is a matter of debate; he put so much time into his work as a magistrate it does not seem possible that he did justice to his spiritual role. Bowles claimed, probably correctly, that reformers, such as Cobbett, should not stereotype all clerical magistrates as unworthy. However, Bowles also claimed, not entirely correctly, that 'the poor know best who is their friend' and that they were aware that 'the Clergy, resident among them [were] succouring their necessities, praying by their sick bed... [and] protecting them'.[25] Bowles wanted greater tolerance towards clerical magistrates and believed that they should be judged individually. Many, however, held clerical magistrates in contempt and believed they had no place in the justice system.

Despite the controversy, clerical magistrates were prominent in the work of the Hampshire bench in terms of attendance at full Quarter Sessions, particularly in the years from 1809 to 1829. The contribution of some of the more active clerical magistrates in Hampshire is shown overleaf in *Table 11*; but, as already demonstrated, their influence waned in the latter part of Wellington's lord lieutenancy.

The named magistrates in *Table 11* were all contemporaneous with the career of Robert Wright and only the years in which they made committals are included. (NB The averages are based on the actual number of years in which committals were made.)

Name	Parish	Number of Committal years	Start Year	End Year	Total Committals	Average per Year
Rev Robert Wright	Itchen Abbas	35	1810	1848	579	16.54
Rev J H Ashworth	East Woodhay	10	1832	1847	161	16.1
Rev W H Newbolt	Morestead	20	1809	1830	262	13.1
Rev E Poulter	Buriton	21	1809	1830	222	10.57
Rev J Worsley	Thorley IOW	13	1818	1833	142	10.92
Rev C Dodson	Penton Mewsey	14	1833	1849	113	8.07
Rev J Harwood	Deane	14	1815	1830	100	7.14
Rev R W White	Wooton IOW	20	1822	1849	141	7.05
Rev T Salmom	Dogmersfield	12	1809	1820	74	6.16
Rev D Williams	Romsey	14	1820	1833	77	5.5

Table 11: *Committals by Hampshire clerical magistrates, 1809–1849. (Source: HRO Printed Calendars of Prisoners)*

St Peter's Fields, 1819: clerical magistrates under attack

On Monday 16 August 1819 a crowd upwards of 60,000 gathered at St Peter's Fields in Manchester to hear Henry 'Orator' Hunt speak about reforming Parliament and obtaining the vote for working people. Those who attended were dressed in their Sunday best and it was a family friendly occasion. Two clerical magistrates, the Reverends Charles Ethelston and William Robert Hay, were instrumental in reading the Riot Act and then giving the orders for Hunt to be arrested. The yeomanry charged through the crowd to reach Hunt, indiscriminately striking innocent individuals in their way. It was carnage, leaving 18 dead and almost 700 injured.[26] Many innocent people were trampled on and others suffered terrible sabre wounds to the arms, legs and heads. William Marsh, for example, aged 57, sustained 'a sabre cut on [the] back of the head, body crushed, bone shattered in [his] left leg'.[27] The authorities were unsympathetic to the plight of the crowd and the Prince Regent actually congratulated the magistrates for 'their prompt, decisive and efficient measures for the preservation of the public tranquillity'.[28] *[Plate 12]*

The event, which became known as the Peterloo Massacre, caused widespread public anger all over the country. The *Hampshire Chronicle* informed its readers:

> The unfortunate occurrence at Manchester continues to occupy the public attention throughout the country. Meetings are daily held in various places at which the conduct of the magistrates is freely canvassed, and the proceedings on the 16th [August] strongly reprobated.[29]

Plate 12: *Manchester Heroes, by George Cruikshank, 1819
(by courtesy of the People's History Museum).*

In Hampshire the leader of the Whigs, the Earl of Carnarvon, instituted a freeholders' requisition for a county meeting to discuss what had happened in Manchester, with particular reference to the Tory government's approval of the way the magistrates had acted. Only the High Sheriff of the county, Henry Compton of Minstead, had the power to call a county meeting, but before he could respond a counter requisition was quickly organised by the Hampshire Tories, arguing that any meeting would be 'unconstitutional' and would undermine the authority of Parliament. Over 400 Tory freeholders, including Robert Wright, signed the counter requisition.[30] Clearly, Wright was more concerned about upholding the establishment than addressing the excessive and disproportionate violence directed towards the innocent people who were present at the Manchester meeting. In the end, the original requisition was withdrawn when it was learned that Parliament would be recalled to debate the issue.

CLERICAL MAGISTRATES AND THE RADICAL PRESS

THE CLERICAL MAGISTRATE.

Plate 13:
The Clerical Magistrate,
by George Cruikshank, 1819
(Private Collection/
Bridgeman Images).

In the ensuing weeks clerical magistrates were attacked in the radical press. In December 1819 William Hone, a radical publisher, collaborated with George Cruikshank to publish *The Political House That Jack Built*, a 24-page booklet lampooning the role of the magistrates at St Peter's Fields.[31] In particular, it attacked the 'religious hypocrisy and the incompatibility of religious and civil authority',[32] and included a satirical Cruikshank cartoon depicting the Reverend Charles Ethelston as representing the 'two faces' of clerical magistrates [Plate 13].

The Political House That Jack Built rapidly sold 100,000 copies and captured the public mood of the time. Peterloo had had the effect of intensifying the hatred between the radical press and the clergy. Dr John Gardner explains the importance of the radical press in the context of St Peter's Fields:

> Most people in Britain had never even been to Manchester, never mind St Peter's Fields, and for them the only way that they could understand what happened there on 16 August 1819 was through representations in the press, in poetry, and in graphic art. Pamphleteers like Hone used poetry and the pamphlet as mediums that could travel quickly, efficiently, and cheaply.[33]

Wright would almost definitely have been aware of the controversial nature of his dual role and of Hone's satirical publication, but he was not to be deflected from his rigid philosophy of life. He was unshakeable in his strongly held view of the way he believed society was designed to work, and for him the maintenance of established order was paramount. Memories of the French Revolution were still fresh in the mind and any threat to the status quo needed to be quashed.

The case of Richard Deller, 1823

Richard Deller was a tenant farmer from Easton whose land bordered the estate of the first Duke of Buckingham and Chandos. On 19 February 1822 Deller went hare-coursing on his rented property accompanied by some friends, one of whom had a number of dogs. Deller was not licensed to indulge in coursing, but his friend with the dogs had a current game certificate and this meant Deller himself was not breaking the game laws. One of the Duke of Buckingham's gamekeepers, however, had spotted the coursing and informed his employer. On 6 March 1822 Deller was again found coursing and this time he was summoned to appear before the Duke, a member of the Hampshire bench, charged with coursing hares without a licence.

In law, there was no case to answer and Deller felt affronted. When he appeared before the Duke at Avington House, Deller claimed that the game preserved by the Duke's gamekeepers damaged his crops and cost him an estimated £30–£40 each year. Unmoved, the Duke would not allow Deller's witnesses to give evidence, and he warned the indignant farmer that a constable would take him into custody if he did not moderate his behaviour. The Duke then proceeded to fine Deller £5 for coursing on his rented land and without the express permission of his landlord.

The situation was exacerbated some months later when one of the Duke's servants, John Grey, trespassed on Deller's land on 10 April 1823. He was challenged by Deller but refused to speak or give his name. Deller then forcibly grabbed Grey and marched him the two miles to Robert Wright's house in Itchen Abbas to make a complaint to the reverend magistrate.

Wright, probably not wishing to offend the Duke, his close associate, refused point blank to hear the complaint and told Deller to go to the Petty Sessions at Winchester the following day, when his clerk would be available to record the proceedings. Deller complied and appeared before Reverend E Poulter (in the chair), William Nevill and Wright. To Deller's astonishment, John Grey accused him of assault and was allowed to put his complaint to the three magistrates. Deller used the 1820 Malicious Trespass Act to defend himself, but the three JPs deemed it inadmissible and bound him over to keep the peace! Grey was acquitted.[34]

The furious Deller drew up a petition of complaint, which was presented to the House of Commons on 25 April 1823. The chronology of events, as contained in the petition, was read to the House. Deller claimed he had not broken the law but rather that the magistrates had not applied it correctly. The petition concluded by demanding, among other things, that the law should be amended so that tenants were allowed to kill any game damaging their crops and a new law should be passed which forbade clergymen from acting as magistrates. Unsurprisingly, the petition was rejected and no new legislation was enacted to prevent clerics from being magistrates.

Reverend Poulter felt that he and his colleagues had been slandered by Deller's petition and he wrote to the press, defending the way the magistrates had conducted the case:

> I trust that I have thus, satisfactorily to the public, vindicated the conduct of the Magistrates acting at Winchester on this occasion; and I think I have cause to complain that the constitutional right of petition ... has been grossly abused in this instance.[35]

William Cobbett, however, was unconvinced and blamed Wright for his initial indecision which had resulted in an unsatisfactory delay to the delivery of summary justice. Cobbett wrote that 'if Wright had ... heard [the case] at his own house there would have been an end [to] it one way or the other'.[36] Wright, for his part, made no public utterance about his part in the affair. When he was the target of criticism he often remained quiet and went about his business as usual. In some ways, this displayed a steely character; had he allowed criticism to worry him he would not have coped with the responsibility of being a county magistrate for over 40 years.

Deller had received financial support from a number of friends which enabled him to pay his legal expenses in the 'notorious game transaction between the Duke of Buckingham and myself'.[37] He placed a letter of thanks to his supporters in the local press and also informed the public that a sum of money left over had been donated to the county hospital in Winchester.

In his book *The Long Affray*, the historian Harry Hopkins expresses the opinion that the first Duke of Buckingham and Chandos was known for having 'an army of gamekeepers, supported by a coterie of magistrates, who seem to have been at perpetual war with tenant farmers'.[38] It seemed, therefore, that Deller had been a victim of different sections of the establishment closing ranks on him. On the other hand, it could also have been the case that the three magistrates had judged Deller correctly, because two years later he was fined £10 for assaulting John Weeks. Deller witnessed this young lad accidentally striking some cattle when driving them along a lane in Easton and proceeded to beat him with a hedge stake.[39]

By August 1826 Deller had given notice to quit his tenancy of the 146 acre farm the following Michaelmas. The farm was advertised and interested parties were informed that 'the estate is surrounded by the property of the Duke of Buckingham, and abounds with game, and would afford excellent sport to a qualified gentleman'.[40] The word 'qualified' carried significant weight in the wake of the events involving Deller!

ROBERT WRIGHT AT PETTY SESSIONS

Petty Sessions enabled magistrates to work together in hearing a variety of cases, many of which legally required two JPs. They also reduced the amount of travel when held locally, and for this reason in July 1830 the number of county divisions was increased from nine to thirteen.[41] Robert Wright applauded this change and believed that all market towns such as Romsey, Alresford and Stockbridge should stage Petty Sessions regularly.

The sketchy surviving records do not allow a calculation of the number of times Robert Wright sat at Petty Sessions, but there are random press reports of local Petty Sessions which show the wide variety of offences upon which he had to pass judgement.

Gleaning at Barton Stacey

On 29 August 1825, 13 women from Barton Stacey were brought before Robert Wright and Sir William Heathcote. The women had been spotted gleaning[42] in a harvested field of barley that belonged to Mr Smith, a 'respectable farmer'. The women were convicted and fined two shillings each for damaging the field. All but two were extremely contrite and apologised profusely for trespassing and said they would not repeat the offence. As a result, they were discharged. The two feisty women who refused to apologise were sent to the bridewell for a week. The women had committed a trivial offence but the sitting magistrates used the case to set an example to others who thought they had the 'right' to trespass into a field to glean cereal crops. The *Hampshire Chronicle* reported:

> It is hoped that the example which the farmers have been called
> upon to make in this instance, will operate as a warning, and

prevent those who have persisted in [gleaning] barley, under an impression that they had a right so to do, from following practices which they will now be satisfied are illegal, and which must ultimately subject them to expense and confinement.[43]

There was some criticism of the action of the magistrates involved in this case. Many argued that a more appropriate action would have been to give the women a lecture before releasing them. The *Morning Herald* was astounded that the case had even been brought before the magistrates and expressed an alternative view:

> In most parts of the country, [gleaning] has hitherto been one of the means a labourer has had of paying his rent, of maintaining his wife and family, and perhaps of fattening a pig for their winter consumption; and though the right has been gravely adjudged not to exist ... there are instances of which this is one, in which it would be as well if both farmers and Magistrates were not quite so ready to 'mark what is amiss'.[44]

On occasions such as this Robert Wright showed how uncompromising he could be in applying the letter, rather than the spirit of the law.

Sympathy for Thomas Hopkins

The other side of Robert Wright's complicated character was illustrated by the case of Thomas Hopkins. Wright and Richard Bethel Cox committed Hopkins for trial at the Quarter Sessions on the evidence of William Henry Attwood, overseer of the poor for Stockbridge. Hopkins had refused to go to his place of work and thus made his family dependent on the parish. The case was heard on 23 May 1829 and Hopkins was sentenced to one month in prison with hard labour. Unfortunately, Hopkins had 'aggravated' his offence by sending a defiant letter to the overseer:

> This is to inform you that I will not work for two shillings and sixpence per day and I will not come before eight oclock [sic] in the morning and I shall leave off at four in the evening. Thomas Hopkins.[45]

Hopkins was transported to the bridewell in Winchester but had served only three days of his sentence when Wright intervened. He wrote a letter to the keeper of the bridewell stating that he had been told that Hopkins' wife was in 'a dangerous state' and 'two of his children [were] sadly afflicted'. Wright said that 'these circumstances ... induced me to request his release'. The order was carried out and Hopkins was discharged.[46] The case clearly showed that the enigmatic Wright did have the ability to empathise with the problems of the labouring class if and when he wanted.

Reverend Richard Daws and the highway rate

On 22 March 1838 Wright sat at the Stockbridge Petty Sessions along with fellow JP John Meggot Elwes. Before them was the Reverend Richard Daws, the vicar of Kings Somborne, who had failed to pay his highway rate, despite several requests. Daws tried to prove that the rate was illegal but failed. He was found guilty and told to pay the rate, plus expenses. However, 'the Magistrates observed, that if the Rev. Gentleman felt himself aggrieved, he might appeal to the next general quarter sessions'.[47]

William Saunders and poaching

On Saturday 11 December 1841 Robert Wright chaired a bench of magistrates which committed William Saunders to the house of correction for two months. Saunders was imprisoned as he was in default of paying a fine of £2-7s-0d for using wires to poach game on the property of Paulet St John-Mildmay at Dogmersfield. At the same sitting, the bench dealt with a number of constables and overseers who had failed to send in their parish jury lists and lunatic returns. The officials, who had been summoned to appear, were admonished and ordered to pay the expenses.[48]

An assault at Easton

On 9 September 1848 the now ageing Wright chaired the Winchester Petty Sessions, assisted by Captain William Nevill, William W Bulpett, Esquire and John Thomas Waddington, Esquire. One case involved a local man, John Dagwell of Easton, who was known to Wright. Charles Langford and John Dollery were convicted of an assault on Dagwell. Langford was fined ten shillings and Dollery five shillings, plus costs; the alternative, if they preferred, was one month's imprisonment.[49]

The eccentric Reverend Herbert Smith

On Saturday 5 August 1848 Robert Wright chaired a Petty Sessions bench in the Grand Jury Room in Winchester which consisted of William Nevill, William Crawley Yonge, William W Bulpett, John Thomas Waddington and Wilson Theophilus Graeme. They found themselves dealing with a case of an 'unpleasant nature'[50] which involved the Reverend Herbert Smith (1800–1876).

Smith had been the curate of Micheldever with East Stratton for a number of years but had left the parish in 1834. The patron of the parish was Sir Thomas Baring and he had often told Smith what he should preach and how he was to carry out parochial duties. Smith resented the interference and argued his case, only to be informed he was surplus to requirements in 1834. Another curate was appointed in his place.[51]

Smith, however, refused to accept this and his anger simmered unabated. On 19 March 1848 he barged into the Chapel of Ease at East Stratton, interrupted the service and became involved in a brawl with Mr Charles Pain, the warden of the chapel. Pain complained and Smith was summoned to attend the Petty Sessions.

The magistrates offered Smith a compromise; if he provided sureties that he would not try to take divine service at East Stratton during the next 12 months he would be acquitted. Predictably, the irate Smith rejected this compromise and demanded to be re-instated to his former post. The sitting magistrates felt they had no choice but to send him to gaol to await trial at the Michaelmas Quarter Sessions.[52] The relevant Calendar of Prisoners completes the story:

> **No 13** The Rev. Herbert Smith, aged 48 … Committed August 5th 1848 by Rev. Robert Wright, Clerk, W. Nevill, Esq. and others, charged with having, on the morning of Sunday the 19th day of March 1848, at the parish of East Stratton, willingly, maliciously, or contentiously … disturbed the performance of Divine Service.[53]

Smith was a confrontational individual who was unable to contain his anger at any perceived personal injustice. Even from his prison cell he continued to insist on his innocence and he wrote a letter to the *Hampshire Chronicle* in which he claimed that he actually had agreed to be bound over. He had agreed, he said, with the following words:

I, Herbert Smith, Curate of Stratton, promise that I will not present myself to perform divine service at Stratton Chapel, for twelve months, without the approval of the Bishop of Winchester.

It was likely that Smith had changed the wording so that it stated he was still the curate of Stratton (incorrect) and he was falsely suggesting that he if he could get the approval of the Bishop of Winchester anytime soon then he would be appearing at Stratton. Smith blamed the 'other party' for not accepting his version of the wording and argued that as a result he had been wrongly imprisoned.[54]

By the time the Michaelmas Quarter Sessions met on 16 October 1848 Smith had already served over two months in gaol and he was therefore discharged by the court. The irony was that a clergyman had been committed on the judgement of a fellow cleric, who also happened to be a magistrate, thereby illustrating how the role of a clerical JP was open to conflict, and even compromise.

THE JOHN HUGHES AFFAIR, 1824–1825

Robert Wright's popular reputation as the 'poor man's friend' has been based largely on the compassion he displayed towards John Hughes (alias Smith), a traveller and compulsive thief. Normally, Wright showed little sympathy for persistent law-breakers.

The exact facts and circumstances of the story of John Hughes have never been fully ascertained. Much of the story is based on oral tradition and uncited assertions. However, using newspaper reports from the time it is possible to reconstruct a chain of events leading to the execution of Hughes.

During 1824 and early 1825 there were three incidents of horse stealing which may all have involved John Hughes. On the night of 11 May 1824 two horses were stolen from Wright's stables in Itchen Abbas,[55] an event also mentioned by Jessie Corrie, who states that 'the thief, a gipsy, was caught in London'.[56] Wright offered a reward of 20 guineas for information leading to the arrest of the culprit. Seven months later, on 20 December 1824, the *Hampshire Chronicle* reported the theft of a riding mare from the premises of Mr Michael Bailey of nearby Totford, and it would appear that a harness and saddle also went missing.[57] Finally, on 24 January 1825 the same newspaper told its readers that John Smith (Hughes) had been committed to the (Hampshire) county gaol 'charged with having stolen a horse, the property of William Burrows, at Harrow on the Hill, Middlesex'.[58]

Hughes must have been transported from Harrow back to central Hampshire, where the original thefts took place, and imprisoned in Winchester to await trial at the Lent Assizes. It was usual for county authorities to liaise with Bow Street in London in the pursuit of criminals and it is likely that this was how Hughes came to be apprehended. At this particular time there was such great concern at the growing level of horse stealing that Bow Street had decided to carry out a purge to bring more horse thieves to justice. Bow Street even had officers at the port of Dover to prevent stolen horses being sent to the Continent. Under these circumstances, it is not surprising that Hughes was captured.[59]

At the Lent Assizes in Winchester on 5 March 1825 Hughes was sentenced to death by Mr Justice Burrough who told Hughes that he needed to make an example of him and that there was no hope of any reprieve. In pronouncing the death sentence, the judge addressed Hughes as follows:

John Smith – You have been convicted of a crime, which, from its frequent occurrence, it has been highly necessary to put a stop to. The crime of horse-stealing prevails to such an extent, that it is absolutely necessary the severest punishment should be inflicted, to deter other persons from the commission of it. I myself have tried 30 or 40 horse-stealers-others have been tried by brother Judges, and those convicted have been sent abroad for life; but this has been found insufficient to check it. An example is necessary to repress this crime, and your case is one of that description, which merits the severest penalty of the law.[60]

Hughes was hanged behind the Jewry Street gaol in Winchester on Saturday 19 March 1825. The scene was reported in detail in the *Hampshire Chronicle*:

This morning the extreme sentence of the law was carried into execution on John Smith, aged 26; James Dawes, aged 30; and Wm Dawes, aged 22. … Smith, whose real name was Hughes, and who had been convicted of horse-stealing, was a gipsy, and had always led a wandering life. He professed to be a rat catcher and basket-maker, but confessed that he had subsisted chiefly on plunder. His depredations were not confined to one county, or to any single species of property, but extended to house-breaking, sheep-stealing, and indeed to every other description of robbery. He acknowledged the offence for which he suffered, and the justice of his sentence... From the time of their condemnation the [three] unhappy men conducted themselves in a manner becoming their melancholy situation. They paid the greatest attention to the instructions of the Chaplain, deeply bewailing their past transgressions, and earnestly seeking forgiveness through their Redeemer.

... We cannot close this report without a just tribute of commendation to the worthy Chaplain, the Rev. Mr Zillwood. His attention was unremitting as his zeal was great, and his feelings on the scaffold afforded the best proof of the deep interest he took in the eternal welfare of the unfortunate sufferers. So great was their reliance on his advice and instruction, that they disclosed all the secrets of their hearts to him. Smith, who was at first least affected by his situation, became truly penitent, and the last words he uttered were, "Almighty God, forgive my offences".[61]

The *Hampshire Advertiser* carried the same report but concluded with the additional information that the men had spent two hours in prayer with Reverend Zillwood before 'their dreadful time was come' and then commented somewhat callously that 'their bodily sufferings did not appear to be of long duration'.[62]

There was no reference in the local press describing Wright's attempt to win a reprieve for Hughes. The body was most probably taken away by relatives, and the next day, Sunday 20 March 1825, Wright officiated at the funeral. Hughes was buried under the yew tree in Itchen Abbas churchyard and a headstone was later erected with a poignant epitaph: 'A faithful friend, a father dear, an unfortunate husband lieth here. The Lord removed his earthly body into the realms of everlasting day'.

Plate 14: *The weathered headstone of John Hughes in Itchen Abbas churchyard (Source: Author).*

How much input Wright had into organising the headstone and choosing the epitaph we do not know. The glowing sentiment expressed, however, suggests that members of Hughes' family were the prime movers, in view of the fact that he was a compulsive robber and constant offender against the law. That Wright had any involvement at all with such a character is bewildering. He personally recorded the details of the burial in the register[63] as detailed below.

Tales of Wright's generosity in trying to win a reprieve for Hughes have been repeated, with embellishment, in numerous places

Name	Abode	Age	When Buried	Officiating Minister
John Smith (alias John Hughes) a Gipsey	*A wanderer*	*26*	*March 20th 1825*	*Robert Wright*

since at least 1899, when Jessie Corrie first published her family history. For example, we are told that Wright made a special journey to London to visit Hughes in gaol, but no citations are given for this claim. We are also often given the impression that Hughes was tried in London and hanged in the capital. This, however, was not the case, as can be evidenced by the reports in the Hampshire press.

Wright's munificence towards Hughes needs to be questioned. Why did he afford a convicted horse thief his charity when his track record generally was one of showing little leniency towards those brought before the courts and found guilty? Jessie Corrie claims that gypsy tribes delivered barrels of smuggled liquor as a token of gratitude, leaving us to ponder if Wright, a county magistrate, deliberately cultivated a friendly relationship with the gypsies in order to obtain contraband. According to Corrie 'Many a keg of smuggled spirits after that would be found in the Rectory garden, the Rector receiving a notice from whence he could easily guess to "look into his cabbages" '.[64]

There is no way of knowing the exact truth, but the Hughes story became part of local folklore and was handed down through generations of villagers. Seventy-four years later Corrie wrote:

> The present [parish] Clerk's wife, old Mrs Shefford, told me she remembered her father-in-law tell how he dug the grave and how the gypsy [Hughes] was found to have been hanged in his finest clothes and every button was made of a silver piece.[65]

Also, according to Corrie, the gypsy community was grateful to Wright for later obtaining a reprieve for a sheep rustler by lobbying the Duke of Wellington. Thus, 'the grateful gypsies flocked by dozens to Hampshire to thank [great] grandfather'.[66]

These stories were obviously repeated to create a favourable image of a caring magistrate who was the friend of the poor, but if we look at Wright's career in general a more varied picture emerges. There are some recorded instances where Wright displayed empathy towards the labouring poor, but it is oversimplifying matters to sum him up as the 'poor man's friend'. His attitude, for example, towards the labourers who were involved in the rioting of 1830 was unforgiving and austere.

Five weeks after the execution of Hughes, two horse thieves were detained in the village of Ropley, seven miles distant from Itchen Abbas, by Robert Wright and John Duthy. The thieves, who were not cited as being members of the gypsy community, had three horses in their possession matching the descriptions given in a newspaper advertisement and it appeared that the horses had been stolen in Uxbridge the previous week and taken to Hampshire.[67] Interestingly, the empathy shown by Wright towards Hughes did not appear to be on offer to other horse thieves.

A 'PASSION' FOR THE REFORM OF LUNATIC ASYLUMS

Private or public provision?

A lesser known aspect of Robert Wright's work as a magistrate was his interest in the care of those with mental disabilities for which Ruscombe Foster claims he had a 'campaigning zeal'.[68] Since 1774 magistrates had been given the responsibility for licensing and inspecting lunatic asylums that admitted patients privately.[69] During the first half of the nineteenth century six such asylums were opened in Hampshire, including Grove Place (near Nursling), Lainston House (near Winchester) and Portsea Island.[70] In 1808 central government passed an 'Act for the better Care and Maintenance of Lunatics, being Paupers or Criminals in England', which allowed the construction of county asylums financed out of the rates.[71] Only nine counties took advantage of the act, and although the topic was discussed, the Hampshire bench decided against erecting a county asylum.

In 1815–1816 there was another exhaustive debate within the Hampshire Quarter Sessions of the desirability of the county building a lunatic asylum. Sir Thomas Baring and William Sturges Bourne were strong supporters of the idea, but a group of ratepayers drew up a petition opposing the move and Robert Wright also declared his opposition, citing the expense, which would be 'an everlasting burden on the county'.[72] The idea was therefore shelved, at least for the time being, and customary practices were continued.

Nevertheless, Wright was concerned about the people who suffered with mental health problems and were sent to local workhouses. In an address to Quarter Sessions in 1819 he declared:

> There was no situation which demanded more our pity and compassion than those unfortunate objects, who laboured under that awful visitation of Providence ... [and] it was some consolation ... to learn that there was a place in the county [Grove Place] capable of receiving the whole of the paupers ... than in any institution they [the County] could have formed.[73]

As a visiting magistrate to Grove Place, Wright said he was impressed with the cleanliness and comfort of the accommodation, which fully justified his opposition to a county asylum. However, another factor was that the county was in the process of spending a sizeable amount of ratepayers' money on making improvements to the county gaol in Jewry Street, Winchester and the magistrates knew that another costly building project would be questioned by the ratepayers.

The Portsmouth case, 1823

On Friday 21 February 1823 Robert Wright gave evidence in the widely publicised Portsmouth case at the Freemasons' Hall in London. A *Commission de lunatico inquirendo* had been established to decide if John Wallop, the Third Earl of Portsmouth (1767–1853), of Hurstbourne Park, near Whitchurch, Hampshire was insane.[74]

Portsmouth was a man of great eccentricity who had learning difficulties. He was prone to behaving in strange ways. For example, he was obsessed with funerals and would join processions as an uninvited 'guest', laughing and making inappropriate comments. He took pleasure in whipping his horses and gratuitously killing animals with an axe in a nearby slaughterhouse. Another habit was asking the servant girls on his estate to bleed him in the pursuit of 'erotic pleasure'. Despite this unusual behaviour, Portsmouth was active in society, attending balls and taking his seat in the House of Lords.[75]

In 1799 Portsmouth had married Grace Norton, who was 47 years of age and 16 years his senior. She was unlikely to have children and therefore did not pose a problem for Portsmouth's heirs. Grace had a calming influence on Portsmouth but she died in 1813. John Hanson, Portsmouth's solicitor, saw an opportunity and arranged for his 23-year-old daughter, Mary Anne, to marry Portsmouth. Newton Fellowes, Portsmouth's brother and heir to the estate, was furious; he knew there was a possibility of Mary Anne bearing children thereby disinheriting him. Thus Fellowes attempted to get his brother declared insane, but the Lord Chancellor initially rejected the case.

Mary Anne proceeded to have an affair with William Alder which was brazenly conducted; the adulterous couple even shared the same bed as the naïve Earl. Elizabeth Foyster writes:

> Portsmouth seemed to have little idea of what Alder and his wife were doing when they were in bed together. Portsmouth appeared to know neither how babies were made nor how long a pregnancy

was expected to last... Sexual innocence was certainly a description that could be applied to Portsmouth.[76]

In November 1822 Portsmouth's nephew, Henry Arthur Fellowes, applied for a new Commission of Lunacy and this time it was approved.[77] How Wright came to be called as a witness at the commission is not known, but he travelled to London and spoke in defence of the Earl of Portsmouth. He told the inquiry that he had been the visiting magistrate of lunatic asylums in Hampshire for the past 12 years and had known the Earl since 1795. He had met him several times and found his 'manners and conduct were gentlemanly ... and his conversation was rational'.[78]

The Freemasons' Hall was packed with excited members of the general public on every single day that the commission was in session. Most were hoping to hear at first hand all the scandal, but for Wright this was an opportunity to have the limelight and enhance his status. There is little doubt that he was at ease and confident when addressing large audiences.

All the witnesses received expenses to appear at the inquiry and the total cost of the suit was rumoured to be £40,000. The inquiry found the Earl to be insane, and as a result his second marriage was annulled. Mary Anne Hanson was ordered to pay the costs and she responded by fleeing the country!

The asylum debate again

The Portsmouth case was probably the reason Wright reignited the campaign for pauper lunatics to be accommodated in private asylums. In May 1824 he spoke out at Quarter Sessions about the unsuitability of workhouse accommodation for people suffering from 'insanity' and described the case of a 'respectable' young woman who went insane during her pregnancy and was placed in a workhouse, along with four fellow sufferers. He related that the pregnant woman was 'fastened with cords' and that 'from the effects of the ligatures her feet subsequently dropped off'.[79] He absolved the parish officers from any blame but regretted that all pauper lunatics were not accommodated in asylums. In his opinion, a private asylum was much cleaner than the filth of a poorhouse.

He told the bench that Dr Twynam had offered to take 'these unfortunate persons' into his private asylum at Lainston House. For 14 shillings each per week, Dr Twynam would provide accommodation, food, clothes and medical support. (It was possible that Wright was representing the interests of Dr Twynam.) The bench declined Wright's suggestion, citing that the legislation already allowed any JP to make an order to send a pauper lunatic to a private asylum. Wright then tried to get a motion passed that ordered an official count of all the lunatic paupers in the county, but this too was defeated and nothing concrete emerged from the discussion.[80]

Nevertheless, Wright maintained his interest in mental illness and, along with Sir Thomas Baring and Sir William Heathcote of Hursley, continued to be a visiting magistrate for lunatic asylums within the county of Hampshire.

The sad affair of Mary Owen

In February 1827 Baring and Wright wrote separately to the Home Office about the plight of Mary Owen, a young woman who had been sent to the bridewell for six weeks for the 'crime' of bastardy. During her incarceration, her behaviour became increasingly violent and uncontrollable. The letter written by Wright shows a degree of empathy and pity for the plight of the young woman:

> *Sir*
>
> *As chairman of the Visiting Justices in this county, I beg to inform you that a Female by the name of Mary Owen, a Prisoner in the Bridewell, has become insane.*
>
> *Our medical attendant giving not the smallest hope of her recovery, the malady continuing to increase rather than diminish.*
>
> *As it is in the power of his Majesty's Minister alone to order the removal of such objects from confinement to a proper Lunatic Asylum, I write to request that your indulgence may be afforded to the unhappy object and that an order to this effect may be as early as possible forwarded to the keeper of the County Bridewell at Winchester.*
>
> *I have the Honour to be sir your obedient servant*
>
> *Robert Wright*
>
> *Winchester Bridewell Feb 15th 1827.[81]*

Mrs Middleton's private asylum at Grove Place in Nursling was nominated as the destination for Mary Owen, and in the absence of any surviving evidence it is assumed that this was where she was taken.

The Madhouse Act of 1828 required visiting justices to send pauper lunatic returns each year to the Home Office detailing numbers admitted to and discharged from asylums. Wright approved of this measure, and in May 1829 he reported to Quarter Sessions that there were 242 'registered' lunatics in the county who were costing the ratepayers over £2,000 per annum, but that in his opinion the number suffering from 'temporary derangement' was even higher. He informed Quarter Sessions that he wanted a reconsideration of how they made provision for these 'unfortunate individuals, either by having an asylum of their own, or by contracting with some [private] lunatic asylum for their care'.[82] Again, no action was taken by the authorities and things continued as before.

Lord Ashley and county lunatic asylums

In 1842 Lord Ashley was instrumental in promoting a movement for lunacy reform at a national level. A national tour of inspection of lunatic asylums was organised between 1842 and 1844. The Hampshire private asylums were heavily criticised, with Lainston House in particular receiving a poor report. Here the inspectors found filthy living conditions and some patients restrained by hand locks and chains.[83] The inspections revealed that visiting magistrates, no matter how well intentioned, did not have the qualifications or knowledge to make judgements about the treatment of lunatics. Dr Twynam of Lainston House complained that the inspection was biased and that Lord Ashley had no experience of what it was like to spend time daily 'among these unfortunate cases'.[84]

By now Robert Wright had come round to believing that a purpose built county lunatic asylum was desirable and he raised the issue at Quarter Sessions. He argued that a county lunatic asylum would be in keeping with the county's reputation for charity and moved that a committee should be formed to report on the matter. Support came from Sir Thomas Baring, John Acworth Ommanney and John Elwes.[85] The motion was carried and a committee set up, only for events to overtake it. In August 1845 Ashley's County Asylum Lunacy Act passed into law, which made it compulsory for counties to build asylums to treat lunatics. The Hampshire authorities acquired land at Knowle, near Fareham, and by 1853 an asylum to house 560 patients had been opened at a cost of £65,000.[86]

Robert Wright's motives in improving provision for mentally ill people are not immediately obvious. He would have seen some very disturbing cases in his role as a visiting magistrate and perhaps he had a degree of altruistic empathy, particularly for those 'unfortunates' who were incarcerated in workhouses. In some ways, though, when considered with his unpitying attitude towards the ordinary labourer, his concern for lunatics was out of character.

One suggestion for his benevolent attitude is the early death of his daughter, Mary Elizabeth, who died at the age of five in 1826. Her mother would have been 45 when Mary Elizabeth was born and she had not been with child for 16 years. It may have been a difficult birth, and if the girl had been afflicted with a mental disability as a result that may help to explain Wright's 'passion' for lunacy reform. However, the birth of Mary Elizabeth postdates Wright's initial interest in the issue and therefore his motives remain a mystery and the subject of speculation.

Poor Law administration

Supervising accounts and removal orders

The overseers' account books for administering poor relief in Itchen Abbas have not survived. The identity of those who served as overseers is therefore not known, but there is the possibility that Robert Wright himself was responsible for distributing relief to the poor, sick and unemployed. When he appeared before the Select Committee on the Sale of Beer in 1833 Wright stated that if anyone needed relief in Itchen Abbas they asked him, suggesting he was in charge, rather than the parish overseer of the poor. It was not unusual for a JP to be a parish overseer, as we know that Samuel Whitbread JP acted as an overseer of the poor for Southill in Bedfordshire between 1806 and 1816.[87]

In his role as a magistrate, Robert Wright, acting with a colleague, was required to administer the Poor Law by auditing overseers' account books. He visited local parishes to verify the accounts. His signature appears several times in the Poor Law accounts book of Avington, confirming the amount of poor rate for the coming year and the accuracy of the figures for the dispensation of relief.[88]

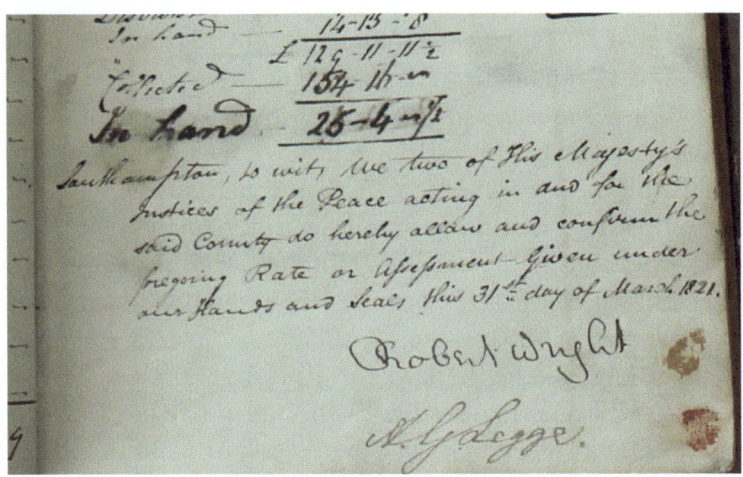

Plate 15: *The signatures of Robert Wright and AG Legge verifying the Avington Poor Law accounts, 31 March 1821 (Source: HRO 22M69/PO2).*

Two magistrates sitting together were also required to supervise the Settlement Laws. JPs were empowered to examine and issue removal certificates to those accused of living in a parish without a right to settlement. There are four removal certificates in the Hampshire Record Office signed by Robert Wright and Walter Long sitting on 31 May 1821 that denied a number of paupers their right of settlement in Ovington and ordered their removal.[89]

Name of pauper	Removed from	Removed to
Harriet Ayling, a single woman	Ovington	East Meon
Charles Stoneadge and Elizabeth his wife	Ovington	Tichborne
James Hunt and Elizabeth his wife	Ovington	Martyr Worthy
Thomas and Sarah Paice and three children	Ovington	Hinton Ampner

Paupers removed from Ovington by Robert Wright in 1821.

The process was de-humanising and harsh, with no pity or sympathy for the victims. Those removed from a parish were summarily carted off to the parish deemed to be their place of settlement and dumped there. Any parish that had to receive paupers in consequence of a removal order had the right of appeal at the Hampshire Quarter Sessions and there are several instances recorded in the order books where removals sanctioned by Wright were appealed. Quarter Sessions JPs would study the evidence presented and either confirm the removal order or overturn it. Wright did not appear to have any difficulty in making some cruel decisions in applying the strict letter of the law.

Allowance scales

Magistrates had the power to regulate allowance scales that decreed the amount of money which parishes could pay to unemployed labourers or to subsidise the wages of those in work. Such scales were usually set according to the price of bread and the size of a labourer's family. In September 1822 eight magistrates met in Winchester and decided to reduce the allowances for the unemployed because of 'the diminished price of every article of life'.[90] Five of the eight magistrates who implemented the reductions were clergymen, namely the chairman, Reverend Edmund Poulter, the Honourable and Reverend Augustus George Legge, the Reverend William Hill Newbolt, DD, the Reverend Francis Wickham Swanton of the Worthys and, predictably, Robert Wright. The prime objective had been to reduce the cost of administering the Poor Law, rather than consider the reasons so many labourers were living in poverty and misery. Protests, even violence, must have been expected as the magistrates asked for members of the yeomanry to attend. The resolutions passed were uncompromising and the final paragraph issued a warning:

> And the Justices do declare, that all paupers maintained and relieved by their parishes, and able to work, shall, for the allowances so to be made to them, be compelled to perform such proper work as the parish officer shall direct or require them; and it is earnestly recommended to the parish officers to providing as far as possible employment for all paupers, and if they neglect or refuse to perform the work found for them, they will be punished as the law directs.[91]

William Cobbett, the radical journalist, who hailed from nearby Botley, knew all about the activities of Wright and there was no love lost between the two men. Cobbett rarely missed an opportunity to lampoon Wright and in the *Political Register* of 21 September 1822 Cobbett wrote sarcastically of the clerical magistrates:

> [They] must, doubtless, be persons of singular merit, seeing the posts which they fill, and the large incomes that most of them derive from their posts... The Rev Robert Wright is Rector of [both] Itchen Abbas and Ovington.[92]

In 1831 the reduced allowances were reaffirmed at a time when the worst of the agricultural riots had just subsided and mistrust between farmers and labourers ran deep. By now, Robert Wright had a reputation for being one of the more rigid magistrates, and he was the subject of a letter to *The Times* in 1831 in which the author criticised him for his harsh treatment of the 'peasantry':

> Thank God, all magistrates have not such feelings, but in too many instances, I fear, a magistrate cannot stand between the vestry and the peasant. I observe the name of the Rev. Robert Wright among the signing magistrates [of the scales of allowance].[93]

Poor rates

Poor rates were increasing during this period, causing great concern to those who had to pay them. In January 1834 the Hampshire Quarter Sessions discussed a petition that had been sent to both houses of Parliament by their Somerset counterparts which complained about 'the heavy pressure on the ratepayers' and 'pray[ed] for a redress of the grievance'.[94] Several voices expressed support for the petition, including Robert Wright, who had an eagle eye for retrenchment and was always looking for an opportunity to reduce spending.[95] The matter, however, was already in hand with a Royal Commission of Inquiry, which had been sitting since 1832. Parliament acted on the report of the commission and passed the Poor Law Amendment Act in August 1834. The New Poor Law attempted to reduce the rates by making it virtually impossible for able-bodied labourers to get outdoor poor relief when they were out of work.

Robert Wright was nothing if not persistent, and in 1843 he expressed his great concern at the number of Irish paupers living in Alresford who 'were a burthen to that parish'.[96] He proposed to Quarter Sessions that a committee should be set up to arrange the removal of these paupers under an Act of Parliament passed ten years previously. There was not much support for the idea and as the terms of the act were due for revision, the bench concluded that it was advisable to await any new legislation before going any further.[97]

WATCHING OVER THE PUBLIC PURSE

Much of the county administration that magistrates were obliged to do was assigned to ad hoc and standing committees. Robert Wright, for example, served on the Finance and Road and Bridge Committees from 1823 until 1849. Most of the work was mundane and time consuming, but Wright displayed some accounting acumen and was willing to audit a variety of accounts. On several occasions he was trusted to present the County Treasurer's quarterly accounts to Quarter Sessions, in which he explained the income, expenditure and rate set for the ensuing three months.

The county rate

Wright was anxious that public spending should provide value for money. In April 1817 he expressed his concern to the Easter Quarter Sessions about the unfair way in which the county rate was calculated. Some parishes which had a total rental of £2,000 per year were paying more to the county rates than those that 'boasted a rental in excess of £8,000'.[98] Calling it no more than 'legal robbery', he demanded deliberations on how to equalise the county rate, especially at a time of long-term agricultural distress. Wright, supported by the Reverend E Poulter, concluded his address by stating: 'The iniquity of the present rate was generally acknowledged, and the burthen ought to be equally divided'.[99]

Twelve months later Wright returned to the same theme and this time was backed by Dr Newbolt, who quoted several counties where the rate had been successfully equalised. Some of the gathered magistrates demurred, and Wright's motion to debate the issue was only just carried, with a majority of three (sixteen to thirteen). Wright told his fellow JPs that his motion had 'truth for its basis, and justice for its end'.[100]

No action, however, was forthcoming on the issue on this occasion.

Yet another example of Wright's desire to see the county rating system reformed occurred in 1829 when he reported to Quarter Sessions that the extra parochial parts of parishes were not rated and paid nothing into the county funds. He succeeded in getting a motion passed that required high constables to make returns of all extra parochial locations within their jurisdiction, thus making it possible to calculate their liability to the county rates.[101]

In 1842 the issue of a fairer rating system was once again brought to the table. In a wide-ranging debate, driven by Sir William Heathcote of Hursley, an adjournment of the Quarter Sessions agreed that a new county rate based on an up-to-date valuation of property would be adopted, despite the concerns of magistrates from the Isle of Wight. [102] The Finance Committee expressed its approval at the Michaelmas Quarter Sessions:

> The Committee congratulated the rate-payers upon the result of the new county rate, which has been brought into operation at a moderate cost, and without an appeal, and which, by bringing under contribution property either not before rated at all, or not rated up to its full value, has supplemented the receipts upon a penny rate from £2,552-7s-8d to £4,487-18s-9d. [103]

Robert Wright had campaigned for this reform for many years and was entitled to take some of the credit for the changes.

Dealing with fraud

In a letter to Sir Thomas Baring in 1821, Wright expressed his outrage that carriers hired to convey vagrants out of Hampshire were abusing the system.[104] He described how he had met a vagrant woman ('a wretched object') at the side of the road near Newbury who had been abandoned by a carrier. She had been given a shilling and told to make her way to Whitchurch, where she would be picked up the next day by a pass cart and conveyed to Dorset (presumably her place of settlement). On his return journey, the next day, Wright met the woman again. The carrier had abandoned her and pocketed his fee without completing the job. Bristling with indignation, Wright informed Baring that he believed such fraud was common practice and that 'the law is violated and the county robbed'.[105]

Wright said he would be happy to help to expose the fraudsters and suggested that the carrier who tendered the most reasonable overall price should be awarded a contract for the carriage of all vagrants through the county. The letter was typical of Wright in that it was straight to the point and laced with indignation. Unfortunately, there is no record of Baring's reply.[106]

In April 1827 Robert Wright angrily complained at Quarter Sessions of county constables abusing the system by getting their bills signed by a magistrate who had not actually committed the accused person for trial. He put forward a motion that constables would not be paid a fee unless the magistrate who had committed the accused for trial had signed their claim bill. Wright must have felt a degree of satisfaction when the motion was carried.[107]

Another complaint followed at the Midsummer Quarter Sessions in 1827 when Wright told how he suspected constables of fraudulently charging the county for an assistant in conveying offenders to prison and for hiring horses. He called such false charges 'premeditated and gross acts of wilful perjury' and wanted offenders dealt with, 'however painful it might be'.[108] His colleague and friend, John Duthy of Ropley, agreed but intimated that the low remuneration the constables received probably contributed to attempts to falsify their expenses.[109]

Wright, however, was not in the mood to entertain such an explanation and he continued to pursue his desire for retrenchment. In April 1830 he presented the Finance Committee's report to Quarter Sessions and proudly declared that the county's spending was lower than any other similar sized county in the land, but it could be reduced even further. It was decided to slash the cost of advertising by using only Hampshire based newspapers in the future.[110] On another occasion, Wright supported Dr Daniel Quarrier of Alverstoke when he complained about the high cost of printing the list of people qualified to vote in elections. After discussion, Quarter Sessions agreed that the job should be offered out for tender.[111]

WRIGHT'S PART IN THE GEORGE HOLLIS SCANDAL, 1823

George Hollis was a long serving county treasurer who supplemented his income by working for turnpike trusts and political groups such as the Hampshire County Club. He had served the county since 1790 and had a wealth of experience; perhaps the job was so routine that by 1823 he had become complacent. Hollis prepared the county accounts each quarter as well as collecting the rates and ensuring that bills were paid on time.

False accounting or an honest error?

When Hollis's accounts for Easter 1823 were scrutinised by the Finance Committee they were signed off as correct by five magistrates, one of whom was Robert Wright. However, a few days later inconsistences were detected in the accounts and an inquiry was launched, led by Sir JWS Gardiner.

At an adjournment of the Quarter Sessions in May 1823, Gardiner said that he hoped the inconsistencies were honest errors rather than embezzlement, but the uncomfortable truth was that Hollis had shown negligence in his handling of public funds and should be dismissed. Some members of the bench believed that Hollis had been such a loyal servant that he should continue in the post and Gardiner's motion was defeated. Wright was a member of Gardiner's committee of inquiry and he voted for Hollis to be dismissed, a decision which was to cause him acute embarrassment in the following weeks.[112]

The dispute goes public

On 30 May 1823 Hollis went public and defended himself in a letter to the *Hampshire Chronicle*.[113] He blamed one of his clerks for not spotting the errors. Furthermore, he continued, he had been visited at his home by Gardiner and Wright on Saturday 19 April 1823 and they had exonerated him of any blame. They thought Hollis's explanation was perfectly acceptable and praised him for his co-operation. This claim was countered by a letter to the *Hampshire Chronicle* dated 4 June 1823 and signed by JWS Gardiner, WH Newbolt and Robert Wright. They accused Hollis of trying to deflect the blame from himself to others:

> We cannot... permit the Treasurer, pending our most important and unfinished examinations of his accounts, to send forth to the public mere garbled extracts from such parts of our first Report... as may appear in the smallest degree to justify him, or the culpable neglect with which he stands charged in the performance of the various duties of his Office... Is it not obvious... that his sole object

was to remove all imputation of blame from himself, and to fix on others?[114]

The fact that the dispute was being played out before the public was creating an unedifying spectacle which threatened the reputation of those involved.

Further revelations

At the Midsummer Quarter Sessions in 1823 there were more revelations from the committee of inquiry. In its report, the committee stated that the estimated deficit to the county was about £4,000 and the way rates were collected was chaotic and lacking in structure. Many constables were late paying in the rates they had collected and appeared to have a casual attitude. Some of the rate payments had been paid into Hollis's own bank labelled as 'cash' and were subsumed into his own personal account. As a result, they 'disappeared' from view, with neither Hollis nor his clerks detecting what had happened. Hollis claimed this was a genuine error rather than any attempt to defraud the county.

A huge row ensued. Some JPs wanted the report to be made public, and Sir Thomas Baring, who was particularly vitriolic in his condemnation of Hollis, called for the money to be made good to the county and for the immediate suspension of the treasurer. Baring, a Whig, may have been politically motivated in his comments given that Hollis was a Tory, but he denied any suggestion that this was the case. Wright said he did not wish the report to be published and kept quiet for the rest of the discussion, no doubt embarrassed by what had happened. The Reverend John Orde, the rector of Winslade, intervened and said that the magistrates who had signed off the accounts as correct also had to take some of the blame. Hollis pronounced that he did not have the personal resources to pay the money back, and more heated exchanges took place with Baring.

The whole thing must have been extremely uncomfortable for Wright, with both his honesty and reliability being called into question. As usual, however, he was able to brush off the criticism and somehow retain his composure.[115]

The scandal drags on

The fallout continued at the Michaelmas Quarter Sessions of 1823. John Woodham was elected as the new county treasurer, winning 42 votes, including Wright's, as opposed to the 23 votes received by Mr Barnard Winter. Wright's pride was sorely challenged when Sir Henry Wright Wilson interrupted him and asked if he was a member of the bench. A mortally offended Wright endeavoured to put Wilson in his place and informed him that he had been a magistrate for 'seventeen years [sic]' and 'as it was the first time he had ever seen the worthy gentleman in court, he might retort the question'. Wright then told Wilson he should not be commenting about something 'he knew nothing about', whereas he himself had served on the committee investigating the issue and had knowledge of all the details.[116] Throughout his career, Wright never accepted criticism of his conduct; he either made a strong retort or ignored it and continued as if nothing had happened.

The Hollis affair dragged on for another eight years without resolution. Hollis angered the bench by making personal comments about individual magistrates in the press and delayed a resolution by disputing the amount of money that had gone missing. He was desperate to protect his reputation and found it difficult to admit any liability in the scandal. In a letter to Sir Thomas Baring, written on 26 September 1829, Wright expressed dismay that Hollis had given the impression to the public that he had been 'injured and persecuted' and that such a 'flagrant and open ... defaulter should not be suffered to vilify the proceeding of the magistracy'.[117]

By 1831, after the King's Court had considered the case, the will to carry on the dispute was exhausted and the matter was closed. It was claimed that £3,000 had been recovered, but as the deficit had been disputed for so long by both sides, the figure was probably exaggerated in an effort to save face.[118] Wright himself did not emerge with any credit from the dispute, but it had now faded from public attention. In any case, one year before the Hollis scandal had concluded, Robert Wright found himself embroiled in another controversy in the south east of the county.

THE HAVANT 'DISPUTE', SEPTEMBER 1830

In the autumn of 1830 differing opinions among magistrates on the Havant bench escalated into a bitter dispute. Captain Henry J Leeke (RN) and the

Reverend John Coles joined together in a war of words against Sir John Theophilus Lee. This spilled over into the courtroom, where the three men argued aggressively in front of the lower classes, thereby, in the view of Dr Daniel Quarrier JP, damaging the good reputation of the Hampshire magistracy.[119] The dispute was referred to the Duke of Wellington by Quarrier and Sir John Fleming, MP for Hampshire. They condemned the behaviour of Leeke and Coles and suggested to the Duke that he ought to remove one or both of these magistrates from the new Commission of the Peace which was in the process of being compiled.

Prior to this, on or about 25 September 1830, a group of county magistrates, including Robert Wright, drew up a petition in support of Captain Henry Leeke and submitted it to the Duke of Wellington:

> [They gave] their entire approbation of [Captain Leeke's] conduct and our perfect confidence in him in every respect for the perfect discharge of his magisterial duties, having on all occasions performed them with great temper, impartiality, and judgment to the satisfaction of all parties.[120]

Apart from Robert Wright other signatories included William Grant JP, William Thresher JP, John S Hulbert JP, G Collins Poore JP and George Thomas Staunton of Leigh Park. They feared that the removal of Leeke from the Havant bench would leave the local population without 'a resident magistrate to redress their grievances'.[121] The petitioners implored the Duke not to remove Captain Leeke from the Commission of the Peace without first carrying out a thorough enquiry into the dispute.

When Daniel Quarrier learned of the petition he was unable to contain his anger. He tended to confront his opponents head on and always promulgated his strong opinions in public. On 23 October 1830, having taken legal advice on the dispute, he wrote a robustly worded letter to Sir John Fleming.[122] Quarrier called for the prosecution of Captain Leeke and Reverend Coles, who, he believed, had acted inappropriately in a case by issuing a summons for Mr Howe, a builder and carpenter from Hayling Island, to appear at Petty Sessions to answer an accusation of assault. Quarrier argued that the magistrates should have entered into arbitration and added: 'Magistrates as arbitrators may use an influence much more beneficial than by inflicting penalties'.[123]

Quarrier then turned his ire on Robert Wright as one of the signatories to the petition. The two men knew each other from attending the Quarter Sessions in Winchester and there appeared to be some friction between them, even though they shared the same ultra-Tory opinions. Quarrier wrote disdainfully that Robert Wright was incapable of acting 'in any case with impartiality'. He felt that the Havant dispute had nothing to do with Wright and wrote that he would never 'condescend to communicate [with] him' on the matter.[124]

It was all rather a waste of time and energy. There appears to be no record of Wright's response, but he would not have been cowed by the anger of Daniel Quarrier. In any case, a much more serious crisis was about to break which would cause him much deeper consternation.

THE 1830 AGRICULTURAL RIOTS

Events in mid-Hampshire

In late November 1830 the Hampshire establishment was shaken to its very core when agricultural labourers rose in revolt, demanding higher wages. It was a defining event in the career of Robert Wright as a magistrate. These disturbances have become known as the 'Swing riots' because labourers in some places sent threatening letters to farmers signed by 'Captain Swing', a fictitious leader. The riots began in Kent and spread to other southern counties very quickly. The fulcrum of the disturbances in mid-Hampshire was the Dever Valley, where mobs roamed the countryside between Barton Stacey, Sutton Scotney, Stoke Charity, Micheldever and East Stratton.

On 19 November the estate of Sir Thomas Baring at East Stratton was attacked amid ugly scenes. William Bingham Baring, nephew of Sir Thomas, confronted the mob and was struck a glancing blow with a hammer by Henry Cook, a 19-year-old ploughman from Micheldever.[125] Baring recovered his composure and summoned the local magistrates to a meeting in Alresford the same evening to discuss their response to the violence. A letter was promptly composed and sent to the Home Office, signed by Robert Wright, Henry Joseph Tichborne and John Duthy.[126] The letter describes a scene of anarchy in which a mob estimated at 1,000 of 'the labouring class' was terrorising the neighbourhood, demolishing threshing machines and demanding money. The letter reveals how vulnerable the magistrates actually were in this situation. They were supposed to keep the peace but did not have the means or the support to confront a crowd of angry labourers. The three magistrates pointed out that the troubles would continue and demanded a military force be despatched to Winchester as soon as possible.

On Monday 22 November a large number of labourers assembled in Itchen Abbas and made their way to nearby Avington House, the Hampshire seat of the first Duke of Buckingham and Chandos. The local tenantry and labourers, however, remained loyal and led by Wright forced the mob to retreat. They took 50 prisoners, and later, troops escorted over half of them to the county gaol at Winchester. The Duke of Buckingham and Chandos described the events of the day in a letter to the Duke of Wellington, the Lord Lieutenant of Hampshire, who was in London:

> The mob broke a Machine in the village [of Itchen Abbas], upon which a hundred of my men, labourers like themselves headed by the Rev Mr Wright a Magistrate and two Police men sent down from the Secretary of State's office and armed only with Bludgeons attacked them, routed them in an instant and took near 50 prisoners... Some Magistrates assembled in my House while the Prisoners were brought and we took Depositions, letting out on their Recognizances those the least guilty but committing to Winchester I think 31 who are just set off escorted by the Dragoons... I am bound... to bear testimony to the spirit and firmness of the Rev Mr Wright who himself headed the attacking Party, and to his Perseverance and determination we owe to having dispersed this assembly.[127]

By 24 November the situation had improved, and Wright and Samuel Wall wrote a letter to Lord Melbourne from the 'County Goal [sic]' to inform him that the area had calmed down.[128] *[Plate 16]*

The Duke of Wellington arrives in Hampshire

Wellington's role in restoring law and order to the county has been condemned by historians. According to Ruscombe Foster, Wellington did not arrive in Hampshire until 23 November, at which point the worst of the trouble was over. The burden of quelling the riots had fallen on the

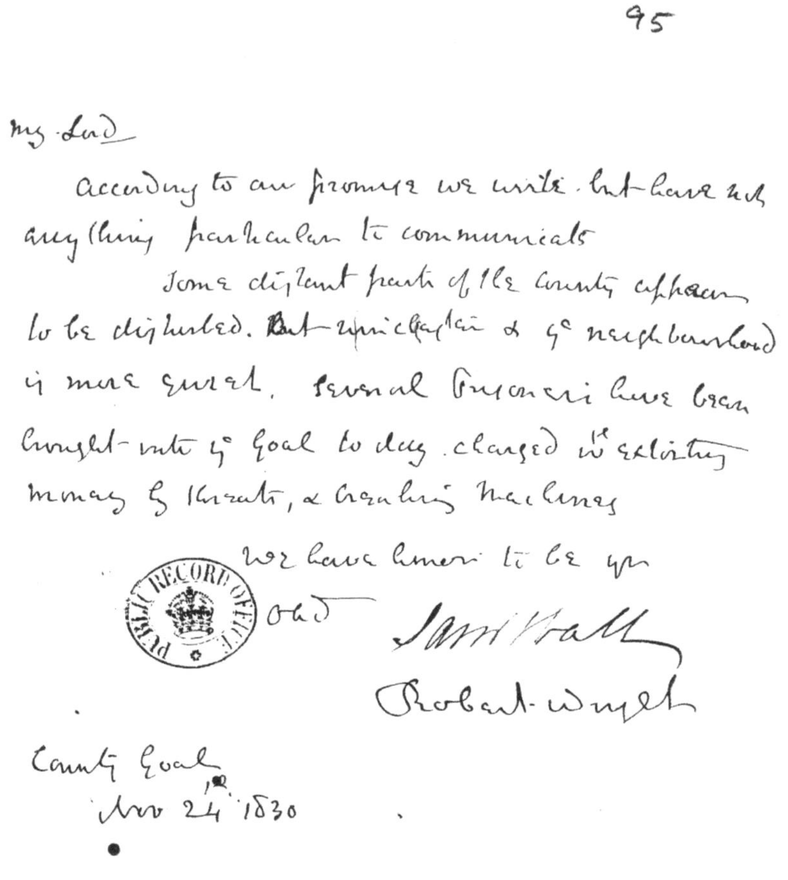

95

My Lord

*According to our promise we write, but have not
any thing particular to communicate*

*Some distant parts of the County appear
to be disturbed. But this Parish & the neighbourhood
is more quiet. Several Prisoners have been
brought into the Goal to day, charged with extorting
money by threats, & breaking machines*

*We have honor to be your
obd*

*Saml Wall
Robert Wright*

*County Goal,
Nov 24 1830*

Plate 16: *Letter from Samuel Wall and Robert Wright to the Home
Secretary, 24 November 1830 (Source: The National Archives).*

local magistrates, whose approach lacked any kind of co-ordination.
Letters from anxious individual magistrates were written in panic, some
to Wellington, some to the Home Secretary, but rarely to both. The recent
disagreements among individual magistrates on the Havant bench mili-
tated against a quick, effective and co-ordinated response to the disorder
in south east Hampshire.

Wellington eventually turned up at the Grand Jury Chamber in Winchester on 25 November 1830 to chair a meeting of county magistrates. The meeting was the idea of Richard Pollen, who managed to bring together 74 magistrates and deputy lieutenants, all of whom were listed on the press release that spelt out a number of 'Resolutions' for the future.[129] Robert Wright was, of course, among those who attended.

In the press release, the public were informed that the magistrates were determined to 'maintain the laws' and 'put down the outrages'; that Wellington was to request a 'Special Commission to be sent to Winchester without loss of time'; and that it was the magistrates' 'anxious wish to relieve the distress and improve the condition of the labouring classes'. The statement concluded with a chilling warning that any future attempts to use violence as a means of achieving an increase in wages would lead to the 'most disastrous and fatal consequences'.

A vote of thanks was given to Wellington for his attendance and 'judicious conduct in the chair'.[130] In truth, however, he should have been on the scene much sooner to direct operations. The meeting had allowed him to take credit he did not deserve, credit that should have gone to frontline magistrates, such as Robert Wright, who had taken decisive, if unco-ordinated, action to restore order.

As it turned out, the resolution to tackle the causes of distress and poor living standards went largely ignored by the authorities and in the main only punishment and retribution followed.

Attempts to pacify the labourers

At the outset of the rioting there were some attempts to placate the rioters. The Andover magistrates, for example, initially appeared to adopt a conciliatory approach. They held a meeting on 20 November and published their resolutions on a handbill. An agreement had apparently been reached with local farmers to pay 12 shillings a week to married men and 9 shillings a week to single men. Seventy farmers put their name to the resolutions and stated they were convinced of 'the impossibility of our Labourers existing on their present rate of Wages'.[131] Unfortunately, events appeared to overtake these good intentions, as the handbill was not printed until 23 November and by that time Tasker's Iron Foundry in Upper Clatford had been attacked and razed to the ground by a tumultuous mob of 300 labourers.

On 10 December 1830 a resentful Dr William Hill Newbolt, county magistrate and the rector of Morestead, wrote a letter to Lord Melbourne justifying his conciliatory manner in attempting to disperse the mob intent on attacking Sir Thomas Baring's estate at East Stratton on 19 November 1830. His anger was in a response to a circular issued by the Home Office which advised magistrates that attempts to appease the labourers had been inappropriate.[132] Newbolt, who was in poor health, had hired a post-chaise and travelled as quickly as he could to East Stratton and then to Sutton Scotney, where he addressed an aggressive mob and agreed to their demands for 12 shillings a week for married men and 9 shillings for single men. Had he not done so, he claimed, they would have wrecked more machinery and damaged property. He told Melbourne he had been a magistrate for 20 years and was one of the most diligent members of the Hampshire bench. His indignation was evident: he felt insulted by the lack of gratitude he thought he deserved.[133]

In a debate in the House of Lords on 9 December 1830 recrimination was in the air. The new Whig government, which had been in power for just three weeks, attempted to argue that the policy of the previous Tory government, headed by Wellington, was the main cause of the rioting. Wellington defended himself by stating that such an argument was 'absurd' and demanded that his detractors supported their accusations with evidence.[134] A degree of sympathy for the plight of the labourers was forthcoming from some peers, but the political will to do anything other than talk was evidently lacking.

THE SPECIAL COMMISSION IN WINCHESTER

Most committals made by JPs

Robert Wright, however, was in no mood to pacify the labourers. Working with other magistrates, he played a significant role in cross-examining prisoners (one of whom was Henry Cook) and committing them for trial at the Special Commission held in Winchester in late December 1830. As might be expected he was the most prolific in this task of any cleric, sending 65 individuals for trial, a number exceeded only by Sir Thomas Baring, who committed 69 offenders [Table 12]. The sentences received by the offenders committed by Wright varied from imprisonment to transportation and, in the case of Henry Cook, death [Graph 3].

Magistrate	Rank	No of offenders committed
Sir Thomas Baring	Baronet	69
Reverend Robert Wright	Clerk	65
Samuel Wall	Esquire	63
Sir William Heathcote	Baronet	58
Stephen Raymond Jarvis	Esquire	49
William Sloane Stanley	Esquire	28
Reverend T C May	Clerk	24
Reverend J Orde	Clerk	22
Sir Lucius Curtis	Baronet	21
Sir C S Hunter	Baronet	21

Table 12: *Committals for trial at the Special Commission made by leading magistrates (Source: HRO Printed Calendars of Prisoners).*

Sentence	Number
Acquitted/Discharged	15
Bound Over	12
Hanged	1
Imprisoned	22
No Bill	1
Transportation	14

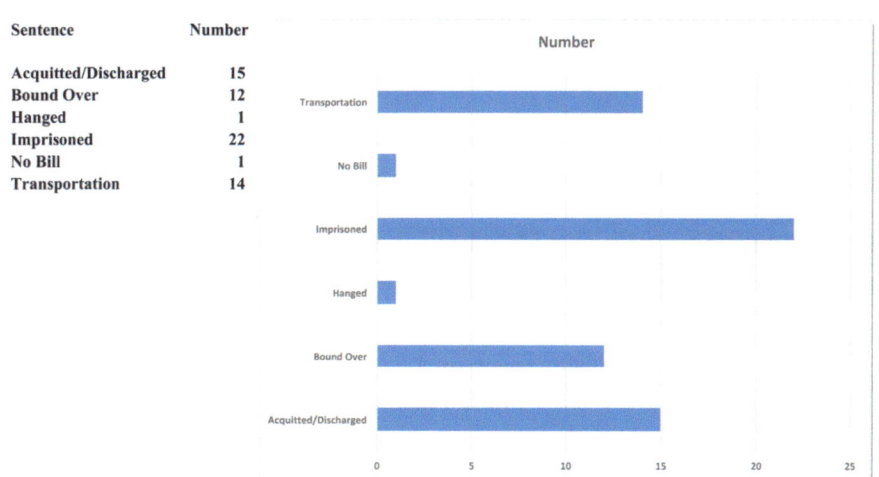

Graph 3: *The 1830 riots: Sentences given to offenders committed by Robert Wright to the Special Commission in Winchester (Source: HRO Printed Calendars of Prisoners).*

Evidence given at the Special Commission

Contemporary newspaper coverage of the Special Commission often contained errors, suggesting that reporters struggled to assimilate and record the deluge of evidence. The errors were compounded when reports in the local Hampshire papers were printed verbatim in other publications the length and breadth of the land.[135]

Both Robert Wright and his son, the Reverend RJW Wright, gave evidence at the Special Commission. RJW Wright had been alongside his father when he confronted the mob in Itchen Abbas, and he made a request to the judge, Mr Justice Parke, that 13 men who had pleaded guilty should be allowed the mercy of the court because of their previous good character. His plea was successful and the men each received the relatively lenient sentence of one month's imprisonment. The judge told the men:

> They might consider themselves very fortunate that the activity of a Magistrate had stepped in between them and the commission of crimes which might place their lives in danger; for if the riotous assembly, of which they formed a part, had not received a timely check, it was probable it would have proceeded to acts of outrage similar to those which had disgraced the country in other instances; and he could not but again express his regret that similar activity had not been evinced by the local magistrates in other instances.[136]

The magistrate referred to was Robert Wright, but he was mistakenly identified in this report as 'Richard Wright'.

The trial of Henry Cook of Micheldever

Cook was found guilty of the attempted murder of William Bingham Baring and also of assault and robbery. He was sentenced to death by hanging. Some writers claim that Baring could easily have been killed when Cook attempted to strike him with a sledgehammer, but others said it was merely a glancing blow. It would appear, however, that Baring was not that seriously injured, as he wrote a letter to Harriet, his wife, (who was staying at 12 Great Stanhope Street, Mayfair), on 21 November 1830, just two days after the incident, stating that he had recovered from 'his wound'. [137] William Cobbett also claimed that Baring was seen 'walking in Winchester's streets' on Saturday 20 November, the day after the confrontation with the mob.[138]

Robert Wright, one of the magistrates who convicted Henry Cook, told the court that the accused had admitted striking William Bingham Baring when he was questioned in prison and had claimed he was encouraged to do so by other members of the mob. Wright did not offer any plea for mercy and the authorities were in no mood to back down. [139] They were intent on making an example of this young, gullible labourer.

Cook was subsequently hanged, on 15 January 1831, alongside James Thomas Cooper, aged 33, who had been found guilty of breaking threshing machines and robbery at Fordingbridge. The hangings took place in front of an estimated crowd of 300 that gathered in a yard at the rear of the gaol in Jewry Street. The report in the local press captured the tension and drama of the occasion:

> Cook's mother and little sister yesterday took their final earthly farewell of him in the condemned cell, and the parting was, indeed, a most heart-rending one ... From an early hour this morning till the time of their execution, [the two men] were engaged in their religious duties with the chaplain, whose attentions have been unceasing. About 10 minutes past eight o' clock, the mournful procession entered the room from whence the platform leads to the fatal drop. The Reverend Chaplain [Zillwood] first entered, and after him followed Cooke, with his arms pinioned: his sobs were truly heart-rending, and he seemed to have lost all fortitude in the overwhelming agony of that dreadful moment. He was dressed in ragged and wretched apparel, and presented a pitiable appearance ... On their being placed under the fatal beam, Cooke's groans were dreadful ... At that part of the service where the Lord's Prayer occurs, both the wretched men accompanied the Rev Chaplain in an audible voice ... At the termination of the service, the drop fell, and a few convulsive struggles closed their earthly career. After hanging the usual time, their bodies were cut down, and delivered to their friends for interment ... Among the prisoners assembled in the prison yard ... we observed that many of them wept unceasingly; and one man fainted from the excess of his emotions.[140]

The case of William Bolter of Martyr Worthy

On 1 December 1830 George Over (aged 34), George Hall (25), William Grantham (36) and William Bolter (60) were committed for trial at the Special Commission. They were charged with assaulting the Reverend Sir Henry Rivers, baronet, at Martyr Worthy on 20 November 1830. They had 'feloniously [stolen] four notes of the Bank of Knapp and Co., of Winchester, of the value of five pounds each' from Rivers and put him in 'bodily fear and danger of his life'.[141] The examining magistrates sitting together in Petty Sessions who made the committals were Sir Thomas Baring, SR James Esq, S Wall Esq, Sir William Heathcote and the Reverend Robert Wright. They further charged the men with 'other misdemeanours' that were to be put before judge and jury.

On Wednesday 22 December 1830 the four men were brought before Mr Justice Alderson. The jury, much to the surprise of the public in the court gallery, found them not guilty, mainly because they did not believe the evidence of Robert Fisher, servant to Sir Henry Rivers.[142] Later in the day, William Bolter and George Over were tried for stealing a sovereign from William Twitchen.[143] Again, the jury passed a verdict of not guilty. Finally, Bolter was brought to the bar for a third time, along with George Coleman, and charged with stealing five shillings from John Dagwell, who was the miller at Itchen Abbas. The mob had demanded a sovereign from Dagwell, who replied that he was a poor man and did not have that sort of money. One of the mob said they would let him off with 'a crown', which Dagwell then borrowed from Twitchen and handed over to the labourers.

The Reverend Robert Wright entered the witness box. He told the court that he had approached the mob with a posse of 70 men and ordered them to disperse. They refused, and Wright said that he was forced to tie up several of them, including William Bolter, and take them into custody. Wright went on to say that Coleman had actually confessed that he was the man who had taken £20 from Sir Henry Rivers. Wright told the court that the prisoner had been cautioned as to the possible consequences of his confession.

This time the jury was convinced by the evidence and returned a verdict of guilty on both Bolter and Coleman. Death was recorded as the punishment for both men, but was subsequently commuted to transportation, seven years for Coleman and fourteen for Bolter. [144]

A sense of injustice

The severity of Bolter's sentence shocked the inhabitants of the upper Itchen Valley. On 9 February 1831 Bolter was taken to Portsmouth and imprisoned on the prison hulk *York*, before being transferred to the *Hardy* three weeks later. Already, however, moves were in progress to get his sentence reduced. Samuel Wall of Worthy Park, one of the original examining magistrates, wrote to Lord Melbourne, the Home Secretary, on 20 January 1831 asking for the sentence to be imprisonment rather than transportation, 'as I understand [Bolter has] lived in Martyr Worthy for 35 years and his honesty was unquestioned'.[145] James Pyle Ashe wrote to Melbourne on 10 February 1832 explaining that Bolter had worked for him as a woodman at Pyle's Farm for 20 years and that his crime was being in the wrong place at the wrong time. Bolter had gone to sharpen his bill-hook when he inadvertently encountered the mob, who compelled him to go with them to be the custodian of any money they managed to purloin.[146]

John Dagwell appeared to be mortified by the whole affair and felt so bad about what had happened to Bolter that he wrote two letters to Melbourne, the second one, dated 26 January 1833, pleading that Bolter should be freed and allowed to go back to his wife and family. A petition addressed to the King, organised locally, collected 65 signatures and called for leniency; it was a moving document:

To the Kings most excellent Majesty

The Petition of certain owners and occupiers of Land residing in the Parish of Martins Worthy and neighbourhood in the county of Southampton

Most humbly sheweth

That **Willm Bolter** *late of Martins Worthy aged 61 years was convicted at the late Special Commission held at Winchester on a charge of an offence sworn to have been committed during the Agricultural Riots, that his Master Mr Edwd Parker of Piles Farm (one of your Majestys present Petitioners) at the time of his trial came forward in Court, and gave the Prisoner the character of a Man of the strictest integrity, stating that during the 34 years that he Willm Bolter had workd on his Farm, he had been a pattern of honesty industry and sobriety up to the Day, when from temporary excitement and (as your Majesty Petitioners firmly believe)* *not from any premeditated plan or design, he was unfortunately led to join others in those unlawful transactions which led to his conviction, and which induced the sentence under which is he now suffering. That your Majestys petitioners having learnt that some fresh arrangements as to the disposal of the Convicts at Portsmouth is about to take place and the said Willm Bolter being there, serving out his sentence of fourtenn years transportation, and your Majestys petitioners having other knowledge or learnt from those who have known the unfortunate Man, his most exemplary conduct, and moreover having known the fact of his breeding up a family of nine children to habits of industry and sobriety without Parochial aid and they do most conscientiously and confidently venture to approach your Majesty praying that your Majesty will in unison with the benevolence of your Majestys Heart extend mercy that brightest prerogative of your Majestys Crown to the unhappy Prisoner, which God like act would not only fill his and Families Hearts with gratitude and joy; but now that the strength of the Law has been shewn, and their dignity supported, now that the salutary effects of Punishment is demonstrated and the tranquility of the Country restored; such an act of your Majestys Royal clemency would diffuse pleasure and satisfaction into Breasts of your Majestys Petitioners and by restoring the unfortunate Prisoner to Liberty and usefulness would confer on his late employer (one of your Majestys Petitioners) a great personal obligation in giving him back a worthy and useful Labourer. And your Majestys Petitioners as in duty bound will ever pray.[147]*

In the end, the pressure paid off and Bolter was granted a free pardon on 16 May 1833, ten days after Palmerston himself had lent his support to the campaign.[148]

In what appeared to be a genuine miscarriage of justice, the silence from the Reverend Robert Wright was deafening. He made no moves to intervene on Bolter's behalf. Perhaps he was too proud to admit that the conviction was unfair, or did he genuinely believe that the woodman was guilty and deserved his punishment? His fellow JP Samuel Wall expressed his deep regret, but Wright, as stubborn as ever, held his ground.

One wonders how this episode affected Wright's standing and relationship with his parishioners, particularly John Dagwell, Andrew Twitchen, James Bignell and Benjamin Bear, all of whom had signed the petition.

All four men were well known and respected in Itchen Abbas and the surrounding area. Twitchen was a tenant farmer, Bear was a small farmer and parish official, Bignell was the village carpenter and Dagwell was the village miller. It is hard to believe that the case of William Bolter did not cause distress among the many of the ordinary folk of the upper Itchen Valley. Wright, however, was unmoved and carried on apparently confident in his judgement.

WHY DID THE VILLAGES OF THE UPPER ITCHEN VALLEY REMAIN 'LOYAL' DURING THE 1830 RIOTS?

The riotous events in the Itchen Valley raise the question as to why the local labourers appeared to stay loyal and showed no desire to join with the mob which arrived in their locality from elsewhere. Trouble to the north west of Winchester, in the Dever Valley, continued for several months, but there was calm in the Itchen Valley to the north east of the county town. Bethanie Afton has put forward the opinion that the first Duke of Buckingham and Chandos was an established landowner in the area and the local population had long benefitted from the paternalistic generosity of the Duke and his popular wife, Lady Anna Brydges.[149] (In comparison, although Sir Thomas Baring also had a paternalistic attitude, his family had only owned land in Hampshire since 1800 and had not yet built up the level of respect afforded to the Duke of Buckingham and Chandos.) Other reasons for the calm were that many of the labourers of Itchen Abbas, Easton and Avington had too much to lose by rioting, and they were probably wary of Robert Wright, who, despite his recent benevolence to John Hughes, was uncompromising in his approach to those who broke the law.

In 1831 the Duke and Duchess put on a feast for 200 of the villagers of Avington, Itchen Abbas and Easton, for their 'steady conduct last year during the unfortunate disturbances in this neighbourhood'.[150] The villagers were provided with an 'excellent and substantial dinner of roast beef, mutton and plum pudding with a suitable supply of the strong beer for which the hospitable mansion of their noble patrons is so justly celebrated'.[151]

Presumably, the villagers invited to the feast were tenants of the Duke who were renting a cottage and/or land. The total aggregated population of the three villages in 1831 was 928, which suggests many missed out, and they may well have felt resentful. It was not such a united neighbourhood as we have been led to believe. Robert Wright claimed there was still a good deal of idleness and he was concerned about the amount of heavy drinking taking place in the local beershops, particularly in Easton.[152]

Sir Thomas Baring sensed the need to build bridges with the labouring fraternity in an effort to gain more respect and authority. In contrast to Robert Wright, he was prepared to be conciliatory to some of the offenders he had committed for trial. He supported petitions to get Thomas Berriman (Senior) and Joseph Carter freed, recognising that both were men of previous good character and that their release would boost morale in their localities of Wonston and Barton Stacey.[153] As the case of William Bolter showed, Robert Wright did not get involved in pleas for clemency and displayed a hard-nosed attitude to those found guilty of rioting.

Some of the labourers of Avington, Easton and Itchen Abbas had the opportunity to rent allotments provided by the first Duke of Buckingham and Chandos, which may also have been a reason for their loyalty. In recognition of his allotment scheme the Duke was awarded the 20 guineas medal given annually by Sir Thomas Baring for good agricultural practice. Baring clearly wished to encourage allotments because they could be of benefit to some of the labouring class.

Arthur Octavius Baker, the Duke's steward, wrote a detailed letter to Baring's agent, dated 6 January 1833, thanking Baring for the award and furnishing details of how the Duke's Cottage Allotment System operated.[154] The scheme was started at Michaelmas 1830 (two months before the riots), and by Michaelmas 1831, 49 acres of quality land had been rented out in the villages of Avington, Easton and Itchen Abbas. Allotments varied in size from half an acre to two acres and were located within walking distance of the labourers' cottages. The rent charged was at two-thirds of the market value and brought the Duke a total of £58-5s-6d. The allotment holders were able to grow food for their families and have a surplus to sell at local markets.

Those who rented an allotment did not find any need to apply for parish relief and they were so content that every one of them paid their rent before the deadline date. Their tenancy agreement was for one year only, which meant there was no 'abuse' of the system. However, Baker also pointedly commented that some labourers were not interested in the scheme and in his opinion this was caused by the way the Poor Law was administered:

Let the magistrates of the County be less liberal in their 'bread allowances' to the Poor and we should find the labourers far more anxious to avail themselves of the Allotment System and this system itself working much greater good. But so long as the Poor have such ready access to the funds of the Parish they have little inducement to look to any means of active industry for support.[155]

The *Labourers' Friend* magazine of 1835 gave further details of the allotment system in the upper Itchen Valley, showing that the crops grown were wheat, barley, beans, potatoes and peas. Full details of 16 individual Easton tenants were given, but only generalised data was provided for Itchen Abbas and Avington. *Table 13* shows the profits made by the allotment tenants in 1832. Although Itchen Abbas had the fewest number of allotments, it still made a healthy profit.[156]

Parish	Number	A/R/P	Produce	Costs	Net Profit
Avington	25	12.0.36	£177-1-6	£37-12-0	£139-9-6
Easton	16	15.0.03	£143-2-0	£47-9-6	£95-12-6
Itchen Abbas	22	09.2.10	£122-0-0	£31-11-9	£99.8.3
Totals	63	46.3.09	£442-3-6	£116.13.3	£325.10.3

Key

A=Acres; **R**=Roods; **P**=Perches   40 Perches = 1 Rood;   4 Roods = 1 Acre

Table 13: *Summary of produce and profit for allotments at Avington, Easton and Itchen Abbas, 1832 (Source: The Labourers' Friend, 1835, pp. 218-222).*

The social historian Harold Perkin estimated that over one third of the population at this time could be categorised as 'the labouring poor' and it is clear that within this number there were varying degrees of poverty and distress.[157] Using the 1841 Census for Easton, it is possible to match ten of the sixteen tenants named in the report that appeared in the *Labourers' Friend* and they are all over the age of thirty, with settled families. Younger labourers did not appear to be renting an allotment, probably because they could not afford the rent, despite it being set at a favourable level. Again, using the 1841 Census, the percentage of labourers renting allotments appeared to be lower in Easton than either Itchen Abbas or Avington. There may well have been some disgruntled labourers in the neighbourhood and it is likely that not everyone was as happy as newspaper reports made out. Robert Wright said he 'did not know of a more distressed parish'[158] than Easton and claimed that the poor rates had increased to a great amount. This was also true of Itchen Abbas where the poor rates had risen from £120 per year to £160.[159] Overall, however, the availability of allotments was likely to have been a factor in explaining the loyalty of many of the labourers in the upper Itchen Valley.

THE DEACLES OF MARWELL TAKE ON THE ESTABLISHMENT

Another example of the fallout from the 1830 riots for Robert Wright was the Deacle affair. During the disturbances, on 24 November 1830, Thomas and Caroline Deacle of Marwell Farm were arrested for allegedly inciting labourers to riot. Robert Wright issued the warrant for their arrest and William Bingham Baring, Francis Baring and, it would appear, RJW Wright, together with a number of constables, turned up at their home to take the pair into custody. The Deacles protested their innocence, but to no effect. Caroline Deacle was handcuffed and roughly handled as she was bundled out of the house and Bingham Baring 'struck Mr Deacle a back handed blow with his stick'.[160] The two prisoners were transported to Winchester in a 'common coal cart [that] had no springs'.[161]

Why RJW Wright was involved in this incident is puzzling. He was not a magistrate and so was probably acting on the orders of his father. Unless he had been sworn in as a special constable, he had no authority to carry out any arrest and he probably felt very uncomfortable with the level of force used by the constables. It was certainly not in RJW Wright's character to relish this kind of confrontation. He had much more empathy with the problems of the labouring class than his father, and his later career supports this assessment.

The Deacles were subsequently cleared of any transgression and released. On 13 July 1831, angry at their treatment, they pressed charges against Baring for assault. He was convicted and ordered to pay £50 in costs, which led him to publish a pamphlet claiming his innocence in the affair.[162] The Deacles, backed by William Cobbett, had landed a small blow against the establishment.

ROBERT WRIGHT CONTINUES THE 'RURAL WAR'

Pursuing the arsonists

After the Special Commission had concluded Robert Wright continued to pursue a number of labourers who had escaped conviction due to a lack of evidence. He was relentless in his work and even financed a small, private police force to go around the local villages collecting intelligence.

Thomas Berriman (Junior) and Henry Hunt were suspected of setting fire to hayricks and buildings belonging to Sir Henry Wright Wilson of Barton Stacey on the night of the 19–20 November 1830. They were taken into custody, but were released on bail, very reluctantly, by Wright, as he was experienced enough to know that the evidence he had at the time would not secure a conviction. Wright was confident they were guilty, though, and continued to examine witnesses.

Twelve months later further arson attacks on Sir Henry Wright Wilson's property on the night of 11–12 December 1831 provided the evidence Wright was seeking.[163] Again, Thomas Berriman (Junior) and Henry Hunt were the suspects, together with James Whitcher. Warrants for their arrest were issued on 26 December 1831. Wright and Colonel William Iremonger interviewed 60 witnesses from Barton Stacey over a period of time in order to build up a 'connecting chain of evidence'.[164] Such was Wright's determination to convict the perpetrators of the crime that he later claimed he sat every day, 'to carry the law into effect'.[165] There must have been much clandestine chat and discussion concerning the event within the cottages of Barton Stacey residents.

On 16 January 1832 a second warrant was issued for the arrest of John Dore, suspected of arson at Sir Henry Wright Wilson's property on 19 November 1830. Wright's dogged pursuit of these men illustrated his fear that the establishment was under a concerted attack and his belief that only ruthless action would restore any sense of normality.

Berriman (Junior), Dore, Hunt and Whitcher went on trial at the Lent Assizes in Winchester on 25 February 1832. The evidence was complicated and much of it circumstantial. Wright gave evidence for the prosecution, together with 40 witnesses from Barton Stacey. Wright affirmed that Hunt had confessed his guilt to John Diddams, the Barton Stacey tithingman who had conveyed him to gaol in Winchester.

All four prisoners were found guilty by the jury and sentenced by Mr Justice Gaselee. He delivered a severe lecture to the men, clearly intended as a warning to others not to commit arson: 'It is my painful duty, after the evidence given against you, to pronounce the awful sentence of the law on you'.[166] Dore and Whitcher had the sentence of death recorded against them, commuted to transportation to Van Diemen's Land. Berriman (Junior) and Hunt were not so lucky; they were sentenced to death, with the executions scheduled for 17 March 1832. The judge told them to spend the time they had left repenting and making peace with their creator. Berriman (Junior) appeared defiant and left the dock saying, 'If any one destroys my body, he can't destroy my soul'.[167]

At 8.00 a.m. on Saturday 17 March, Berriman (Junior) and Hunt were taken out to a 'platform over the back entrance to the county gaol',[168] where a large crowd had gathered to witness the hangings. The *Hampshire Chronicle* reported that both men were contrite and had made written confessions. Berriman blamed his demise on 'a disregard of the Sabbath, drunkenness, and keeping dissolute company'. Hunt, according to the newspaper, expressed similar regret at his crime.[169] The *Hampshire Advertiser* described their final demise as follows:

> At the appointed signal the drop fell, and they seemed to die with little bodily suffering. Their bodies were received by their friends, placed into two coffins brought for the purpose, and taken to their native village for internment.[170]

For his part, Robert Wright may well have felt a quiet contentment that his hard work had brought the criminals to justice. In such turbulent times, he clearly valued the maintenance of the status quo more highly than any attempt to improve the miserable living conditions of many of the labouring poor. He also, no doubt, would have noted that the men had been frequenters of the local beershops, which he blamed for the recent rioting. There was not the slightest sign that Wright had any sympathy and his hard-line approach illustrated a resolute inner character. The concluding words of the *Hampshire Chronicle* report were a loud warning to other labourers and could well have come from the mouth of Robert Wright:

> It is hoped that these deluded men will now take warning by the sad end of their more abandoned leaders, and desist from such

horrible practices, a perseverance in which will not only lead to the certain forfeiture of their own lives, but will cause great distress in the country at large. Some of them are so well known, and their conduct so narrowly watched, as to induce a belief that any other offence they may hereafter commit will be followed by speedy and retributive justice.[171]

The Winchester Political Union

The tension between labourers, farmers and the authorities continued unabated following the conclusion of the Special Commission in Winchester; there was 'unfinished business' for both sides. Political unions to lobby for the reform of Parliament and the extension of the franchise sprang up across the country. They first appeared in the large industrialising cities such as Birmingham, Leeds and Sheffield but soon infiltrated into rural areas, including Hampshire and Sussex.

On 7 November 1831 a public meeting of the Winchester National Political Union was held on Oram's Arbour to formulate an address to the King which called for 'Universal Suffrage, Annual Parliaments, Vote by Ballot and no Property Qualifications'.[172] Special constables and the cavalry flanked the meeting in readiness for trouble, but as the *Poor Man's Guardian* reported, 'the whole proceedings went off, as they always will when the working people are left to themselves, in an orderly and peaceful manner'.[173]

The Winchester Political Union was linked to smaller 'satellite' unions that were established in villages such as Barton Stacey. They were well organised, with a written constitution, and meetings were held in an accommodating local beershop. Labourers paid an initial subscription of a few pence and then an entrance fee at each gathering they attended. Furthermore, their activities were reported by the radical press, particularly the *Poor Man's Guardian*, which was openly available at Daniel Snagg's shop in Middle Brook Street, Winchester. The *Poor Man's Guardian* was extreme in its condemnation of the authorities, and its threatening language alarmed the magistracy within the mid Hampshire locality. To them, the activities of the political unions went hand in hand with the continuing threat of arson, particularly in the Dever Valley. Robert Wright, Colonel William Iremonger, Sir Lucius Curtis and Sir John Pollen were the four most prominent magistrates attempting to silence the unions and they were directly targeted by the *Poor Man's Guardian*. It was a state of rural war which exposed the fears and feelings of both sides.[174]

'Tyranny and oppression' at Wonston

On Saturday 29 September 1832 a letter appeared in the *Poor Man's Guardian* signed by five farm labourers claiming cruel treatment from their employer, William Saunders of Cranborne Farm in Wonston.[175] The letter was in perfect English and most probably crafted on behalf of the five men by an unknown 'correspondent'. The men said they wished to tell of 'the tyranny by which we are governed on the one hand, and the injustice we are treated with by the magistrates on the other'.[176]

On the 16 August the men had worked from 4.00 a.m. to 11.00 p.m. unloading barley. No food or water was provided, so at one point during the day, they walked the one mile into Sutton Scotney for beer and bread and cheese. Nothing was said to them on their return to the farm. The next day, however, William Saunders came into the yard and beat the boy who was looking after the horses for no other reason than the horses were drinking water. Saunders travelled to the Castle in Winchester and returned with two summonses from two JPs for the men to appear before them. The charge was 'nothing more nor less than for refreshing ourselves at our own expense, after working from four in the morning till 11 at night'.[177] The men went off to Winchester to answer the charge supported by a number of witnesses willing to speak in their defence. However, they reported that 'a Mr Wright, a magistrate and a minister of Christ's gospel, so he professed at least, ordered that no witness should be examined for us, and he committed us for one month's imprisonment to hard labour'.[178]

The case was heard in Petty Sessions but unreported in the mainstream media. Perhaps this was as well for Robert Wright, as the charge appeared to be 'trumped up' and the men were innocent of any law-breaking. They had quite simply been used to illustrate that the magistracy would not tolerate any acts of 'disobedience'.

Go and starve!

On Saturday 1 December 1832 another story of 'rural tyranny' appeared in the *Poor Man's Guardian*.[179] The article alluded to the strength of the Winchester Political Union in terms of a growing membership and funds.

The labouring men, according to the article, were 'abject slaves of the magistrates and parsons', and the authorities were intent on ending their right to belong to such an organisation.

In Chilbolton, 13 men had been dismissed by their employers for being members of the local political union. One of the farmers who had dismissed men happened to be the overseer of the poor in the village, and when the men applied for poor relief, they were refused. In desperation, they went to Andover and appealed to the magistrates (Pollen, Curtis and Iremonger) to issue an order to the overseer to provide 'work or relief'. The appeal was refused, causing one of the labourers with a family of five children to ask what he should do to feed them. Sir John Pollen allegedly answered, GO AND STARVE![180]

The men continued to apply for relief each week but the answer was the same. Such an act of oppression, the *Guardian* argued, needed to be publicised and the men defended from the 'Moloch of Aristocracy'.[181] The divisions in rural society were widening but there was no sign of the two sides discussing the situation and arriving at a compromise. Wages remained low and, as we have seen, allowances were reduced. No sort of agreement was on the horizon, and the politicisation of the situation did not help. Most labourers merely wished for a living wage, but the authorities felt threatened and under attack. No one, least of all Robert Wright, wanted to show any sign of weakness in the struggle.

Wright's surveillance network

Robert Wright was fully aware that political unions had the potential to destroy many of the values he believed in. Thanks to the survival of some letters in the Wellington Papers, we are able to build a picture of how Wright operated a sophisticated network of surveillance across the locality. The first Duke of Buckingham and Chandos wrote to the Duke of Wellington on 20 November 1832 urging him to arrange a meeting with Wright, who had a wealth of knowledge about the activities of the political unions. Buckingham and Chandos stated that Wright had set up a 'system of espionage' and this was how he obtained his information. Wright informed Wellington that the Winchester Union met on Tuesday nights, usually under some pretence of being 'an amateur concert' rehearsal and up to 700 members would march in the street in an orderly procession.[182] A more detailed letter to Wellington, dated 1 January 1833, described a meeting attended by Wright's undercover spies. He wrote that the meeting was 'employed in exciting tumult'[183] in response to some members complaining they had been refused relief because they were paid up members of the union (clearly, this must have been the Chilbolton men). The complaining men were given 12 shillings each but told they had to repay it when they found a job. This, Wright claimed, 'occasioned discontent' among the members.

The union members then discussed some ideas received from other unions as a way of formulating a policy of their own. They agreed a resolution 'to watch the conduct of those Members of Parliament who had been supported by the [union to check that] … they advocated the vote by ballot, annual parliaments, abolition of tithes [and the] repeal of the assessed taxes, etc'.[184]

Wright went on to say that he had in his custody six members of the union who were suspected of setting fire to an 'oat rick' in the parish of Chilbolton. He had no doubt they were guilty but he did not have enough evidence to convict them. His 'emissaries' were out trying to gather more evidence with the intention of securing a conviction. Judging from another letter written by Robert Wright to the Duke of Wellington on 10 March 1833, one man was convicted but found not guilty by the jury.[185]

This seemed to shake Wright's confidence, and he sought the Duke's counsel on another issue that emerged from the case. Wright thought that the political union had paid for the defence of the alleged arsonist, but he could not prove it. In addition, he claimed that some members of the union had made statements on oath affirming that the steward of the union had 'promised them eight shillings per day to attend the city and county elections to make disturbances and oppose the Conservative candidates'.[186]

Wright appeared to have lost his ability to assess evidence and he wanted the Duke to tell him how to proceed. Wellington, however, told Wright to make his own decisions according to the evidence in front of him. He also told Wright that he needed to obtain copies of the statements alleging that men had been paid to disrupt elections. 'If they could be [produced]', he wrote, 'they would afford the ground for proceeding against the steward of the [union]. But I must say that in these times no step can be taken without being supported by proof.[187] Wellington's tone was one of exasperation. He complained that it was difficult to read Wright's handwriting and it was impossible for him to make any judgement on the issues. It was up to Wright to decide whether evidence was sufficient to proceed.

Robert Wright had become obsessive in pursuing arsonists and the activities of the political unions. He was troubled that the establishment was under threat, and he was so determined to defend his beliefs that his decision-making was temporarily impaired. Although he was a man under stress, his remarkable durability and energy kept him going.

THE SELECT COMMITTEE ON THE SALE OF BEER (1833): A WINDOW INTO THE TROUBLED MIND OF ROBERT WRIGHT

In the spring of 1833 a Parliamentary Select Committee was set up under the chairmanship of the Marquis of Chandos (to become the second Duke of Buckingham and Chandos in 1839), friend of Robert Wright, to investigate the working of the 1830 Beershops Act. Under the act anyone could open a beershop on the payment of £2 to the Excise, meaning that, unlike public houses, they did not have to obtain a licence from the local magistrates. The intended purpose of the act was to reduce the consumption of spirits, especially gin, which was prevalent at the time. Hampshire magistrates were convinced that the rapid establishment of beershops in rural areas was one of the main causes of the rioting in the county in the last weeks of November 1830. They believed that radical reformers were active in these establishments politicising labourers into calling for the reform of Parliament and living conditions.

On 24 April 1833 Wright appeared as the very first witness before the Select Committee. The Marquis of Chandos asked Wright 294 questions. The line of questioning was designed to elicit answers that showed the beershops to be evil institutions. Asked about the 1830 riots Wright stated, 'I believe that I shall feel the riots to the day of my death; the blow that I got then I shall never recover [from]'.[188] When this statement is placed in the context of Wright's fight to bring the rioters to justice, it looks as if he had been through a period of trauma and anxiety. He was adamant the riots were not down to low wages and poverty but were politically motivated and inspired by menial journeymen and craftsmen meeting in beershops. Chandos asked him:

Question 10: You have seen therefore the effect of those beerhouses upon the population of the district in which you have resided?

Answer: I have.

Question 11: Will you state to the Committee what has been the effect you have witnessed from those beerhouses?

Answer: I think the Committee ought to be informed first of the character of the people who keep those beerhouses; they are generally men who do not work; a little kind of petty tradesmen, who will rather get their bread by any other way than by hard labour; during the riots, those beerhouses were the focus for the meeting of the different parties, and there all the mischief commenced and was carried on by the delegates; crime has increased very considerably in our county; I frequently assist as chairman of the Quarter Sessions, and we never used to have more than one or two cases of assault; and within the last three months there has been no less than 38 committals for punishment for offences of assaults arising from those beerhouses.[189]

Wright also claimed that the men who suffered the severest penalties for their actions in the riots had begged him 'to use every exertion I had in my power to put a stop to beerhouses'.[190] It is nigh impossible to check whether Wright's statistics are accurate, but he could be economic with the truth if it suited his purpose, so caution is advised. His opinions were firmly set and unshakeable. He did not wish to acknowledge that labourers in work were being paid a wage they could not live on. He could not be blamed for wishing to keep the peace, but his sympathies lay with the farmers, rather than the labourers, and his opposition to the importation of cheaper foreign corn is evidence of this view.

Wright provided a further insight into his analysis of the detrimental effects of beershops in his reply to Question 46 when he claimed that the cheap beer was not the only reason for the beershops' popularity:

> It is not altogether the beer, but the fellowship they meet with, and the conversation they get into, and the petty publications which are continually carried round to those houses, and which they get to read; I think as long as they can get to those houses mischief will ensue.[191]

In reference to the spate of arson attacks in mid-Hampshire since 1830, Robert Wright had no doubt at all why they had occurred:

I do not think there is a single fire in our neighbourhood or county, that has not originated from the beershops, and where they have not started [off] from the beershops to commit the crime. ... From the confession of the criminals, after sentence of death passed, I should think that 50 of the persons in the parish where the conflagration took place, and the villages round, were all leagued together ... [Before the Beer Act of 1830] we had no incendiaries, and the other crimes were different from that, and did not require their meeting so much, because it was merely for their sole and self advantage.[192]

Unsurprisingly, there were no beershops in Itchen Abbas, but there were several in nearby villages, Itchen Stoke and Easton included. Wright told the Select Committee that he had a paid group of undercover men who frequented the beershops in search of individuals discussing reform and political change. He blamed beershops for a perceived increase in drunkenness and domestic violence, which in turn led to a rise in the poor rates. The idea that poverty and poor living standards may have produced this behaviour did not seem part of his thinking. In contrast, the Reverend Samuel Best (1802–1873), rector of Abbotts Ann, displayed a much greater degree of empathy with the plight of the poor, arguing that the real social evil of the times was not the beershop but the lack of decent cottages. Best said labourers visited beershops because 'they can be seldom said to have a home'.[193] Both Wright and Best came from privileged 'middling' back-grounds, so it is interesting that the latter genuinely wanted to improve the lives of the labouring poor and the former showed little understanding of their plight.

When giving his evidence to the Select Committee Wright provides us with an insight into his relationship with the lower orders of Itchen Abbas. A woman visited him to ask for parish relief, explaining that her husband was ill and unable to work. Wright visited the labourer 'in his capacity of clergyman' and found that most of his possessions had been pawned at the 'pop shop'.[194] Wright was amazed that a labourer who was said to earn 10 shillings a week was having to raise money by pawning his posses-sions and drew the conclusion that he was using the money to fund his drinking. The reverend gave the man a blanket but had little sympathy for

Plate 17: *The Home of the Rick Burner, a cartoon from Punch, 1844.*

his predicament, as he believed it to be caused by alcohol. Before the advent of beershops, Wright told the Select Committee, the labourer in question had a reputation for being a good worker, but Wright no longer considered him to be a respectable individual because 'he seldom comes near the church' and spent all his wages on drink.[195]

We do not know the identity of this man or exactly where he lived in Itchen Abbas. At this time, however, many labourers lived in substandard temporary cottages on Itchen Down which were constructed of daub, flints and thatch. They were probably little better than the squalid hovel depicted in the famous *Punch* cartoon drawn by John Leech in 1844.

Wright undoubtedly regarded himself as a person of great importance within the local community. With obvious satisfaction, he told the Select Committee that Itchen Abbas was 'more clear' of crimes than other parishes and that there had not been 'an illegitimate child born for these twenty years'.[196] In his own parish, he said, 'there is no police but myself' and he proudly claimed there was no scale of allowances. He told the committee that any man who 'has not sufficient to maintain his family ... comes to me and I order him relief'.[197] Wright repeated his view that even the labourers themselves believed that beershops were the root of all evil and wanted them abolished:

> The man who struck Mr Bingham Baring two days before he died, begged and entreated me to use all the influence I possessed to get the beer-houses put down; and the other men did the same; of ninety-seven that were put in our Bridewell, I do not think there were five that did not tell me that they owed their misery to the beer-houses.[198]

Questioned about the working of the Poor Law in the neighbourhood, Robert Wright lamented the fact that Easton operated an allowance scale which gave poor relief according to the number of children in a family. Itchen Abbas, however, had no set way of dealing with requests for help from the parish. He told the Select Committee:

> I have no regular system [of allowance], because I go according to what I conceive to be the wants of the people; but I can state what the allowance is in the neighbouring parishes, it is a gallon of bread to each person, and if they have four children, sixpence a head besides.[199]

Robert Wright was obviously making the point that he thought allowance scales were too generous and that encouraged idleness. In Itchen Abbas, however, it appeared that poor relief was less 'generous' and this, he argued, made most of the labourers more diligent. As he was obsessive in his wish to keep spending out of the rates to a minimum, it is highly likely that the expenditure on poor relief in Itchen Abbas was relatively low compared to many parishes.

Robert Wright told the Select Committee that he thought beershops should be rated to the poor rates for at least £15 per year (more in London and urban areas) and that any individual intending to open a beershop should have to provide references as to their character.[200] Both these suggestions were included in the report of the Select Committee when it was published in June 1833.

Wright's evidence reveals his philosophy towards the poor and his modus operandi. He was almost paranoid in his belief that the status quo was about to be turned upside down, and he saw himself as a sort of overlord of the local area, an authoritarian figure not to be challenged. The 1830 riots had hardened his attitude towards the poor and he had come to distrust many of the labouring class. Also, a theme running through the answers he gave was his sense of self-importance and lack of empathy for the conditions that many had to endure. He believed he was 'conscientious [and] performing [his] duty to the best of [his] abilities'.[201] It was a clash between the 'old world' and the irresistible force of change threatening to overwhelm traditionalists such as Robert Wright.

Just two weeks before giving evidence to the Select Committee,

Robert Wright had written and presented a petition to the Hampshire Quarter Sessions in which he called for the Beershops Act to be repealed. In his inimitable style, Wright argued:

> We are fully sensible that this Act was passed with a benevolent intention; but regret from the constant complaints which are made, and the frequent cases which come before us, the demoralising effects it has upon the lower orders of society. Our bridewell for some time past has not been without 200 persons under confinement for petty offences and 267 individuals have been committed to the prison since the last Quarter Sessions [held in early January 1833].[202]

Again, the statistics appear to be arbitrary, and they do not agree with those Wright quoted to the Select Committee! However, the petition met with the approval of his fellow magistrates and was submitted to the House of Commons. In its report, however, the Select Committee did not go as far as recommending the repeal of the Beershop Act, but instead opted for a more stringent enforcement of licensing and opening hours. Wright would have been disappointed with this outcome, because he clearly felt beershops were evil and a source of political agitation for extending the franchise and, as such, a grave threat to the establishment.

WRIGHT ATTEMPTS TO REASSERT
THE CREDIBILITY OF THE ESTABLISHMENT

On Monday 19 November 1832 Robert Wright attended a dinner at the Grosvenor Arms Hotel given by the electors of Stockbridge and district in honour of the Marquis of Douro, the son of the Duke of Wellington. After a sumptuous meal, Baring Wall, the chairman, of Norman Court, proposed a toast to the Reverend Robert Wright and praised his 'magisterial exertions'.[203] Wright stood up to give his thanks and proceeded to comment on the ecclesiastical and political situation of the day. He was unhappy at reformers attacking the practices of absenteeism and pluralism within the established Church. He blamed the press, which he said, was 'cankering with its force and pestilential mouth the very principles of the church of England'.[204] Perhaps Wright was referring to newspaper reports of the activities of the Society for the Extinction of Ecclesiastical Abuses, which had as one of its aims 'to put an end to the existing union between Church and State; that is, the consequent annexation of political power to episcopal rank'.[205] Wright remarked that the clergy carried out their duties conscientiously and that the reformers were in danger of bringing down both the Church and the state. Thus, 'it was necessary for friends of the established church to be on their guard'.[206]

Wright rejected the reform of Parliament and rebuked Charles Lefevre, a Whig and fellow magistrate, for supporting the extension of the franchise and shorter parliaments. This was anathema to Wright, who exclaimed that the recently passed Great Reform Act was 'oppressive and tyrannical'.

Wright concluded his defence of the establishment by declaring that farmers should be given greater protection from foreign grain imports: 'If we granted sufficient protection to agriculture, it would enable the farmer to get a fair return for his capital, and also to pay his labourers well, and to bring more land into cultivation'.[207] The counter argument – that tariffs and duties on imports of grain kept the price of bread artificially high and wages in general did not keep pace with these prices – was not Wright's concern. William Huskisson, as President of the Board of Trade from 1823 to 1827, had devised a sliding scale of duties on imported corn so that 'when the home price of corn was high, duty on foreign corn was reduced'.[208] This had been bitterly opposed by farmers and landowners alike, but momentum for the complete abolition of duties on imported grain was building and Wright consistently sided with the farmers rather than the labouring class.

Two weeks after this tirade, the *Reading Mercury* reprinted an article from the *Morning Herald* that delivered a fierce attack on Robert Wright.[209] The *Morning Herald* said it denied 'this gentleman's unfounded imputations [about the press], and [threw] back the slander in his teeth'. The article also condemned the abuses that were deeply 'rooted in the establishment'. Such abuses included the unfair division of Church property; the large number of preferments on certain favoured families at the expense of others; and the manner in which the clergy involved themselves in secular activities, 'to the great detriment of religion', most probably a reference to the unpopularity of clerical magistrates. The article concluded with a stinging retort to Robert Wright:

The great majority of the clergy, we are persuaded, feel and act differently; and are, we are convinced, grateful to the Press for the line which it is taking, and are only scandalised by the conduct of its assailant.[210]

It was common for local newspapers at the time to repeat articles from other publications. In this instance, however, not one of the mainstream Hampshire newspapers reprinted the *Morning Herald's* article. Even if one had, Robert Wright would have been completely unmoved.

In 1835 Wright provided further insights into his philosophy of life when he made a speech at a dinner for James Buller East (Tory MP for Winchester) held at St. John's House in the cathedral city. His views on politics, religion and society showed no signs of changing:

It has become necessary for the friends of the church and the monarchy to show themselves prepared to defend their institutions when that frantic and democratic seal for every fanciful or destructive innovation is exhibited abroad; when the withering blast of destruction is working with its foul and pestilential breath, the subversion of the church and the throne. If ever it was necessary to rally round the throne and the altar, it was the present period- (loud applause). Gentlemen, I am not one of those bigoted enthusiasts who disclaim everything for the profession to which they belong. I am desirous of granting liberty of conscience to everyone, and to allow all to worship God in the manner most agreeable to their feelings. Such too is the general desire of the clergy of the Established Church. But we believe the throne and the altar to be closely united together that whatever destroys one will leave the other a rude and shapeless mass of ruin.[211]

Wright was being disingenuous; in real life, his opinions changed in accordance with the audience he was addressing. He was known to have no time for Calvinism, thereby contradicting his own statement about 'liberty of conscience'.

Wright's strong words were a reaction to a changing atmosphere in which the Anglican Church felt threatened and under attack. Evangelicals and supporters of the Oxford Movement were calling for a return to spiritualism and an improvement in 'clerical discipline' and pastoral care of parishioners. These 'reformers' had little time for clerical magistrates or clergymen who regarded themselves as both parson and squire. No wonder Wright was anxious to counter these developments. In addition, non-conformity was growing and Roman Catholics were enjoying greater civic freedom thanks to the Catholic Relief Act of 1829. WM Jacob sums up the concerns of the Anglican clergy at this time:

> Many feared for the continuation of the established Church as they knew it, as reformers began to question the endowments of the Church, the utility of the clergy, the payment of tithes and church rates ... and the Church's role as sole celebrant of marriages and provider for burial of the dead.[212]

Add to this the reforms of the Whig government such as the 1832 Great Reform Act, the centralisation of the Poor Law in 1834, the Municipal Corporations Act of 1835 and the introduction of the Ecclesiastical Commission in 1836, and it is not difficult to see why a traditionalist such as Robert Wright was feeling insecure. His anger would have increased when he learned of the Ecclesiastical Commissioners' intentions to curb pluralism and non-residence. He did not appear to suffer adversely from the requirements of the Tithe Commutation Act of 1836, but would have found the Registration Act of 1836 a downgrading of the status of the Anglican Church. This act set up the civil registration of births, marriages and deaths, 'independent' of the parish registers kept by the clergy.[213] There was a lot happening to trouble Wright. Everything he believed in was under attack amid a sea of change. His answer was to lash out at his critics.

WRIGHT AND THE 'GHOST' OF 1830

As late as June 1837, seven years after the agricultural riots, Hampshire magistrates were still worried about the possibility of further rioting and tumult in Hampshire. At the Midsummer Quarter Sessions a Mr Gauntlett addressed the bench, saying he had been sent by the inhabitants of Waterloo Vill (now Waterlooville), an extra parochial settlement to the north of Portsmouth. Gauntlett reported that the inhabitants were nervous that their settlement was about to be engulfed in rioting and violence. An extra-parochial township had few rights and lacked a constable to keep the peace, forcing Gauntlett to plead with Quarter Sessions to appoint a special constable for a limited period which, he said, would be paid for by the local inhabitants.[214] He was told that the court could not appoint a temporary special constable on this basis and there was no possibility of the costs being met out of the rates. Temporary special constables could only be appointed for one off events such as the fair at Magdalen Hill in the parish of Chilcombe, after which the temporary special constables were paid a fee and dismissed.

Wright claimed that he was fully aware of the law, but nevertheless he and fellow magistrate George Haines Jones decided to appoint John Hawkins as the special constable for Waterloo Vill 'adjoining the parish of Southwick' for the 'space of six months now ensuing [from] the 14 day of November 1837'.[215] This information was sent to the Duke of Wellington, with an accompanying letter from Robert Wright to explain the decision. Wellington was not impressed, and on 3 December 1837 he wrote to John Woodham, Clerk of the Peace for Hampshire, issuing a severe censure:

> These two magistrates have appointed a constable for six months. If they can appoint one [underlined], they can a hundred; if for six months, they can for a year. My impression is that the power is given to them in order to provide for an emergency [underlined] and that appointment can be made only for the emergent occasion. Only conceive giving the man 45 pounds for such service for six months.[216]

Woodham replied to the Duke agreeing with his assessment but attempting to defend the indefensible. He stated that 'the magistrates consented to the appointment on the inhabitants of the "ville" agreeing to pay the constable a salary'.[217]

On 10 December 1837 Woodham wrote an admonishing letter to Robert Wright telling him that 'it would be more regular for them to apply to the magistrates in Quarter Sessions'.[218] Worse was to follow, in that Wellington wrote directly to Wright on 12 December 1837 and told him that he did not have the power as a JP to appoint special constables 'permanently'.[219]

Wright had admitted that he was aware that the legislation did not empower him to appoint John Hawkins for an extended length of time, so why did he do it? It may have been a sense of hubris and he thought it would be overlooked, but more likely he was worried that his nearby parish of Southwick was under threat from rioting. His experience of the 1830 riots was still very fresh in his mind and he was nervous of a repeat. Wright liked praise and had an inflated opinion of his own popularity, so a lecture from the Lord Lieutenant was humiliating and a blow to his pride.

On 12 October 1837 Robert Bray, aged 45, of Over Wallop, a pauper in the Stockbridge Union workhouse, set fire to two hayricks at James Cooper's farm also in Over Wallop. He was convicted by Robert Wright and John Newington Hughes and sent for trial at the Lent Assizes in Winchester in March 1838.

In court, Cooper said that the hayricks were situated a mile from his house and on the morning of 12 October 1837 he had found them burned down. He offered a reward of £50 for information leading to the arrest of the offender. The culprit, however, had quickly confessed to the master of the Stockbridge Union workhouse. Bray stated that he had committed the crime out of spite because Mr Cooper had starved him of food (presumably, Bray had been working on Cooper's farm on a daily basis as part of an arrangement with the Poor Law authorities). On 13 October 1837 Bray absconded from the Stockbridge workhouse, but he was found and arrested the following day by a constable from Winchester. In court, Bray offered no defence but said he fled the Stockbridge Union because they did not provide sufficient victuals.

The jury applied the letter of the law and found Bray guilty of arson No mercy was shown by the judge who sentenced him to transportation for life.[220] On 19 March 1838 Bray was taken from Winchester gaol to await transportation aboard the prison hulk *Leviathan* in Portsmouth harbour. He was obviously undernourished and as a result died on board the hulk on 3 April 1838.[221] A sad end to a sad case.

It looks as though the 'ghost 'of 1830 had influenced Robert Wright again. Ever since Wright had relentlessly pursued arsonists with the aim of convicting and making an example of them. It could not be denied that he was doing his duty as a magistrate in keeping the peace, but by now any empathy he might have had for the plight of people of the labouring class such as Robert Bray had long since disappeared.

Changing times for the Hampshire bench

The Rural Police Act 1839

On 27 August 1839 the Rural Police Act was passed into law by the Whig government. It gave county magistrates the power to establish and organise a trained, uniformed police force funded out of the local rates along with a 25 per cent grant from central government. The first county to take advantage of the act was Wiltshire, followed in December 1839 by Hampshire. Significantly, both counties had suffered badly during the 1830 disturbances.

Ever since 1830 the Hampshire authorities had feared another outbreak of violence, and as a precaution volunteer yeomanry troop regiments had been reintroduced. Magistrates looked at the increasing number of prisoners in the county gaol and drew the conclusion that petty crime was on the increase. This, too, was at a time when the Hampshire bench was losing any confidence it may have had in the local parish constables, many of whom were not doing the job properly.[222] Some, in fact, were more interested in 'fiddling' their expenses, an issue that Robert Wright had been complaining about for years.

It was no surprise, therefore, that the vast majority of the Hampshire bench was in favour of introducing a regular police force, but the public would have to be convinced that this was a wise move. At the Michaelmas Quarter Sessions in October 1839 the issue of a regular police force was discussed and there were petitions from Lymington, Petersfield and the Isle of Wight calling for the immediate 'establishment of a Constabulary force'.[223] There was a comprehensive debate and it was clear that there was a great deal of support for the measure, but Robert Wright slowed things down by proposing that all 14 Petty Session divisions of the county should be consulted and that a committee should be set up to report back at the Epiphany Sessions in January 1840.[224] The suggestion was taken up but the committee was ordered to report one month sooner, at an adjournment meeting on 3 December 1839.

Robert Wright opposes the new county police force

At this adjournment the chairman of the committee, the Rt. Hon. William Sturges Bourne, said that 'nearly all the magistrates in each division were in favour' of establishing a county police force in Hampshire. He proposed a motion to this effect, seconded by Sir Thomas Baring.[225]

The loudest dissenting voice came from Robert Wright, who said that 'if he left the room without protesting against it, he should do violence to his own conscience, and an act of injustice to the ratepayers'.[226] Wright had spent nine years fretting about the perceived rise in crime and in fear of a repeat of the 1830 riots, yet he still remained sceptical about the introduction of a professional police force in the place of amateur law enforcement. As a staunch Tory, Wright may have feared that the 1839 act was part of a Whig conspiracy to curb the power of local magistrates and eventually to bring the police under the control of a centralised board, as had happened with the Poor Law. This was patently not the case, as the size of the new force and the rules and regulation were all to be under the direction of the county magistrates. Crucially, they were also responsible for appointing the chief constable.

Wright was not going to give in easily. He claimed that a regular police force would cost the ratepayers £12,000 per year. It would be better, he argued, to abolish beershops, which would have the undoubted effect of reducing the crime rate. Wright was also of the opinion that the number of recommended regular constables for the force, 106, was too low. He produced a petition with numerous signatures opposing the proposed change.

The Rt. Hon. CS Lefevre, however, stated that Wright was incorrect about the cost of a regular police force and that the true cost would be only £7,000 per year. Wright was subsequently outvoted, and the meeting concluded with an agreement to send a report to the Secretary of State which said that:

> [The] Justices for the Peace for the county had come to a resolution that the ordinary force for preserving the peace, the protection of the inhabitants and for the security of property, was not sufficient; and that 106 constables should be appointed at the salaries recommended in the resolution.[227]

At the Epiphany Quarter Sessions in January 1840, Captain George Robbins was elected as the first chief constable of the new county police force and a committee was set up, consisting of Sir Thomas Baring, Sir Raymond Jarvis, Mr Waddington and Mr Yonge to decide on clothing and equipping the new force of 106 men.[228]

The new police force was a huge step forward in the maintenance of law and order in the county, yet it had been opposed by Robert Wright who had always worked consistently hard to bring offenders to justice. When it came to the crux, Wright's long held belief in entrenchment came to the fore, but his opposition was also indicative of his deep distrust of any sort of reform that eroded his own traditional beliefs.

For the next 16 months Wright remained silent, but he resurrected his opposition in 1841 in the hope that Quarter Sessions would rescind the decision to form a county force. At the Easter Quarter Sessions, he presented between 30 and 40 petitions from parishes that did not want the new police. Included among them, unsurprisingly, were Itchen Abbas, Easton, Ovington, Cheriton, Bighton, Ropley, Old Alresford and Bishop's Sutton. All these places were local to Wright and he most probably had been lobbying them to raise petitions. In his presentation to his fellow JPs Wright argued that he had 'conscientiously opposed the formation of a Constabulary Force in the county, on the ground that it was unnecessary, uncalled for and oppressive'.[229]

Wright considered the force unnecessary because the county was now quiet and peaceable and also because no district had petitioned directly for a new police force. Furthermore, there were anomalies in the financing of the new system whereby villages of 200 or 300 people were paying more to the police force than towns with populations of thousands. He went on to say that he

greatly regretted differing so widely from many of his brother magistrates, especially from those gentlemen with whom he had the honour to act; but he could not force his conscience to agree to a measure which was never solicited and, apparently, unnecessary.[230]

Wright believed a constabulary police force was a financial burden which should be 'alleviate[d] as soon as possible'.[231] Unfortunately, no one spoke in support of his opposition. Daniel Quarrier, William Hughes and William Yonge all made powerful arguments in favour of the new force, and in doing so forced the debate to a close, leaving Wright isolated and frustrated.

At the Epiphany Quarter Sessions of January 1842 Wright made yet another attempt to get the county police force abolished when he contradicted a claim by Sir William Heathcote that crime in the county was decreasing. Wright referred to two new petitions from Titchfield and Petersfield, where crime had risen. In Titchfield, for example, there had been 35 cases of sheep stealing, many of which, Wright claimed were not even known to the police. Ultimately, the powerful arguments of Heathcote, William Yonge and the Chief Constable, Captain Robbins, forced Wright to admit defeat.[232]

Wright now went completely silent on the issue. The police force was too well established and any attempt to disband it required the county to give the Secretary of State a notice period of six months. It was not a practical option, and instead Wright diverted his efforts into the campaign to build a county lunatic asylum and, in politics, to fighting the threat of the Anti-Corn Law League.

A new county gaol

Another major issue came to the fore in 1845. For some time there had been concerns about the inadequacies of the facilities at the Winchester bridewell in Hyde. As a result, Sir William Heathcote, the chairman of the Hampshire bench, volunteered to consult architects to draw up plans to enlarge the building. At the Epiphany Quarter Sessions in January 1845 Heathcote presented a more radical solution to the problem with a plan for the construction of one large county prison that incorporated both the gaol and bridewell. He suggested the formation of an ad hoc committee of 15 magistrates to consider the idea and to report back with their findings. As a visiting JP to the county gaol and bridewell with many years of experience, it was no surprise that Robert Wright was invited to join the committee. He was only too aware of the overcrowding problem in both of the institutions.[233]

The committee duly presented its report for consideration at the Easter Quarter Sessions in 1845. It declared that the gaol in Jewry Street, designed by John Howard in 1788, had ill-arranged accommodation which made it virtually impossible to classify the prisoners, with debtors, for example, having to mix with criminals. (This was despite a new building for debtors being added in 1805.) In addition, the bridewell, built in Hyde in 1787, was similarly outdated and the committee recommended its abolition. Although the county had carried out some renovations in the early 1820s, the gaol and bridewell were no longer fit for purpose.

Plate 18: *The County Gaol, Jewry Street, Winchester in the early 1840s*
(© Hampshire County Council collections;
provided by Hampshire Cultural Trust).

Major Jebb, a government inspector of prisons, believed it would cost a total of £35,000 to renovate both the gaol and bridewell. However, the bridewell was located on low-lying damp ground, which contributed to frequent outbreaks of diarrhoea and fever, and modernising a building that stood on an unsuitable site was pointless.

A much more radical solution was needed, and it was recommended that the county should build a completely new prison to replace the Jewry Street gaol and the Hyde bridewell, rather than attempt an upgrade of the two existing prisons. The estimated cost was £57,000, funded out of the rates and a central government loan.

There was inevitable opposition from some magistrates, who thought it was too costly and unnecessary, but Sir Thomas Baring argued convincingly that one new prison would be the 'truest economy' and stated that the committee could oversee the planning and building of the new establishment.[234] Baring and Heathcote appeared to be the prime instigators

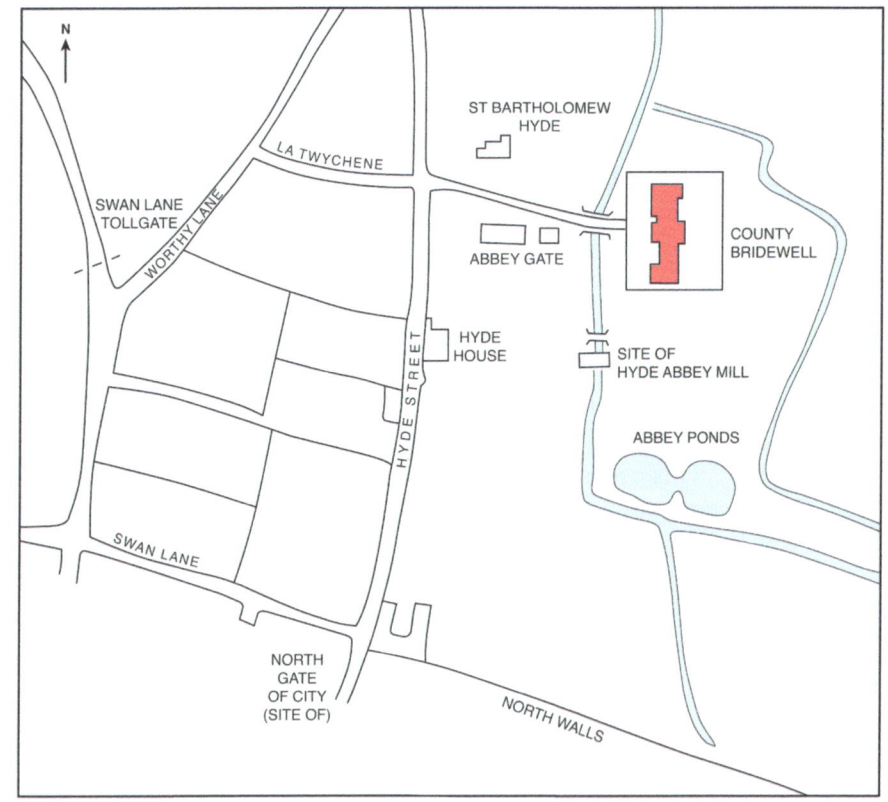

Figure 10: *Location of the County Bridewell, Hyde,
a northern suburb of Winchester, in 1800.*

of this important decision. Although we do not know exactly how much
Wright contributed to the deliberations of the committee, we know at
least that he did not publicly oppose the new prison, as had been the case
with the county police force. When the assembled magistrates voted on
the motion 'that a county prison be erected on a new site' it was carried
without difficulty.[235]

Initially, the contract to build the new prison was awarded to the experienced Charles Pierce, but some way into the job he was dismissed and a
local builder, Thomas Stopher, was called in to finish the construction.[236]
Ill health had forced Sir Thomas Baring to withdraw from the new prison
committee, but nevertheless the new building situated on Romsey Road,

Winchester was completed and by the end of September 1849 was ready to receive prisoners.

The movement of prisoners into the new gaol from the bridewells in Winchester, Gosport, Southampton and Portsmouth then began. The proximity to the railway station should have facilitated the quick transfer of inmates to their new surroundings, but it took until December to complete the task.

The **'Plans of the New Prison at Winchester'** appeared in the *Second Report of the Surveyor-General of Prisons* in 1847 and gave the following details:

This prison, now in the course of erection, is designed to contain 400 separate cells, viz:

312 males
20 male debtors
6 Misdemeanants
60 Female prisoners
2 Female debtors
Total 400

The design is by Mr C. Pierce, and the cost of the building, including all fittings, has been £43,716, or about £153 per cell. The area enclosed by the boundary wall is about 3 acres 3 roods 1 perch. The chapel contains 250 separate stalls for prisoners.

The new prison had the most up-to-date design, with a central tower or hub from which radiated wings, enabling the wardens to view the whole prison from one location. Alan Constable has researched the history of the building, and provides a vivid description of the new building:

Every cell had its own gas burner, and in total the prison had 500 gas burners to augment the natural light from the windows ...

Water for the prison was drawn from a well in the grounds which was 217 feet deep' ... The prison was ventilated through the centre tower, and a system of ducting was installed to supply fresh air and remove stale air from the building.[237]

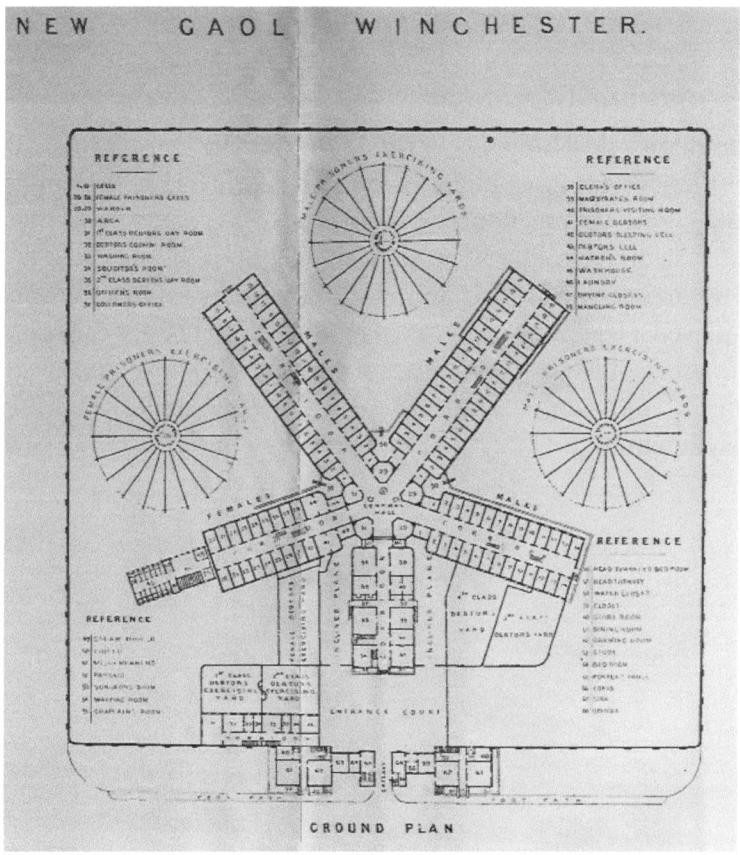

Plate 19: *Plan of the new County Gaol, Winchester (from the Second Report of the Surveyor-General of Prisons, 1847)*

A contemporary Victorian guide book to the city of Winchester considered the new prison to be 'a model establishment almost too comfortable for the purpose of correction'.[238]

RJW Wright was able to move his young family into the brand-new chaplain's house which fronted the prison.[239] His neighbour was the prison governor, Henry Barber, but two years later the two men were to find themselves locked in a bitter dispute. The Hyde bridewell was demolished and the stones made available as 'recycled' building material.[240] The gaol in Jewry Street was advertised for sale by auction in June 1850[241] and the old governor's house came into public use in November 1851 as a library and museum.[242]

A new county lunatic asylum

The other major development of the 1840s was the construction of a new county lunatic asylum, an obligation brought about by Lord Ashley's Lunacy Act of 1845. The ageing Robert Wright, however, was not in attendance at Quarter Sessions in July 1849 when the decision to build a new county lunatic asylum at Knowle was announced by Henry Combe Compton, but he had played a leading role in campaigning for the better care of lunatics over a number of years.[243] He most probably would have approved of the decision, but unfortunately he did not live long enough to see the opening of the asylum in 1853.

NOTES

1   Foster, Ruscombe, *The Politics of County Power*, Harvester Wheatsheaf, 1990, p. 25.

2   *Ibid.*, p. 25.

3   Shurlock, Barry, 'Francis Wickham Swanton (1746–1823), of Worthy, Hampshire, and Long Stratton, Norfolk: Plural Curate, Plural and Absentee Rector, Magistrate, Landlord, and Man of his Time', *Proceedings of the Hampshire Field Club and Archaeological Society*, Volume 63, Hampshire Studies, 2008.

4   The phrase *dedimus potestatem* translates as 'We have given the power'.

5   HRO, Q27/3/144, Justice's certificate of qualification: Rev. Robert Wright, 1808.

6   Foster, Ruscombe, *op. cit.*, p. 27.

7   White, Philippa, *Quarter Sessions Records in the Hampshire Record Office*, Hampshire County Council, 1991, pp. 3–5.

8   Gregory, Jeremy and Stephenson, John, *The Routledge Companion to Britain in the Eighteenth Century 1688–1820*, Routledge, 2007, pp. 265–270.

9   Calendars of Prisoners for Quarter Sessions were published four times a year. The Hampshire Record Office states that 'They contain for each Session, a list of prisoners tried … with details of their crime and a note of the verdict and the sentence passed'. They also include the names of the magistrates who committed the prisoners.

10 HRO, Quarter Sessions Order Books, Q1/27 (1806–1809), Q1/28 (1810–1812), Q1/29 (1812–1814), Q1/30 (1814–1817), Q1/31 (1817–1819), Q1/32 (1819–1821), Q1/33 (1822–1823), Q1/34 (1823–1825), Q1/35 (1825–1827), Q1/36 (1828–1831), Q1/37 (1831–1834), Q1/38 (1835–1837), Q1/39 (1837–1840), Q1/40 (1840–1843), Q1/41 (1844–1847), Q1/42 (1847–1851).

11 Statistics for Table 5 compiled by using the Quarter Sessions Order Books (HRO), *Hampshire Chronicle, Hampshire Advertiser, Hampshire Telegraph* and the *Salisbury and Winchester Journal* (www.britishnewspapersarchive.co.uk).

12 HRO, Printed (Quarter Sessions) Calendars of Prisoners, photocopied files on the open shelves of the Search Room, 1803–1849. (NB The years 1826, 1828, 1837, 1838 and 1844 are missing.)

13 *Ibid.*

14 *Ibid.*
15 Cirket, Alan F (Ed.), *Samuel Whitbread's Notebooks, 1810–11, 1813–14,* Bedfordshire Historical Record Society, 1971, *passim.*
16 HRO, 23M69/PW10, Itchen Abbas Churchwardens' Accounts, 1821–1916.
17 House of Commons Parliamentary Papers, *Report from the Select Committee on the Sale of Beer with The Minutes of Evidence,* 1833, No 416, Volume XVI, p. 16 (www.proquest.com).
18 HRO, Printed Calendars of Prisoners, *op. cit.*
19 HRO, Quarter Session Order Books, *op. cit.*
20 *Ibid.*
21 Hartley Library, University of Southampton, MS61 Wellington Papers 1/7/13/1, Letter from Arthur Wellesley, first Duke of Wellington, to the Duke of Buckingham and Chandos, 29 June 1822.
22 Brougham and Vaux, Baron Henry, *Speeches of Henry Lord Brougham,* Volume 1, Lea and Blanchard, 1841, p. 543 (www.books.google.co.uk).
23 Virgin, Peter, *The Church in an Age of Negligence: Ecclesiastical Structure and Problems of Church Reform, 1700–1840,* James Clarke, 1989, p. 115.
24 Bowles, WL, Rev, *A Word on Cathedral-Oratorios and Clergy Magistrates Addressed to Lord Mountcashel,* John Murray, 1830 (www.books.google.co.uk).
25 *Ibid.*
26 The Peterloo Memorial Campaign (www.peterloomassacre.org).
27 Bates, Stephen, 'The Bloody Clash That Changed Britain', an article in *The Guardian* newspaper, Thursday 4 January 2018.
28 *Ibid.*
29 *Hampshire Chronicle,* Monday 27 September 1819, p. 4.
30 *Ibid.,* Monday 18 October 1819, p. 4.
31 Hone, William and Cruikshank, George, *The Political House that Jack Built,* 1819, British Library Historical Collection reprint.
32 Grimes, Kyle, *Romantic Circles* (www.rc.umd.edu).
33 Gardner, John, 'William Hone and Peterloo', in Poole, Robert (Ed.), *Return to Peterloo,* Manchester Region History Review, 2012, p. 92.
34 *Cobbett's Weekly Political Register,* Volume 46, No 7, Saturday 17 May 1823, *passim*; and the *Kentish Weekly Post,* Tuesday 29 April 1823, p. 4.
35 *Salisbury and Winchester Journal,* Monday 19 May 1823, p. 4.

36 *Cobbett's Weekly Political Register*, Volume 46, No 7, *op. cit.*, p. 430.

37 *Hampshire Chronicle*, Monday 12 January 1824, p. 2.

38 Hopkins, Harry, *The Long Affray*, Secker and Warburg, 1985, p. 222.

39 *Hampshire Chronicle*, Monday 16 January 1826, p. 3.

40 *Ibid.*, Monday 28 August 1826, p. 3.

41 *Ibid.*, Monday 19 July 1830, p. 1.

42 Gleaning was the practice of gathering left over grain after a cereal crop had been harvested.

43 *Ibid.*, Monday 29 August 1825, p. 3.

44 *Devizes and Wiltshire Gazette*, Thursday 1 September 1825, p. 3.

45 TNA, HO17/2/202, 13 May 1829.

46 *Ibid.*

47 *Salisbury and Winchester* Journal, Monday 26 March 1838, p. 4.

48 *Hampshire Telegraph*, Monday 13 December 1841, p. 1.

49 *Hampshire Advertiser*, Saturday 16 September 1848, p. 5.

50 *Hampshire Chronicle*, Saturday 12 August 1848, p. 1.

51 Preston, Richard, 'The Eccentric and Reverend Mr. Smith: The Reverend Herbert Smith 1800–76', *Journal of the Southampton Local History Forum*, Summer 2007, pp. 9–22.

52 *Salisbury and Winchester Journal*, Saturday 12 August 1848, p. 4.

53 HRO, Calendars of Prisoners, 1848, *op. cit.*

54 *Hampshire Chronicle*, Saturday 12 August 1848, p. 1.

55 *Ibid.*, Monday 17 May 1824, p. 4.

56 Corrie, Jessie Elizabeth, *op. cit.*, p. 35.

57 *Hampshire Chronicle*, Monday 20 December 1824, p. 2.

58 *Ibid.*, Monday 24 January 1825, p. 3.

59 *Ibid.*, Monday 31 January 1825, p. 4 and Monday 4 April 1825, p. 2.

60 *Ibid.*, Monday 7 March 1825, p. 3.

61 *Hampshire Chronicle*, Monday 21 March 1825, p. 3.

62 *Hampshire Advertiser*, Monday 21 March 1825, p. 3.

63 HRO, 23M69/PR15, Itchen Abbas Burial Register, 1813–1993.

64 Corrie, Jessie Elizabeth, *op. cit.*, p. 36.

65 *Ibid.*, pp. 35–36.

66 *Ibid.*, p. 36.

67 *Hampshire Chronicle*, Monday 25 April 1825, p. 3.

68 Foster, Ruscombe, *op. cit.*, p. 153.

69 Ayers, Gwendoline M, *England's First State Hospital*, 1971, Wellcome Institute for the History of Medicine, 1971 (www.sochealth.co.uk).

70 Burt, Susan Margaret, 'Fit Objects for an Asylum: The Hampshire County Asylum and its Patients 1852–1899', unpublished PhD thesis, University of Southampton, 2003, pp. 53–54.

71 Balchin, Andrew Timothy, 'The Justice of the Peace and County Government in the East Riding of Yorkshire 1782–1836', unpublished PhD thesis, University of Hull, 1990, p. 362.

72 *Hampshire Chronicle*, Monday 16 January 1815, p. 4.

73 *Ibid.*, Monday 26 April 1819, p. 3.

74 *Ibid.*, Monday 24 February 1823, p. 4.

75 Foyster, Elizabeth, *The Trials of the King of Hampshire: Madness, Secrecy and Betrayal in Georgian England*, One World, 2016, *passim*.

76 *Ibid.*, p. 206.

77 *Ibid.*, p. xviii.

78 *Hampshire Chronicle*, Monday 24 February 1823, p. 4.

79 *Ibid.*, Monday 3 May 1824, p. 3.

80 *Salisbury and Winchester Journal*, Monday 3 May 1824, p. 4.

81 TNA, HO17/2/68.

82 *Hampshire Chronicle*, Monday 4 May 1829, p. 4.

83 *The 1844 Report of the Metropolitan Commission in Lunacy*, Section 4.9.8 (www.studymore.org).

84 Burt, Susan Margaret, *op. cit.*, p. 54.

85 *Hampshire Telegraph*, Saturday 19 October 1844, p. 3.

86 Foster, Ruscombe, *op. cit.*, p. 33.

87 Cirket, Alan (Ed.), *op. cit.*, p. 9.

88 HRO, 22M69/PO2, Avington Overseers' Account Book, 1818–1853.

89 HRO, 32M69/PO8/PO9/PO10/P11, Ovington Removal Orders, 1821.

90 *Hampshire Chronicle*, Monday 9 September 1822, p. 3.

91 *Ibid.*

92 *Cobbett's Weekly Political Register*, Saturday 21 September 1822, *passim*.

93 *The Times*, Friday 5 August 1831, p. 6.

94 *Hampshire Chronicle*, Monday 6 January 1834, p. 1.

95 *Ibid.*

96 *Hampshire Advertiser*, Saturday 8 April 1843, p. 2.

97 *Ibid.*

98 *Hampshire Chronicle*, Monday 21 April 1817, p. 2.

99 *Ibid.*

100 *Ibid.*, Monday 6 April 1818, p. 3.

101 *Ibid.*, Monday 19 January 1829, p. 1.

102 *Hampshire Telegraph*, Monday 8 August 1842, p. 3.

103 *Hampshire Advertiser*, Saturday 22 October 1842, p. 4.

104 HRO, 92M95/F2/15/93, Wright to Sir Thomas Baring, 1821.

105 *Ibid.*

106 *Ibid.*

107 *Hampshire Chronicle*, Monday 30 April 1827, p. 1.

108 *Ibid.*, Monday 16 July 1827, p. 1.

109 *Ibid.*

110 *Ibid.*, Monday 26 April 1830, p. 1.

111 *Hampshire Advertiser*, Saturday 4 January 1834, p. 2.

112 *Hampshire Chronicle*, Monday 26 May 1823, p. 4.

113 *Ibid.*, Monday 2 June 1823, p. 4.

114 *Ibid.*, Monday 9 June 1823, p. 4.

115 *Ibid.*, Monday 21 July 1823, p. 4.

116 *Ibid.*, Monday 20 October 1823, p. 4.

117 HRO, 92M95/F2/19/194, Letter from Robert Wright to Sir Thomas
     Baring, 1829.

118 *Hampshire Chronicle*, Monday 24 October 1831, p. 1.

119 Hartley Library, University of Southampton, MS61, Wellington Papers,
     WP4/2/1/23, Letter from Dr. Quarrier to John Fleming, MP,
     c. 27 September 1830.

120 Ibid., WP4/24/19/1, Letter and Petition to Arthur Wellesley,
     first Duke of Wellington, c. 25 September 1830.

121 *Ibid.*

122 Hartley Library, University of Southampton, MS61, WP4/24/19/14,
     Letter from Dr. Quarrier to John Fleming, MP, 23 October 1830.

123 *Ibid.*

124 *Ibid.*

125 The agricultural riots in mid-Hampshire have been discussed in detail
     in a number of papers and articles, including: Kent, David, *Popular
     Radicalism and the Swing Riots in Central Hampshire*, Hampshire Papers,
     No 11, Hampshire County Council, 1997. Afton, Bethanie, 'A Want of

Good Feeling', in *Proceedings of the Hampshire Field Club and Archaeological Society*, Volume 43, 1987, pp. 237–254. Afton, Bethanie. 'The Motive Which Has Operated on the Minds of My People: 1830 The Propensity of the Hampshire Parishes to Riot,' in *Proceedings of the Hampshire Field Club and Archaeological Society*, Volume 44, 1988, pp. 107–118.

126 TNA, HO52-7-44, Letter to Home Office, 19 November 1830.

127 *Ibid.*, HO52-7-95, Letter from the Duke of Buckingham and Chandos to the Duke of Wellington, 22 November 1830.

128 *Ibid.*, HO52-7-95, Letter to Lord Melbourne, 24 November 1830.

129 Foster, RE, *The Duke of Wellington in Hampshire, 1817–1852*, Hampshire Papers, No 30, Hampshire County Council, 2010, pp. 7–8.

130 TNA, HO52-7-137, Resolutions of a Meeting of the Lord Lieutenant and Magistrates of the County of Hants, 25 November 1830.

131 *Ibid.*, HO52-7-106, Poster advertising resolutions made by the Andover magistrates, 20 November 1830.

132 *Hampshire Chronicle*, Monday 6 December 1830, p. 2.

133 TNA, HO52-7-151, Letter from Newbolt to Lord Melbourne, 10 December 1830.

134 *The Times*, Friday 10 December 1830, p. 1.

135 The reporting of the trials at the Special Commission sometimes contains inaccurate names and places or has confused chronology. For example, RJW Wright is frequently confused with his father, Robert Wright.

136 *The Morning Post*, Thursday 30 December 1830, p. 4.

137 HRO, 100M70/F1, Letter from William Bingham Baring to Lady Harriet Baring, 21 November 1830.

138 *Cobbett's Weekly Political Register*, Saturday 23 July 1831, p. 194.

139 *Salisbury and Winchester Journal*, Monday 5 January 1831, p. 3.

140 *Hampshire Advertiser*, Saturday 15 January 1831, p. 3.

141 HRO, 14M50/2, Calendar of Prisoners for Trial at the Special Commission of Assizes, Saturday December 18th 1830, p. 17.

142 *The Times*, Thursday 23 December 1830, p. 3.

143 The newspaper reports cites the name, 'William' Twitchen, but this person was most likely Andrew Twitchen, a farmer of Itchen Abbas.

144 Chambers, Jill, *Hampshire Machine Breakers: The Story of the 1830 Riots*, Jill Chambers Publishing, 1990, pp. 177–178; and *The Times*, Thursday 23 December 1830, p. 3.

145 TNA, HO17/46/C641124, Letter from Samuel Wall to Lord Melbourne, 20 January 1832.

146 *Ibid.*, Letter from James Pyle to Lord Melbourne, 10 February 1832.

147 *Ibid.*, Petition on behalf of William Bolter.

148 *Ibid.*, Free pardon, 16 May 1833.

149 Afton, Bethanie, 'A Want of Good Feeling', *op. cit., passim.*

150 *Hampshire Chronicle*, Monday 14 November 1831, p. 3.

151 *Ibid.*

152 *Report from the Select Committee on the Sale of Beer*, 1833, *op. cit.*, p. 2.

153 TNA, HO17/46 and Chambers, Jill, *op. cit.*, p. 2.

154 HRO, 92M95/F2/19/174, Letter from Arthur Octavius Baker to Sir Thomas Baring's agent, 6 January 1833.

155 *Ibid.*

156 *The Labourers' Friend*: 1835, pp. 218–222 (www.books.google.co.uk).

157 Perkin, Harold, *The Origins of Modern English Society 1780–1880*, Routledge and Kegan Paul, 1969, p. 19.

158 *Report from the Select Committee on the Sale of Beer*, 1833, *op. cit.*, p. 2.

159 *Ibid.*

160 *Cobbett's Weekly Political Register*, Saturday 23 July 1831, p. 196.

161 *Ibid.*

162 *Hampshire Chronicle*, Monday 18 July 1831, p. 3.

163 Chambers, Jill, *op. cit.*, p. 175.

164 *Hampshire Chronicle*, Monday 19 March 1832, p. 1.

165 *Report from the Select Committee on the Sale of Beer*, 1833, *op. cit.*, p. 1.

166 *Hampshire Chronicle*, Monday 19 March 1832, p. 1.

167 *Ibid.*, Monday 5 March 1832, p. 1.

168 *Ibid.*, Monday 19 March 1832, p. 1.

169 *Ibid.*

170 *Hampshire Advertiser*, Saturday 17 March 1832, p. 2.

171 *Hampshire Chronicle*, Monday 19 March 1832, *op. cit.*

172 The *Poor Man's Guardian*, Saturday 3 December 1831, p. 8.

173 *Ibid.*

174 *Ibid.*, Saturday 25 August 1832, p. 8.

175 *Ibid.*, Saturday 29 September 1832, pp. 7–8.

176 *Ibid.*

177 *Ibid.*

178 *Ibid.*

179 *Ibid.*, 1 December 1832, pp. 4–5.

180 *Ibid.*

181 *Ibid.*

182 Hartley Library, University of Southampton, MS61 Wellington Papers 4/4/3/44, Letter from Reverend Robert Wright to Arthur Wellesley, first Duke of Wellington, 5 November 1832.

183 *Ibid.*

184 *Ibid.*, Wellington Papers 4/5/3/1, Letter from Reverend Robert Wright to Arthur Wellesley, first Duke of Wellington, 1 January 1833.

185 *Ibid.*, Wellington Papers 2/2/73, Letter from Reverend Robert Wright to Arthur Wellesley, first Duke of Wellington, 10 March 1833.

186 *Ibid.*

187 *Ibid.*

188 *Report from the Select Committee on the Sale of Beer*, 1833, *op. cit.*, p. 1.

189 *Ibid.*

190 *Ibid.*

191 *Ibid.*, p. 9.

192 *Ibid.*, pp. 18-19.

193 Geddes, Alastair, *op. cit.*, pp. 16–17.

194 *Report from the Select Committee on the Sale of Beer*, 1833, *op. cit.*, pp. 11–12.

195 *Ibid.*

196 *Ibid.* p.16.

197 *Ibid.*

198 *Ibid.*, p. 17.

199 *Ibid.*, p. 16.

200 *Ibid.*

201 *Ibid.*

202 *Hampshire Chronicle*, Monday 15 April 1833, p. 1.

203 *Hampshire Advertiser*, Saturday 24 November 1832, pp. 2–3.

204 *Ibid.*

205 *Ibid.*

206 *Ibid.*

207 *Ibid.*

208 Taylor, David, *Mastering Economic and Social History*, Macmillan, 1988, p. 345.

209 *Reading Mercury*, Wednesday 5 December 1832, p. 2.

210 *Ibid.*

211 *Hampshire Advertiser*, Saturday 2 May 1835, p. 1.

212 Jacobs, WM, *The Clerical Profession in the Long Eighteenth Century, 1680–1840*, Oxford University Press, 2007, p. 21.

213 *Ibid.*, p. 22.

214 Hartley Library, University of Southampton, MS61 Wellington Papers, WP4/27/46(i), A notice addressed to the Secretary for Home Affairs, 14 October 1837.

215 TNA, HO52-34, 14 November 1837. On the actual document the original month was given as 'October' but this was struck out and replaced with 'November'.

216 Hartley Library, University of Southampton, MS61 Wellington Papers, 4/28/24, Letter from Arthur Wellesley, first Duke of Wellington to J Woodham, 3 December 1837.

217 *Ibid.*, MS61 Wellington Papers, 4/28/28, Letter from J Woodham to Arthur Wellesley, first Duke of Wellington, 8 December 1837.

218 *Ibid.*, MS61 Wellington Papers, 4/28/30, Letter from J Woodham to Rev. Robert Wright, 10 December 1837.

219 *Ibid.*, MS61 Wellington Papers, 4/28/30(i), Arthur Wellesley, first Duke of Wellington, to Rev. Robert Wright, 12 December 1837 (written in the hand of a secretary).

220 *Hampshire Advertiser*, Saturday 10 March 1838, p. 4.

221 TNA, HO9/14, Prison Hulk Registers, 1802–1849 (www.ancestry.co.uk).

222 Foster, Ruscombe, *op. cit.*, pp. 91–93.

223 *Hampshire Chronicle*, Monday 21 October 1839, p. 3.

224 *Ibid.*

225 *Ibid.*, Monday 23 December 1839, p. 4.

226 *Ibid.*

227 *Ibid.*

228 *Hampshire Advertiser*, Saturday 4 January 1840, p. 3.

229 *Hampshire Chronicle*, Monday 19 April 1841, p. 4.

230 *Ibid.*

231 *Ibid.*

232 *Salisbury and Winchester Journal*, Monday 10 January 1842, p. 3.

233 *Hampshire Advertiser*, Saturday 4 January 1845, p. 5.

234 *Hampshire Telegraph*, Saturday 12 April 1845, p. 1.

235 *Hampshire Chronicle*, Saturday 12 April 1845, p. 4.

236 Constable, Alan, *Five Wings and a Tower: Winchester Prison 1850–2002*, HMP Winchester, 2002, p. 1.

237 *Ibid*, p. 7.

238 *Ibid*, p. 1.

239 TNA, HO107/1674, 1851 Census for Winchester (www.ancestry.co.uk)

240 Grover, Christine, *Hyde from Dissolution to Victorian Suburb*, Victorian Heritage Press, 2012, p. 124.

241 *Hampshire Chronicle*, Saturday 15 June 1850, p. 1.

242 *Ibid.*, Saturday 15 November 1851, p. 4.

243 *Hampshire Advertiser*, Saturday 7 July 1849, p. 3.

The End of an Era

SIGNS OF ERRATIC BEHAVIOUR

By the mid-1840s Robert Wright was displaying signs of erratic behaviour. On 25 November 1843 Grantham Smith, the Poor Law relieving officer for Micheldever, wrote an informal letter to Sir Thomas Baring in which he stated 'the Rev Mr Wright under a summons was fined last Friday by the City Magistrates 5 shillings for evading the payment of tolls at the New Corn Exchange'.[1] No records survive to confirm this incident, but there were times when Robert Wright broke the law, such as taking wood without the permission of the manor of Itchen Abbas and (allegedly) receiving contraband, so Smith's claim was probably accurate.

Another illustration of eccentricity was Wright's behaviour at an event in Winchester on Monday 5 February 1844. Wright called a meeting at the Corn Exchange in support of the farming interest. By this time the campaign to get the Corn Laws repealed was gathering momentum, driven by Cobden and Bright's Anti-Corn Law League. The organisation of Wright's meeting was chaotic. The elderly magistrate stood at the entrance to the Corn Exchange admitting landowners and farm tenants but turning away anyone he suspected of being in favour of repealing the Corn Laws! The meeting began late because no one was sure of the starting time, but the local press claimed that 2,000 people were crammed into the building to hear the arguments in favour of continuing the policy of keeping cheap foreign corn out of the country.[2] Robert Wright was devoting a lot of energy to this particular cause, and he was also active in the formation of the Alresford Society for the Protection of British Agriculture in 1844, which was affiliated to the County Society.[3] Wright clearly felt free trade was detrimental to the farming interest and he would do virtually anything to maintain a policy of protection, even if it denied the labourers cheap bread.

During the 1840s the various parish registers show that Wright no longer officiated at ceremonies in Southwick and Boarhunt, suggesting that the travelling was becoming a burden and there was a need to prioritise his workload. By 1849 his attendance at Quarter Sessions was becoming less frequent. Now he was aged 77, his health was apparently failing and he was certainly slowing down. Wright's last attendance at full Quarter Sessions was in January 1849, ending a quite remarkable attendance record going back to 1809.

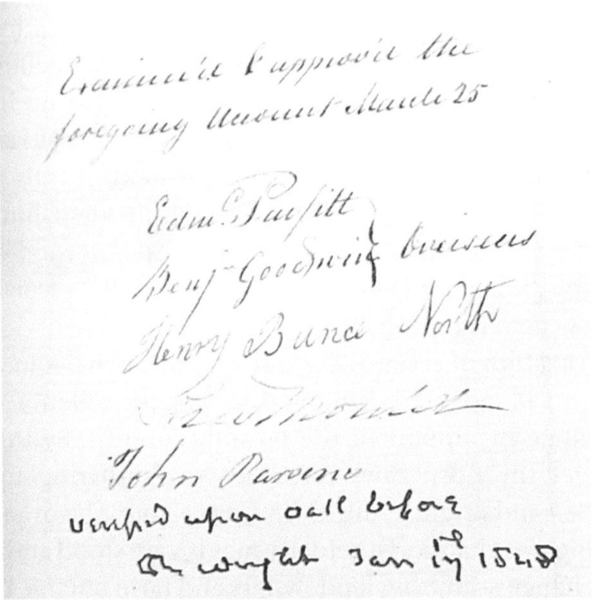
Examined & approved the
foregoing Account March 25

Edmd. Parfitt
Benjn. Goodwin Overseers
Henry Bunce North

John Parsons
verified upon oath before
R Wright Jan 17 1848

Plate 20: *Wright's shaky signature in the Avington Poor Law accounts book, 17 January 1848 (Source: HRO 22M69/PO2).*

FAMILY AND FINANCIAL CONFUSION

Robert Wright had always enjoyed a close professional relationship with his son Robert John William, employing him as a curate at Itchen Abbas and Ovington and providing a glowing reference for his successful application in 1835 for the post of chaplain at the Hampshire county gaol and bridewell. There were differences of opinion between the two men, with RJW Wright having a more empathetic approach towards the lower classes. Nevertheless, they had co-operated closely in carrying out parish duties, allowing Robert Wright to commit himself fully to his role as a county magistrate. From 1836 RJW Wright lived with his family in a staff house near the gaol in Winchester, but he still acted as a locum for his father in taking services at Itchen Abbas. As late as 1849 he chaired two Itchen Abbas parish vestry meetings in the absence of his possibly indisposed father.[4]

Behind the scenes, however, a storm appeared to be brewing. Robert Wright's last will and testament, dated 14 January 1847, made no direct reference to RJW Wright or the advowson being passed on to him.[5] A legacy of £1,000 was made to Margaret Bush, Wright's eldest daughter, which was to be paid on the death of her mother, Elizabeth Wright, and without interest. Although not directly mentioned in the will, Itchen Cottage and The Elms had earlier been placed in trust for William Wynne, the husband of Harriet, Wright's second daughter. Thus, it appears that the two daughters received legacies of approximately equal value and the remainder of the estate was bequeathed to Robert Wright's elderly widow, Elizabeth, who was named as executrix, with sons-in-law William Wynne and John Bush the executors. Perhaps at the time the will was made, RJW Wright was still due to be given the lucrative advowson in keeping with the agreement that had been made in 1836. If so, it would suggest that he was given more favourable treatment than his sisters. In a dramatic turn of events, however, the advowson was snatched from the hands of RJW Wright three months before the death of his father.

On 3 January 1850 RJW Wright surrendered his right to inherit the advowson of the parish of Itchen Abbas when it was legally handed back to his father in a grant agreed between father, son and Harry Comper of Chichester.[6] Robert Wright still owed £2,800 of the capital he had borrowed from Comper in 1830. There was little chance of this substantial amount of money being paid back, as Robert Wright's health was failing. He must have sensed he was near to death, and he knew RJW Wright would have to take on the mortgage debt if he inherited the advowson. To become the new rector of Itchen Abbas, RJW Wright would have had to resign as chaplain at the gaol and live on a stipend of about £480. With a family of five children at the time, he would probably not have had the resources to pay off the capital and interest on his father's debt. In addition, the rectory house would have needed costly renovations to accommodate his large family. The only solution to this dilemma seemed to be to surrender the advowson and remain in Winchester. It must have been a desperate decision for both RJW Wright and his father.

On 4 January 1850 the advowson was sold to John William Spicer of Esher Place, Surrey for the handsome sum of £7,000.[7] Robert Wright was a subscriber to the *Ecclesiastical Gazette*, which advertised the sale of advowsons. An advertisement on Tuesday 11 December 1849 looked suspiciously like it pertained to Itchen Abbas:

The Advowson of a Living in Hampshire
Worth £500 per annum, with a very superior parsonage.
Population small. Possession Immediate.[8]

Spicer proceeded to present his son, William Webb Spicer, to be the new rector at Itchen Abbas and then, on 20 June 1850, conveyed the advowson to him.

The death of Robert Wright, 26 March 1850

Just three months later after the sale of the advowson, Robert Wright passed away at Itchen Cottage, leaving many unanswered questions.

The main question arising from all of his financial dealings is: what happened to the £7,000 received from John Spicer? Presumably, £2,800 would have been used to pay off the mortgage with Comper and a further £1,000 kept in hand for Margaret Bush's legacy. But there was no mention of any pecuniary legacy for RJW Wright, so what happened to the remaining £4,200? Theoretically, it should have gone to Elizabeth Wright, but on 22 June 1850 she applied to be paid half the pension allowed to the 'Widow of an Officer who had died'.[9] The officer in question was Robert Wright, who, she said had been chaplain to General Hunter of the 133rd Regiment of Foot. Elizabeth claimed that she had 'no Pension, Allowance of Provision from Government or other means of support' making out she was virtually destitute.[10] Jessie Corrie also comments on this event saying: '[Great] Grandmother was one of the last widows who drew an army chaplain's Widow's Pension'.[11]

If his widow was in such dire financial trouble, it may have been possible that Robert Wright had other substantial debts and had been living beyond his means in order to impress his gentry friends. If this analysis is correct, it illustrates the complex character of Wright; in favour of retrenchment in his public life, but apparently unable to manage his own private financial affairs satisfactorily.

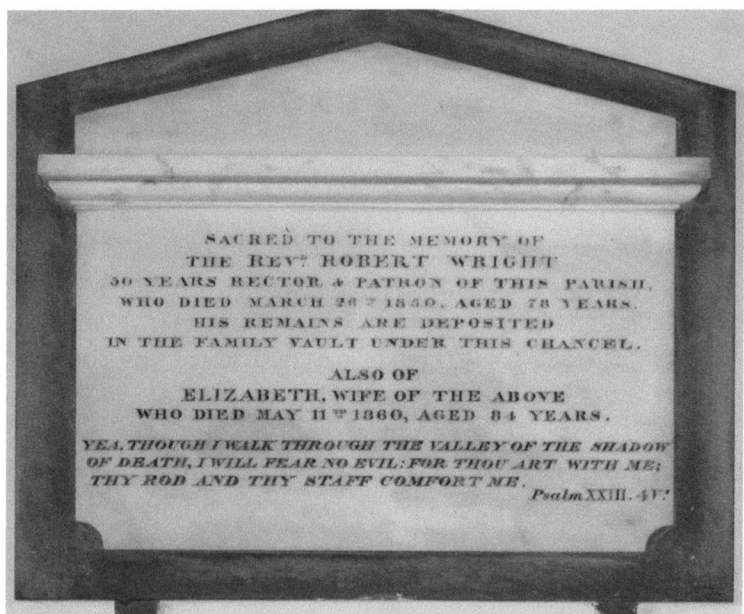

Plate 21: *Memorial plaque to Robert and Elizabeth Wright in Itchen Abbas Church (Source: Author).*

The 1851 Census showed Elizabeth Wright was living at Itchen Cottage with her sister, and she informed the enumerator she was a 'Gentleman Annuitant' giving the impression she was comfortably off.[12] One wonders if she had been 'economic' with the truth when she applied for the widow's army pension? The whole affair is a mystery and we can only speculate as to the true story!

The apparent 'victim' of this financial conundrum was RJW Wright. He had seemingly been abandoned and excluded from executing his father's will. Something was not quite right. He continued in his post as prison chaplain for another three years, until a dispute with the governor, Henry Barber, resulted in his abrupt departure.

A SAD ENDING TO LIFE IN WINCHESTER FOR RJW WRIGHT

In October 1853 press reports began to appear suggesting that the regime at the new county gaol at Winchester was inhumane and cruel. At an inquest into the death of a former inmate, William Jones, a witness, told how the prisoners were subjected to a terrible diet that was totally devoid of any kind of meat and consisted only of small amounts of gruel, bread, cheese and potatoes. Debtors were given the same treatment as convicted criminals, and if they had failed to repay their debts after an initial period of 14 days, they. were incarcerated in 'D" wing, which was where the 'felons' were kept.[13] The authorities at Winchester gaol strenuously denied these claims, saying they were based on untruths. A Home Office inspector visited the gaol and found everything to be satisfactory.

The issue would have ended except for an incident involving the use of a straitjacket. One day RJW Wright heard loud screaming coming from a darkened cell and asked a female turnkey to let him into the cell to investigate. There he found a female inmate, who had verbally abused prison staff, trussed up in a straitjacket with her arms in such a position that she was in danger of dislocating her shoulders. RJW Wright was so distressed by the scene that he wrote a letter to the chairman of the Visiting Magistrates' Committee stating that such use of a straitjacket was tantamount to torture. In his letter, RJW Wright alleged:

> The apparatus is a frame of leather and iron to fasten round the body of the prisoner, with the iron sockets at the hips, into which are inserted iron uprights or crutches, to be fixed higher or lower at the pleasure of the office ... [The prisoner] was rolling on the floor, with her arms back, and entirely cold, owing to the circulation being stopped.[14]

The turnkey who had given RJW Wright access to the cell reported the incident to the governor, but worse was to come when RJW Wright's letter to the visiting magistrates was leaked to the *London Daily News* and the issue entered the public domain. The authorities were swift to act and they turned on the hapless chaplain. The governor denied any allegation of torture or cruelty and said the straitjacket had been obtained from the county hospital, where it was used to restrain patients who were mentally unstable. A Home Office inquiry was rapidly convened under the chairmanship of Captain Williams, Inspector of Prisons. Witnesses were called and questioned with the obvious aim of proving that the governor had not broken any rules and was running a humane prison. RJW Wright was put under great pressure by some aggressive questioning. Unlike his father, he did not have a thick skin and he crumbled under the onslaught. He was instructed to write an open letter of apology for his conduct and he was suspended, before being asked to resign his position. In a letter to the *Hampshire Chronicle* RJW Wright wrote:

> My ideas, after the evidence given this week under the Government Inspector, I confess to be totally erroneous, and I acquit with the greatest pleasure both the Governor and the Matron of any idea of inhumanity either in ordering the [straitjacket's] application or of impropriety, or want of Christian feeling in bringing it into the New Prison. I have most ignorantly and unintentionally done them much injustice, and I beg to express my most sincere sorrow for it. The great mischief has been done by the unauthorised publication of my letter.[15]

RJW Wright had suffered the full weight of the establishment. The investigation was a cleverly organised damage limitation exercise and cover up. It must have been little consolation to him that at least some of the public remained sceptical about the conduct of the prison governor. John L Jardine, a house surgeon at the county hospital, denied that such a straitjacket had ever been used as a means of restraining patients, throwing doubt on the governor's explanation of the incident.[16] An anonymous correspondent to the *Daily News*, 'Vigil', stated that the public would never fully side with RJW Wright because he had shown 'weakness' and 'vacillation'. However, in a tribute to the chaplain, 'Vigil' went on to say:

> We all know the preponderance of fear, but there is a public testimony recorded of the assertion of a county magistrate, that his zeal in the performance of his duty equalled the work of 'three curates'. Therefore it is hoped that such a man, with a family and very limited means, will not be hardly dealt with, after a servitude of many years, without a pension for past services.[17]

The irony of the incident was that Robert Wright, the chaplain's late father, had served as a visiting magistrate for many years at the old gaol in Jewry Street, Winchester, but now the current leader of this very group, Lord Henry Cholmondely, together with Sir William Heathcote and Henry Coombe Compton (who had both sat with Robert Wright), had conspired to condemn the actions of his son. Robert Wright had consistently upheld the establishment which had now closed ranks to humiliate a member of his family.

It was a distressing end to RJW Wright's 17-year career as a caring and humane prison chaplain. His last entry in the chaplain's journal, made on 25 October 1853, confirms he had been suspended from duty while the investigation took place. His last contribution was routine and mundane, belying all the good work he had done as chaplain:

> On Duty 7.15 a.m. Read prayers and Scripture with exposition till 8.00 am. Visited Prisoners committed and to be discharged. Catechised in the school. Visited in B and C Division. *R Wright.*[18]

His replacement, the Reverend R Foster Rogers, who arrived from the Westminster House of Correction, made his first entry in the chaplain's journal on 15 January 1854.[19]

RJW Wright left Winchester immediately after the scandal and obtained a curacy at Holy Trinity Church, Queenshead, near Bradford in West Yorkshire, where he stayed for two years.[20] In 1856 he was presented as the new vicar of Selston, a mining village in Nottinghamshire, where he was able to resurrect both his career and reputation until his death in 1887.

Whether he ever made any return to Itchen Abbas is not known, but when he left Hampshire in 1853 he was in effect abandoning his elderly mother, Elizabeth Wright. She died in 1860 and was buried at Itchen Abbas by her husband's successor, the Reverend William Webb Spicer.[21]

NOTES

1   HRO, 92M95/NP2/S/16/40, Grantham Smith to Sir Thomas Baring, 25 November 1843.
2   *Salisbury and Winchester Journal*, Saturday 10 February 1844, p. 3 and the *Hampshire Telegraph*, 12 February 1844, p. 3.
3   *Salisbury and Winchester Journal*, Saturday 4 May 1844, p. 1.
4   HRO, 23M69/PV1, Itchen Abbas Vestry Minute Book, 1849–1921.
5   HRO, 23M69/E/T28, Last Will and Testament of Robert Wright, 14 January 1847.
6   HRO, 23M69/E/T27, The Next Presentation to the Living of Itchen Abbas, Grant of 1 January 1836 with Endorsed Re-Grant, 3 January 1850.
7   HRO, 23M69/E/T29, Conveyance of the Advowson of Itchen Abbas, 4 January 1850.
8   The *Ecclesiastical Gazette*, Tuesday 11 December 1849, Number 138, p. 156.
9   TNA, HO42/50, War Office Form 122339, 22 June 1850 (www.ancestry.co.uk).
10 *Ibid.*
11 Corrie, Jessie Elizabeth, *op. cit.*, p. 37.
12 TNA, HO107/1673, 1851 Census for Itchen Abbas (www.ancestry.co.uk).
13 *Morning Post*, Friday 14 October 1853, p. 4.
14 *London Daily News*, Tuesday 25 October 1853, p. 4.
15 *Hampshire Chronicle*, Saturday 29 October 1853, p. 4.
16 *London Daily News*, Monday 31 October 1853, p. 2.
17 *Ibid.*, Saturday 19 November 1853, p. 2.
18 HRO, Q13/2/8, Chaplain's Journal, County Gaol and Bridewell, 3 July 1842–26 April 1854.
19 *Ibid.*
20 *Crockford's Clerical Directory 1868*, p. 739 (www.ancestry.co.uk).
21 HRO, 23M69/PR15, Itchen Abbas Burial Register, 1813–1993.

Conclusion

The Reverend Robert Wright was undeniably a 'pillar of the establishment'. He was a product of late Georgian England and came from a privileged 'middling' family, a background that moulded his attitude and instilled in him a burning desire to preserve the establishment. The French Revolution and the insecurity that resulted from the wars against France (1793–1815) would also have influenced this attitude. Supported by his father, Robert Wright sought the life and status of a country gentleman in the guise of a pluralist clergyman. There is little doubt that he enjoyed the role of magistrate and relished socialising with the landed gentry and aristocracy, with Palmerston, Wellington and the Dukes of Buckingham and Chandos among his acquaintances.

It was a world he wished to preserve, and no doubt he subscribed to the view that the poor needed religion so that they would be aware of their place in society and respect those whom God had placed above them in life's pecking order. The world around him, however, was changing. Britain was fast industrialising, and from the mid-1830s the county bench began to lose some of its control as central government intervened in the organisation of the Poor Law in 1834, passed legislation to reform municipal corporations in 1835 and introduced measures to improve public health in 1848. Set this within the context of the demand for parliamentary reform and moves to improve the image of the Church of England and it is clear that Wright was clinging to a disappearing social order.

In addition, the number of clerical magistrates was declining as the clergy became more involved in pastoral work within their parishes. Wright was succeeded as rector of Itchen Abbas by William Webb Spicer and then, from 1874, by Septimus Gillson. Spicer had a keen interest in flora and fauna, which was to bring him fame beyond the boundaries of Itchen Abbas, but he was a successful and popular rector who rebuilt St John's Church between 1861 and 1863. He was also the (reluctant) prime mover in setting up the Itchen Abbas School Board in 1873, although he did not stay long enough to see the new school opened in 1875.[1] Instead, he emigrated to Tasmania in 1874, where he studied the local flora and fauna and wrote a number of important books and articles.[2] Gillson was also very active in the parish, organising clothing clubs, publishing an excellent magazine and assiduously managing the School Board.[3]

Plate 22: *Itchen Abbas Board School, opened in 1875 and extended in 1895.*

Wright was conscientious in his administrative role as a magistrate, whether it was visiting the prisons and lunatic asylums, licensing public houses or auditing the county's finances. His work as a judicial magistrate, however, conflicted with his role as a rector. The evidence shows that he officiated at christenings, marriages and burials in four of his parishes but he appeared to show little true empathy for the poor. He passionately believed that drinking and crime caused their misery, and his real concern was to keep the poor rates down to a minimum.

Many of Wright's colleagues in the Church of England were increasingly coming to the opinion that the role of a clerical magistrate broke the 'paternalistic connection' with the parishioners. Wright was so absorbed in his magisterial work that he left important parish duties to his curate son. The Reverend Robert John William Wright took on responsibility for attempting to build new school rooms in Itchen Abbas and Ovington and increasing the number of seats in Itchen Abbas Church by organising the construction of a new gallery. However, the evidence suggests that he failed to secure a grant to finance a new schoolroom and the fabric of the old church was left in a state of permanent decay.[4]

The 1830 agricultural riots hardened Wright's attitude towards the labouring class and he became a virtual despot in his own neighbourhood, illustrated by his evidence to the Select Committee on the Sale of Beer in 1833. Frightened by any mention of reform or change to the 'old world', Wright was even prepared to organise what amounted to his own private police force. He had a 'do as I say, not as I do' attitude. For example, he was able to get away with stealing wood from the manor of Itchen Abbas, an action for which he was known to punish labourers when he was dispensing justice. In addition, in a letter written to Sir Thomas Baring dated 25 November 1843, Grantham Smith of Micheldever describes how Wright had evaded paying the toll.[5]

Wright sometimes displayed a paternalistic attitude by contributing to charity and making donations to appeals, and he was able to show compassion, as evidenced by the John Hughes affair and the case where he lobbied to get a woman transferred from the bridewell to a lunatic asylum. His campaigning zeal to improve such asylums should also be remembered.

Overall, however, Wright's reputation as the 'poor man's friend' has to be questioned. His modus operandi was to preserve his privileged world and keep the poor in their place. Wright could be truculent and stubborn and he found no difficulty in making an example of law-breakers. In 1896 an old woman from Southwick told Jessie Corrie that Wright was remembered as 'a white haired, ruddy faced rector and [he was] quite as much magistrate as parson [who] sent a lot of folks to prison'.[6] Corrie seems not to have realised that the old lady's comments were a damning indictment of Wright's career. Almost 50 years after his death, ordinary people remembered him more for his uncompromising treatment of people who broke the law than for this spiritual work.

Jessie Corrie demonstrates that within his own family Wright was regarded as a generous father figure who performed acts of kindness, often travelling long distances to officiate at family baptisms, marriages and burials. There was, however, financial confusion at the end of his life that suggested a possible rift with his son, RJW Wright.

In sum, it would have been difficult to find a more dedicated magistrate in terms of administering the county with an almost perfect attendance record at Quarter Sessions – and without such contributions, the county would not have functioned. Yet although Wright may have regarded himself as the 'poor man's friend', many of the labouring class may have had a less complimentary view of his long career as a clerical magistrate.

The fact that no public tribute was paid to Wright after his death is puzzling, but at least there is now a brief record of his complex life. Others may look at his record from a different perspective and arrive at an alternative interpretation of his career; after all, this is the essence of history. If additional source material comes to light in the future to fill in some of the many lacunas in the story, then our knowledge will be suitably enriched.

NOTES

1   HRO, 23M69/PV1, Itchen Abbas Parish Vestry Minute Book, 1849–1921, Meeting of 24 April 1875.

2   Rozefelds, Andrew C, 'A Four-Year Antipodean Odyssey: The Reverend William Webb Spicer, MA, in Tasmania 1874–1878', in *Kanunnah*, January 2005, pp. 33–46, Tasmanian Museum and Art Gallery.

3   HRO, 23M69/PW2, Parish Accounts for Itchen Abbas No. 2, 1885–1916.

4   HRO, 23M69/PW10, Churchwardens' Account Book for Itchen Abbas, 1821–1916.

5   HRO, 92M95/NP2/S16/2/40, *op. cit.*

6   Corrie, Jessie Elizabeth, *op. cit.*, p. 17.

Select Bibliography

MANUSCRIPTS

Hampshire Record Office
Ashburton Papers
Baring (Northbrook Family) Papers
Bolton (of Hackwood) Papers
Shelley-Rolls Papers
The National Archives
HO 52 Counties Correspondence
HO 17 Criminal Petitions
Quarter Sessions and Parish Records (Hampshire Record Office)
Quarter Sessions Order Books Q1/27–Q1/42
Itchen Abbas (23M69)
Ovington (32M/69)
Southwick and Boarhunt (68M/81)
Church of England Record Society
Incorporated Church Building Society
National Society Archives

NEWSPAPERS AND PERIODICALS

Cobbett's Weekly Political Register
Devizes and Wiltshire Gazette
Ecclesiastical Gazette
Hampshire Advertiser
Hampshire Chronicle
Hampshire Telegraph
Kentish Weekly Post
London Daily News
Morning Post
Oxford Chronicle and Reading Gazette
Oxford University and City Herald
Poor Man's Guardian

Reading Mercury
Salisbury and Winchester Journal
The Times

CONTEMPORARY PAMPHLETS

Baker, Arthur Octavius, *Considerations on the Present State of the Peasantry of England with Suggestions for the Improvement of Their Condition*, nd.

Bowles, WL, Reverend, *A Word on Cathedral-Oratorios and Clergy Magistrates Addressed to Lord Mountcashel*, 1830.

Hone, W, *The Political House That Jack Built (The Clerical Magistrate)*, 1819.

Lefroy, Christopher Edward, *Letter to Sir T. Baring on the Subject of Allotments of Land to the Poor, Containing his Experiences of that System for Four Years*, 1834.

Poulter, E, *Address and Report on the Enquiry into the General State of the Poor, Instituted by Order of the Last Epiphany General Quarter Sessions for the County of Hampshire*, 1795.

PARLIAMENTARY PAPERS

Report from the Select Committee on the Sale of Beer with the Minutes of Evidence, House of Commons Parliamentary Papers, No 416, Volume XVI, 1833.

BOOKS

Ayres, Jack, (Ed.), *Paupers and Pig Killers: The Diary of William Holland, a Somerset Parson 1799–1818*, Alan Sutton, 1984.

Beckett, John, *The Rise and Fall of the Grenvilles, Dukes of Buckingham and Chandos, 1710–1921*, Manchester University Press, 1994.

Beckett, JV, *The Aristocracy in England 1660–1914*, Basil Blackwell, 1986.

Belchem, John, *'Orator' Hunt: Henry Hunt and English Working-Class Radicalism*, Breviary Stuff Publications, 2012.

Biddell, Barbara, *The Jolly Farmer? William Cobbett in Hampshire 1804–1820*, Hampshire Papers No. 15, Hampshire County Council, 1999.

Brown, David J, *Palmerston, South Hampshire and Electoral Politics, 1832–1835*, Hampshire Papers No. 26, Hampshire County Council, 2003.

Burchardt, Jeremy, *The Allotment Movement in England, 1793–1873*, The Boydell Press, 2002.

Cannadine, Sir David (Gen. Ed.), *Oxford Dictionary of National Biography* (www.oxforddnb.com).

Carpenter, Kenneth (Adv. Ed.), *The Aftermath of the 'Last Labourers' Revolt', Fourteen Pamphlets 1830–31*, Arno Press, 1972.

Carpenter Turner, Barbara, *A History of Winchester*, Phillimore, 1992.

Chadwick, Owen, *The Victorian Church, Part I*, Adam and Charles Black, 1970.

Cirket, Alan F (Ed.), *Samuel Whitbread's Notebooks, 1810–11, 1813–14*, Bedfordshire Historical Society, 1971.

Crittall, Elizabeth, *The Justicing Notebook of William Hunt 1744–1749*, Wiltshire Record Society, 1982.

Clarke, Peter L, Dever and Down: *A History of the Villages in and around the Dever Valley in Hampshire*, Dever Publications, 2011.

Constable, Alan, *Five Wings and a Tower: Winchester Prison 1850–2002*, HMP Winchester, 2002.

Corrie, Jessie Elizabeth, *Records of the Corrie Family, AD 802–1899, Part II*, Mitchel and Hughes, 1899.

Davey, BJ, *Rural Crime in the Eighteenth Century*, University of Hull Press, 1994.

Davey, BJ and Wheeler, RC, (Eds.), *The Country Justice and the Case of the Blackmoor's Head: The Practice of Law in Lincolnshire, 1787–1838*, Lincoln Record Society, Volume 102, The Boydell Press, 2012.

Davis, Richard W, *Political Change and Continuity 1760–1885: A Buckinghamshire Study*, David and Charles, 1972.

Duthy, John, *Sketches of Hampshire: The Architectural Antiquities and Topography of the County Adjacent to the River Itchen from Alresford to Southampton*, Jacob and Johnson, 1839. (Reprinted by Laurence Oxley, 1972.)

Dyck, Ian, *William Cobbett and Rural Popular Culture*, Cambridge University Press, 1992.

Eccles, Audrey, *Vagrancy in Law and Practice Under the Old Poor Law*, Ashgate, 2012.

Finn, Peter and Johnson, Pamela, (Eds.), *A History of the Worthy Villages*, Worthy Local History Group, 1999.

Foster, Ruscombe, *The Politics of County Power: Wellington and the Hampshire Gentlemen, 1820–52*, Harvester Wheatsheaf, 1990.

Foster, RE, *The Duke of Wellington in Hampshire 1817–1852*, Hampshire Papers No. 30, Hampshire County Council, 2010.

Foyster, Elizabeth, *The Trials of the King of Hampshire: Madness, Secrecy and Betrayal in Georgian England,* One World Publications, 2016.

Gardner, John, *Poetry and Popular Protest: Peterloo, Cato Street and the Queen Caroline Controversy,* Palgrave Macmillan, 2011.

Gibson, William, *The Church of England 1688–1832: Unity and Accord,* Routledge, 2001.

Gregory, Jeremy and Stevenson, John, *The Routledge Companion to Britain in the Eighteenth Century 1688–1820,* Routledge, 2007.

Griffin, Carl J, *The Rural War: Captain Swing and the Politics of Protest,* Manchester University Press, 2012.

Grover, Christine, *Hyde: From Dissolution to Victorian Suburb,* Victorian Heritage Press, 2012.

Haydon, Colin, *John Henry Williams (1747–1829), 'Political Clergyman': War, the French Revolution and the Church of England,* The Boydell Press, 2007.

Hilton, Lisa, *Mistress Peachum's Pleasure: The Life and Times of Lavinia, Duchess of Bolton,* Weidenfeld and Nicolson, 2005.

Hobsbawm, EJ and Rudé, George, *Captain Swing,* Pimlico Edition, 1993.

Hopkins, Harry, *The Long Affray: The Poaching Wars in Britain 1760–1914,* Secker and Warburg, 1985.

Jacob, WM, *The Clerical Profession in the Long Eighteenth Century, 1680–1840,* Oxford University Press, 2007.

Jones, Kathleen, *Lunacy, Law, and Conscience 1744–1845,* Routledge and Kegan Paul, 1955.

Kent, David, *Popular Radicalism and the Swing Riots in Central Hampshire,* Hampshire Papers No. 11, Hampshire County Council, 1997.

Knight, Frances, *The Nineteenth-Century Church and English Society,* Cambridge University Press, 1995.

Lee, Robert, *Rural Society and the Anglican Clergy, 1815–1914: Encountering and Managing the Poor,* The Boydell Press, 2006.

Le Faye, Deidre (Ed.), *Jane Austen's Letters,* Oxford University Press, 2011.

McClatchey, Diana, *Oxfordshire Clergy, 1777–1969,* Oxford at the Clarendon Press, 1960.

McGarvey, Michael (Ed.), *The King's Peace: The Justice's Notebooks of Thomas Horner, of Mells, 1770–1777,* Frome Society for Local Study, 1997.

Moir, Esther, *The Justice of the Peace,* Penguin, 1969.

Moir, Esther, *Local Government in Gloucestershire, 1775–1800,* Bristol and Gloucestershire Archaeology Society, 1969.

Osborne, Bertram, *Justices of the Peace 1361–1848: A History of Our Magistracy over Five Centuries*, The Sedgefield Press, 1960.

Perkin, Harold, *The Origins of Modern English Society 1780–1880*, Routledge and Kegan Paul, 1969

Poole, Robert, *Return to Peterloo*, Manchester Centre for Regional History, 2014.

Pugh, RK (Ed.), *The Letter Books of Samuel Wilberforce, 1843–1868*, Buckingham Record Society and Oxfordshire Record Society, 1970.

Rule, John and Wells, Roger, *Crime, Protest and Popular Politics in Southern England 1740–1850*, The Hambledon Press, 1997.

Sanderson, Isobel, *Itchen Stoke: A Small Parish in the Upper Itchen Valley*, Hampshire, Laurence Oxley, 1975.

Satchell, Veront M, *Hope Transformed: A Historical Sketch of the Hope Landscape, St Andrew, Jamaica, 1660–1960*, University of West Indies Press, 2012.

Shurlock, Barry, *The Speaker's Chaplain and The Master's Daughter: A Georgian Family and Friends*, Scholarly Sources, 2015.

Silverthorne, Elizabeth, *Deposition Book of Richard Wyatt, JP, 1767–1776*, Surrey Record Society, Volume XXX, 1978.

Skinner, John, *Journal of a Somerset Rector 1803–1834*, Oxford University Press, 1971.

Slinn, Sara, *The Education of the Anglican Clergy, 1780–1839*, The Boydell Press, 2017.

Smith, Mark (Ed.), *Doing the Duty of the Parish: Surveys of the Church in Hampshire 1810*, Hampshire Record Series, Volume XVII, Hampshire County Council, 2004.

Snell, KDM, *Annals of the Labouring Poor: Social Change and Agrarian England 1660–1900*, Cambridge University Press, 1985.

Soloway, RA, *Prelates and People: Ecclesiastical Thought in England 1783–1852*, Routledge, 1969.

Spence, Margaret, *Hampshire and Australia 1783–1791: Crime and Transportation*, Hampshire Papers No. 2, Hampshire County Council, 1992.

Steedman, Carolyn, *An Everyday Life of the English Working Class: Work, Self and Sociability in the Early Nineteenth Century*, Cambridge University Press, 2013.

Stone, Michael (Ed.), *The Diary of John Longe, Vicar of Coddenham, 1765–1834*, The Boydell Press, 2008.

Sutton, Alan (Ed.), *The Complete Diary of a Cotswold Parson: The Magistrate,* Volume 3, The Amberley Press, 2008.

Taylor, David, *Mastering Economic and Social History,* Macmillan, 1988.

Taylor, David, *The New Police in Nineteenth-Century England: Crime, Conflict and Control,* Manchester University Press, 1997.

Thompson, FML, *English Landed Society in the Nineteenth Century,* Routledge and Kegan Paul, 1963.

Tindal Hart, A, *The Curate's Lot: The Story of the Unbeneficed English Clergy,* The Country Book Club, 1971.

Tomalin, Claire, *Jane Austen: A Life,* Penguin, 2012.

Vernon, James, *Modern Britain, 1750 to the Present,* Cambridge University Press, 2017.

Victoria History of the Counties of England: Hampshire and the Isle of Wight, Volume IV, Dawsons of Pall Mall, 1911.

Virgin, Peter, *The Church in an Age of Negligence: Ecclesiastical Structure and Problems of Church Reform 1700–1840,* James Clarke, 1989.

Watt, Ian A, *A History of the Hampshire and Isle of Wight Constabulary 1839–1966,* Phillimore, 2006.

White, RJ, *Waterloo to Peterloo,* Penguin, 1957.

Young, Penny, *Two Cocks on the Dunghill: William Cobbett and Henry Hunt: Their Friendship, Feuds, and Fights,* Twopenny Press, 2009.

Ziegler, Philip, *The Sixth Great Power: Barings, 1762–1929,* Collins, 1988.

ARTICLES AND PAMPHLETS

Afton, B, 'A Want of Good Feeling: A Reassessment of the Economic and Political Causes of the Rural Unrest in Hampshire, 1830' in *Proceedings of the Hampshire Field Club and Archaeology Society,* Volume 43, pp. 237–254, Hampshire Studies, 1987.

Afton, B, 'The Motive Which Has Operated on the Minds of My People, 1830: The Propensity of the Hampshire Parishes to Riot' in *Proceedings of the Hampshire Field Club and Archaeology Society,* Volume 44, pp. 107–118, Hampshire Studies, 1988.

Bates, Stephen, 'The Bloody Clash That Changed Britain', in the *Guardian,* Thursday 4 January 2018.

Bell, Alan, S, *Sydney Smith, Rector of Foston 1806–1829,* Borthwick Papers, No. 43, St Anthony's Press, York, 1972.

Biddle, Martin (Ed.), *An Historical Map of Winchester from Medieval Times to 1800*, The Historic Towns Trust, 2016.

Claisse, Penny and Taylor, David, *St John the Baptist in Itchen Abbas: A Short History of a Church and its Community in the Upper Itchen Valley*, Parochial Church Council of St John the Baptist, 1992.

Cooper, JM, 'Leisure and Society in Georgian Winchester' in *Proceedings of the Hampshire Field Club and Archaeology Society*, Volume 54, pp. 127–145, Hampshire Studies, 1999.

Evans, Eric J, 'Some Reasons for the Growth of English Rural Anti-Clericalism, c.1750–1830' in *Past and Present*, No. 66, February 1975.

Evans, Eric J, *Tithes and the Tithe Commutation Act 1836*, Standing Conference for Local History, 1978.

Geddes, Alastair, *Samuel Best and the Hampshire Labourer*, Andover Local History Society, 1981.

Hay, Douglas, 'Patronage, Paternalism, and Welfare: Masters, Workers and Magistrates in Eighteenth Century England' in *International Labor and Working-Class History*, No. 53, 1998, pp. 27–48.

Holt, HME, 'Assistant Commissioners and Local Agents: Their Role in Tithe Commutation, 1836–1854' in *Agricultural History Review*, Volume 32, No. 2, 1984, pp. 189–200.

Latimer, James, 'The Apprenticeship System in the British West Indies' in *The Journal of Negro Education*, Volume 33, No. 1, Winter 1964, pp. 52–57.

Lewin, Sarah, *Records of the Diocese of Winchester in the Hampshire Record Office*, Hampshire County Council, 1991.

Preston, Richard, 'The Eccentric and Reverend Mr. Smith: The Reverend Herbert Smith 1800–1876', in *Journal of the Southampton Local History Forum*, Summer 2007, pp. 9–22.

Rozefelds, Andrew, C, 'A Four-Year Antipodean Odyssey: The Reverend William Webb Spicer, MA, in Tasmania 1874–1878', in *Kanunnah*, January 2005, pp. 33–46, Tasmanian Museum and Art Gallery.

Shurlock, Barry, 'Francis Wickham Swanton (1746–1823) of Worthy, Hampshire and Long Stratton, Norfolk: Plural Curate, Plural and Absentee Rector, Magistrate, Landlord, and Man of his Time' in *Proceedings of the Hampshire Field Club and Archaeology Society*, Volume 63, pp. 58–75, Hampshire Studies, 2008.

Spring, David and Spring, Eileen, 'The Fall of the Grenvilles 1844–1848' in *Huntington Library Quarterly*, Volume 19, No. 2, February 1956, pp. 165–190.

White, Philippa, *Quarter Session Records in the Hampshire Record Office*, Hampshire County Council, 1991.

Woodward, Nicholas, 'Horse-stealing in Wales, 1730–1830' in *Agricultural History Review*, Volume 57, Part 1, 2009.

Zangerl, Carl, HE, 'The Social Composition of the County Magistracy in England and Wales, 1831–1887' in *Journal of British Studies*, Volume 11, No. 1, November 1971, pp. 113–125.

UNPUBLISHED THESES AND DISSERTATIONS

Austin, MR Rev, 'The Church of England in the County of Derbyshire, 1772–1832', unpublished PhD thesis, University of London, 1969.

Balchin, Andrew Timothy, 'The Justice of the Peace and County Government in the East Riding of Yorkshire 1782–1836', unpublished PhD thesis, University of Hull, 1990.

Bowes, David John, 'The Church of England in East Yorkshire from 1743–c.1840, with Particular Reference to Economic Matters', unpublished PhD thesis, University of Hull, 2006.

Burt, Susan Margaret, 'Fit Objects for an Asylum: The Hampshire County Asylum and its Patients 1852–1899', unpublished PhD thesis, University of Southampton, 2003.

Taylor, David, 'Itchen Abbas 1800–1900: A Community in the Upper Itchen Valley, Hampshire', unpublished dissertation for the Diploma of Local History, University of Portsmouth (formerly Portsmouth Polytechnic), 1989.

Index